Praises for this volume

COVID-19 pandemic and digital innovation are making unprecedented disruption to the global higher education landscape. These disruptions have increased academic discussion on how to reimagine the future of higher education after post-COVID 19. Thus, the book, *Global Higher Education During COVID-19: Policy, Society, and Technology* problematized these realities from a global policy context with policy recommendations on issues of racial justice, funding, technology among others. Therefore, I would like to congratulate the editors: *Joshua S. McKeown*, *Krishna Bista*, and *Roy Y.* Chan for this excellent publication.

Dr. KS Adeyemo, Senior Lecturer, University of Pretoria,
South Africa

Global Higher Education During COVID-19: Policy, Society, and Technology is a highly recommended resource for higher education institution policymakers and educators around the globe. Not only does this book provide invaluable insights from higher education institution policymakers, educators, and students during the COVID-19 pandemic, but it also offers useful suggestions on dealing with possible challenges and seeking opportunities in future higher education.

Dr. Misty So-Sum Wai-Cook, Centre for English Language
Studies, National University of Singapore

It's a timely book reporting the most recent responses of international higher education across the world during the Covid-19 pandemic. Besides providing the theoretical contributions, the book also offers practical implications for stakeholders, including policymakers, education managers and practitioners, international students, and parents.

Dr. Hiep Pham, Director, Center for Research and Practice on
Education, Phu Xuan University, Vietnam

Global Higher Education During COVID-19: Policy, Society, and Technology is timely and relevant providing a critically engaged reflective account of geographically diverse higher education institutions' response and practice during the COVID-19 pandemic. This book illuminates some of the current impediments to higher education internationalization within the context of COVID-19 and provides insights into shared learning experiences that address new challenges to internationalisation imposed by the pandemic. A must read for international higher education specialists, practitioners, scholars and researchers.

Dr. Tasmeera Singh, Advisor, International Office,
University of KwaZulu-Natal, South Africa

A worldwide phenomenon: Strategies and inspiration to address the challenges and opportunities for the new normal in the field of global higher education. I cannot recommend it highly enough.

Dr. Daisy Kee Mui Hung, Associate Professor,
Universiti Sains Malaysia, Malaysia

The movement of people across borders furthered the spread of Covid-19. This inevitably impacted international higher education, which although not reducible to student mobility is its primary form. *Global Higher Education during COVID-19: Policy, Society, and Technology* is therefore a timely edited collection that begins to unpack the multifaceted impact the pandemic has had on higher education worldwide. It adds to the growing conversation on reimagining higher education. The collection will be valuable to current and future scholars of higher education, offering an important snapshot of policy and practice during the pandemic.

Dr. Will Brehm, Lecturer of Education and International
Development, UCL Institute of Education, UK

With the COVID-19 crisis having upended higher education around the world, this timely book provides a deep and much-needed analysis of the roles and responsibilities of universities going forward. It sheds light not only on the shared challenges countries have faced, but also reveals how the impact of the pandemic has varied in important ways across countries.

Dr. Rajika Bhandari, Author/Advisor,
STAR Scholar Network, USA

Case studies provide valuable baseline information for practitioners of higher education as the world begins to emerge from the pandemic. A must-read for those looking to understand how various regions reacted, and how institutional systems changed their models to survive.

Dr. L. Amber Brugnoli, Assoc Vice-President and
Executive Director for Global Affairs
West Virginia University, USA

This book presents a comprehensive and rigorous worldwide account of Covid-19 impact, challenges and new opportunities. It stands out as a ground-breaking valuable companion for all those involved in the future of internationalization in higher education.

Dr. Elena de Prada Creo, Vice Dean for International Affairs
Facultad de CC. Empresariales y Turismo, Spain

The STAR Scholars Network Titles

We seek to explore new ideas and best practices related to international and comparative education from the US and around the world, and from a wide range of academic fields, including leadership studies, technology, general education, and area and cultural studies. STAR Scholars publishes some titles in collaboration with Routledge, Palgrave MacMillan, Open Journals in Education, Journal of International Students, and other university presses. At STAR Scholars Network, we aim to amplify the voices of underrepresented scholars, epistemologies, and perspectives. We are committed to an inclusion of a diversity of racial, ethnic, and cultural backgrounds and are particularly interested in proposals from scholars who identify with countries in the Global South.

We value linguistic diversity. Although many of the volumes that we publish are written in English, we welcome proposals in any language. More information at https://starscholars.org/open-access/

Recent Titles Include:

Cross-Cultural Narratives: Stories and Experiences of International Students
Edited by Ravichandran Ammigan

Delinking, Relinking, and Linking Writing and Rhetorics
By Marohang Limbu

Education in the Global Context: Exploring Contemporary Issues and Challenges COVID-19 and Higher
Edited by Ravichandran Ammigan, Roy Y. Chan, and Krishna Bista

Global Higher Education During COVID-19: Policy, Society, and Technology
Joshua S. McKeown, Krishna Bista, and *Roy Y. Chan*

Global Higher Education During COVID-19

Policy, Society, and Technology

Global Higher Education During COVID-19: Policy, Society, and Technology explores the impacts of the novel coronavirus (COVID-19) for institutions of higher education worldwide. Specifically, this book responds to the growing need for new insights and perspectives to improve higher education policy and practice in the era of COVID-19. The sub-theme that runs through this book concerns the changing roles and responsibilities of higher education leaders and the demand to rethink global higher education post-COVID. Topics in this book include: international student experiences, pedagogical innovations through technology, challenges to existing organizational cultures and societal roles, international academic relations, and shifting national policy implications for global higher education.

With the increasing threat of COVID-19 on all aspects of the global economy and workforce, this book serves as an opportunity for teacher-scholars, policymakers, and university administrators to reconsider and reimagine their work and the role of higher education in a global context. The ultimate goal of this book is to provide a critical reflection on the opportunities and challenges brought by COVID-19 and how tertiary education systems around the world learn from each other to address them.

Joshua S. McKeown, PhD, is Associate Provost for International Education & Programs at SUNY Oswego and International Education Leadership Fellow at the University at Albany, USA.

Krishna Bista, EdD, is Professor of Higher Education in the Department of Advanced Studies, Leadership and Policy at Morgan State University, Maryland, USA.

Roy Y. Chan, PhD, is Assistant Professor of Education and Director of the Doctor of Education (EdD) program in Leadership and Professional Practice in the Helen DeVos College of Education at Lee University, Tennessee, USA.

Global Higher Education During COVID-19

Policy, Society, and Technology

Editors
Joshua S. McKeown
Krishna Bista
Roy Y. Chan

STARSCHOLARS
N E T W O R K

★ STARSCHOLARS
N E T W O R K

First Published 2022
by
STAR Scholars
In collaboration with
Open Journals in Education and
Journal of International Students

Category
Education/Higher Education

Series
Comparative and International
Education

Typeset in Baskerville

Series Editor: Krishna Bista

Project Advisor: Chris Glass

Copy Editor
CodeMantra

Cover Design
Srdjan Marjanovic

Printed in the United States of America

Editors
Joshua S. McKeown | Krishna Bista |
Roy Y. Chan

ISBN: 978-1-7364699-6-5

© STAR Scholars

**Library of Congress Control
Number**: 2021943758

COVID-19 and Higher Education
in the Global Context: Exploring
Contemporary Issues and Challenges
Subject: Education/Higher Education –
United States | International
Education | Student Mobility |
Comparative Education
Krishna Bista (series editor)

Library of Congress US Programs,
Law, and Literature Division

Cataloging in Publication Program
101 Independence Avenue, S.E.
Washington, DC 20540-4283

In memory of those who lost their lives during the COVID-19 global pandemic (as of August 2021):

4.38 Million

And to the 204 million heroes worldwide who recovered from the disease.

Contents

Figures

Tables

Tables

Foreword

Yingyi Ma

COVID-19 is upending daily life, and its impact on global higher education (HE) is seismic. How to understand the impacts and improve policy and practice in the field of international HE during and post-COVID? Colleges and universities around the world are wondering about the above questions, and this book has provided a much-needed discussion for those questions.

The editors of this book have done a tremendous job in assembling a wide range of in-depth studies, both in terms of substantive topics and geographic regions. The topics range from the role of HE in society, crisis and innovation through technology in HE, international student experiences navigating the pandemic, national policies, international academic relations, public and private university responses, and the innovative engagement efforts of global HE institutions. Despite the expansive topics, various articles share the theme of exploring the traditional and changing roles of HE in society. Part I presents a few studies grounded in diverse national contexts that show how HE operates and adapts to society changed by the pandemic.

I commend the editors for their efforts to include a wide variety of contexts of HE institutions in different countries. While the impacts of COVID-19 on HE may be uncertain, what is certain is the increasing inequality among countries in dealing with the pandemic due to the unequal access to resources, technologies, and public health management. Part II in this book, in particular, focuses on the Global South (lower-income countries). The studies have shown the devastating impact on HE in countries of the global south due to the faltering economy during the pandemic as well as the incredible resilience of faculty and students in these countries to lessen the hardship through impressive innovations.

Technology-powered online education has been the quintessential innovation of 21st-century HE. Technology is liberating as much as limiting. COVID-19 has forced global HE to confront, leverage, and manage the power of technology to engage with students, experiment, and explore new pedagogy. The editors of this book have presented a wide range of empirically based studies in different HE settings to show that technology is indeed the double-edged sword, and it is incumbent on global HE leaders and educators to figure out innovative ways to use technology well, while fully recognizing and managing its limitations. Part III has been devoted to this theme.

This book is for anyone who is interested in HE in the global world, including but not limited to scholars, teachers, administrators, and students, and for any concerned citizens to reimagine and redesign the global HE in a new era.

Bio

Yingyi Ma is an Associate Professor of Sociology and Director of Asian/Asian American Studies. She is the Provost Faculty Fellow on internationalization at Syracuse University (New York), carrying the term between 2020 and 2022, where she leads and supports culturally responsive pedagogy and programs for international education and partnership. She received her Ph.D. in sociology from Johns Hopkins University in 2007. Ma's research addresses education and migration in the U.S. and China and she has published about 30 peer-reviewed articles and book chapters, in addition to books. She is the author of *Ambitious and Anxious: How Chinese College Students Succeed and Struggle in American Higher Education* (Columbia University Press, 2021). This book has won multiple awards from the Comparative and International Education Association and has been featured in national and international news media such as *The Washington Post* and *Times Higher Education*. She is the co-editor of *Understanding International Students from Asia in American Universities: Learning and Living Globalization* (2017), which has won the honorable mention of the Best Book Award from the Comparative and International Education Association's Study Abroad and International Students Section.

E-mail: yma03@syr.edu

Acknowledgments

We are most grateful to colleagues at the STAR Scholars Network. We also appreciate the support of colleagues with whom we have worked over the years at the Open Journals in Education, a consortium of the professional journals, the Comparative and International Education Society's Study Abroad and International Students SIG, and the *Journal of International Students*.

We would also like to acknowledge the help of all the scholars who were involved in this project and, more specifically, to the authors and reviewers that took part in the review process. Without their support, this book would not have become a reality. At Morgan State University, Dr. Bista would like to thank his colleagues for their encouragement and support including graduate students and graduate assistants in the Department of Advanced Studies, Leadership and Policy. At Lee University, Dr. Chan would like to thank his Ed.D. students for their comments and feedback in this project.

Special thanks to the following reviewers who assisted us in reviewing manuscripts received for this book. It would not have been possible to finalize the selected chapters without their evaluations and constructive feedback.

List of Chapter Reviewers

Adam Thomas Grimm, Michigan State University, U.S.A.
Amit Mittal, Chitkara University, India
Andrea Shelton, Texas Southern University, U.S.A.
Antony Kinyua, South Eastern Kenya University, Kenya
Chris Glass, Boston College Center for International Higher Education, U.S.A.
Crystal Green, University of California, Los Angeles, U.S.A.
Dewi Kurniawati, Universitas Islam Neger, Indonesia
Elizabeth Buckner, University of Toronto, Canada
Joshua S. McKeown, State University of New York at Albany, U.S.A.
Krishna Bista, Morgan State University, U.S.A.
Louisa Hill, University of Leeds, United Kingdom
Mary McConer, Christian Brothers University, U.S.A.
Melisa Valentin, University of Louisiana Monroe, U.S.A.
Mercedes Mareque, University of Vigo, Spain
Mingxuan Liang, Al Afaaq School, Abu Dhabi, United Arab Emirates

Norah Almusharraf, Prince Sultan University, Saudi Arabia
Ramashego Mphahlele, University of South Africa, South Africa
Ravichandran Ammigan, University of Delaware, U.S.A.
Roy Y. Chan, Lee University, U.S.A.
Ryan Allen, Chapman University, U.S.A.
Shawn Conner-Rondot, Indiana University, U.S.A.
Siyin Liang, University of Regina, Canada
Suvas Chandra Ghimire, Tribhuvan University, Nepal
Yang Liu, University of Maryland, U.S.A.
Yingyi Ma, Syracuse University, U.S.A.
Yuko Ida, University of Hawai'i at Mānoa, U.S.A.
   We would like to thank the following colleagues for their feedback on the
early draft of this book as well for their endorsements:

- Dr. Daisy Kee Mui Hung, Associate Professor, Universiti Sains Malaysia,
  Malaysia
- Dr. Elena de Prada Creo, Vice Dean for International Affairs, Facultad
  de CC. Empresariales y Turismo, Spain
- Dr. Hiep Pham, Director, Center for Research and Practice on Education,
  Phu Xuan University, Vietnam
- Dr. KS Adeyemo, Senior Lecturer, University of Pretoria, South Africa
- Dr. L. Amber Brugnoli, Associate Vice-President and Executive Director
  for Global Affairs, West Virginia University, USA
- Dr. Misty So-Sum Wai-Cook, Centre for English Language Studies,
  National University of Singapore
- Dr. Rajika Bhandari, Author/Advisor, STAR Scholar Network, USA
- Dr. Tasmeera Singh, Advisor, International Office, University of
  KwaZulu-Natal, South Africa
- Dr. Will Brehm, Lecturer of Education and International Development,
  UCL Institute of Education, UK

Editors

Joshua S. McKeown, PhD, is Associate Provost for International Education & Programs at SUNY Oswego and International Education Leadership Fellow at the University at Albany (SUNY). Under his leadership SUNY Oswego has earned national awards for international education from the American Association of State Colleges & Universities (AASCU), the Institute of International Education (IIE), Diversity Abroad, and achieved multiple top rankings in the annual Open Doors survey for education abroad enrollment. McKeown is a scholar-practitioner who authored *The First Time Effect: The Impact of Study Abroad on College Student Intellectual Development* (SUNY Press, 2009), several book chapters including *Education Abroad: Bridging Scholarship and Practice* (Routledge, 2021) and NAFSA's *Guide to Education Abroad* (NAFSA, 2014), and numerous articles and presentations worldwide including in the *Journal of Contemporary China*. He was a Fulbright-Nehru International Education Administrators recipient for India, a mentor with the IIE's Connecting with the World Myanmar program, and has served professional organizations like the Forum on Education Abroad, CAPA, and Phi Beta Delta Honor Society for International Scholars. He holds a Ph.D. and bachelor's from Syracuse University, master's from Clarkson University, and teaches in the undergraduate Global & International Studies program at SUNY Oswego and the graduate program in International Education Management & Leadership (IEML) at UAlbany. E-mail: joshua.mckeown@oswego.edu

Krishna Bista, EdD, is Vice President of the STAR Scholars Network and a Professor of Higher Education in the Department of Advanced Studies, Leadership, and Policy at Morgan State University, Maryland. Dr. Bista is the Founding Editor of the *Journal of International Students*. His research interests include comparative and international higher education issues, global student mobility, and innovative technology in teaching and learning. His recent books include *Online Teaching and Learning in Higher Education* (Routledge, w/Chan and Allen), *Global Perspectives on International Student Experiences* (Routledge), *Higher Education in Nepal* (Routledge, w/Raby and Sharma), *Rethinking Education Across Border* (Springer, w/Gaulee & Sharma), and *Inequalities in Study and Student Mobility* (Routledge, w/Kommers).

Dr. Bista serves on the editorial review boards for *Kappa Delta Pi Record, Teachers College Record, Journal of Leadership and Organizational Studies,* and *International Journal of Leadership in Education.* Dr. Bista has organized more than 70 professional development workshops on a variety of topics related to college student experience, international student/faculty mobility, internationalization and exchange programs, and cross-cultural studies; he has published 15 books, and more than 80 articles, book chapters, and review essays. He is the founding Chair of the Comparative and International Educational Society (CIES) Study Abroad and International Students SIG and the editor of the Routledge Global Student Mobility Series. Previously, Dr. Bista served as the director of Global Education at the University of Louisiana at Monroe, where he was also Chase Endowed Professor of Education in the School of Education. He holds a doctoral degree in Educational Leadership/Higher Education, a specialist degree in Community College Teaching and Administration, both from Arkansas State University, an M.S. in Postsecondary Education/Higher Education from Troy University, Alabama. E-mail: krishna.bista@morgan.edu

Roy Y. Chan, PhD, is Assistant Professor of Education & Director of the Doctorate of Education (Ed.D.) program in Leadership and Professional Practice in the Helen DeVos College of Education at Lee University. Previously, Dr. Chan served as the Director of TRIO Student Support Services (SSS), where he managed a budget of $1.3 million funded by the U.S. Department of Education. His research interests include cross-border and transnational higher education, study abroad, global education policy, and educational philanthropy. Dr. Chan currently serves as Chair-Elect of the Comparative and International Education Society (CIES) Study Abroad and International Students (SAIS) Special Interest Group, and previously served as an advisor to the Forum on Education Abroad's Data Committee. His latest books include *Online Teaching and Learning in Higher Education during COVID-19: International Perspectives and Experiences* (Routledge, 2021), *The Future of Accessibility in International Higher Education* (IGI Global, 2017), and *Higher Education: A Worldwide Inventory of Research Centers, Academic Programs, Journals and Publications* (Lemmens Media, 2014). Dr. Chan holds a Ph.D. in History, Philosophy, and Policy in Education from Indiana University Bloomington, an M.A. in Higher Education Administration from Boston College, an M.Ed. in Comparative Higher Education from The University of Hong Kong, and a B.A. from the University of California, Irvine. E-mail: rchan@leeuniversity.edu

1 COVID-19 and Higher Education

Challenges and Successes during the Global Pandemic

Joshua S. McKeown, Krishna Bista, and Roy Y. Chan

Abstract

This introductory chapter identifies attempts by scholars and practitioners worldwide to analyze and present responses to the global COVID-19 pandemic by higher education institutions (HEIs). In addition to initial reactions to the crisis, there are important new insights and perspectives on how to improve higher education policy and practice in the era of COVID-19. Specifically, this chapter gives an overview of the book and draws an outline of the impacts of the pandemic on teaching and learning, institutional leadership, and the transformation of society through technology in the field of comparative and international higher education. We highlight institutional responses within national frameworks, the diverse and not always apparent roles played by HEIs that COVID-19 revealed, the existential threat the pandemic presents to many HEIs particularly in the Global South (lower-income countries), and the challenges and opportunities for new programs, policies, and systems that best utilize resources to align with national needs, institutional priorities, and student learning and well-being.

Keywords

International students, student mobility, higher education, global pandemic, higher education policy

Introduction

In this book, scholars and practitioners of international education have made an attempt to explore the impacts of the novel coronavirus (COVID-19) on global higher education. Specifically, this book responds to the growing need for analysis of the ways COVID-19 has impacted higher education institutions (HEIs), students, and faculty while also pointing in the direction of new insights and perspectives to improve student mobility, higher education organization and administration, and government policies and institutional practices in the era of COVID-19. The sub-theme that runs through this book concerns the changing roles and responsibilities of HEIs in societies upended by the pandemic, and how international education leaders can respond to the new educational environment. Topics in this volume include national policies and international academic relations, international student experiences, HEIs in society, crisis and innovation, public and private university responses, and how HEIs globally found new ways to engage with students through available technology.

As HEIs around the world shut down normal operations following the World Health Organization's (WHO) declaration of a pandemic in March 2020, what followed varied widely based on several factors. For some, it was an urgent but fairly orderly transitional process reflecting the resource and policy environments within states that were more adept at crisis response, including having dealt with disease outbreaks before. University sectors elsewhere, particularly societies with divisions and disparities due to region, privilege, and access, faced more existential challenges. The role of technology has been especially important. To some degree technology was the common denominator for HEIs in all parts of the world, as abrupt transitions to remote teaching occurred regardless of readiness or resources (Chan et al., 2021). In some societies, particularly those with better technology, literacy and infrastructure, the pandemic allowed healthy experimentation and advances to occur including those pushed along that may have been waiting for the right moment. In other places, however, the gap in technology access and usefulness rendered higher education delivery severely curtailed.

Similarly, the way HEIs organize themselves around concepts of shared governance, faculty freedoms and privileged positions, and private vs. public sector revealed much about how organizational and structural assumptions made pre-pandemic were not able to hold up during COVID-19. Rapid and unexpected changes demanded responses that existing higher education often could not easily accomplish, such as student needs for curricular flexibilities, training in learning management systems (LMS), and stability in a markedly disrupted employment environment that impacted students' ability to remain in class. Private HEIs, whose very need was often to fill existing gaps in the equitable distribution of higher education access, suffered particularly because of tuition revenue loss, underlying their lack of state support despite recent growth.

Finally, it became clear during the pandemic that HEIs around the world hold prominent places in their societies and that, as COVID-19 forced them to close, the absence of them and the roles they had come to play meant disruptions beyond merely teaching and learning. Communities who looked to HEIs for information and resource dissemination did not always get it; societies that relied on higher education not only to educate youth but also to instill values and social norms faced uncertainty in that assumed process; students who had previously felt marginalized and discriminated against felt that intensity grow, often fueled by racist rhetoric and distrust of outsiders; and academic relations between states came under new pressure and scrutiny as the pandemic made previously strained international relations harsher and more tense, with HEIs suffering state-imposed restrictions borne of broader suspicions.

Crisis and Opportunity for Post-Pandemic Global Higher Education

The COVID-19 pandemic has taught many lessons to reassess pedagogical tools and organizational resources, to re-evaluate approaches and perceptions of human organization and communication, and other lessons focused on how best to foster teaching and learning in unprecedented times of unimaginable disruption and stress. It has also provided an opportunity to test the possibility of developing new innovative tools and technologies to bridge the gap between existing and new paradigms of learning (Chan et al., 2021). For global higher education as a whole and international education, in particular, there is a need to explore new ways of virtual learning and exchange programs as well as inclusive programs and resources for post-pandemic learning. Recent surveys indicate "ever-deepening anxiety among higher education leaders about the future of international education and exchange" (Glass et al., 2021, p. 2), due to the steady decline in enrollments for some institutions and the global pandemic lockdown for over a year. This has prompted calls from policymakers and institutional thought-leaders to develop national policies to address what has become a global crisis.

However, despite the COVID-19-induced crisis in global higher education, kernels of evidence suggest that the sector is moving into a new era. The profound changes and reactions to the crisis do not mean that international education is irrevocably harmed. Rather, students, faculty, and HEIs have shown resilience, pivoting quickly and necessarily towards new models of delivery and focus, demonstrating that the sector will survive and even thrive with adaptability to these new circumstances. The ways that the sector and its stakeholders have responded to such a widespread global calamity reflect the combined wisdom and experience based on what had been built before and will guide actions towards the next growth era in global higher education.

Organization of the Book: Themes and Issues

This volume is organized into three parts. The contributors in the **first part** examine the role HEIs have played in their societies before and during COVID-19, and look to new roles beyond it. The pandemic, in some instances, altered those roles due to political constraints; in other instances, it highlighted opportunities to amplify traditional educational roles, as well as larger ones in service to society as a whole; and invariably these chapters portray global higher education as always residing within distinct policy environments. Indeed taken together, these first chapters illuminate the balanced and nuanced situation in which global higher education often finds itself, on the one hand, a conveyor of national interests and priorities while on the other hand embedded in particular communities who have needs, sometimes urgent ones, that defy overly narrow organizational definitions. Experiences of HEIs vary based on where they are located and within what national frameworks they reside, but they have in common the expectation to fulfill vital societal functions that may not have always been associated with core higher education activities, all the while trying to fulfill their core functions of research and developing students to their fullest potential. Finally, higher education during COVID-19 was often caught in the frenzy of border closures and international entanglements between powerful states, lacking predictable cross-border educational movements and those free from rancorous and antagonistic rhetoric.

In the introductory chapter, *Joshua S. McKeown, Krishna Bista,* and *Roy Y. Chan* provide an overview and framing of the book and respond to the growing need for new insights and perspectives to identify and improve policies and implementation of global higher education in the era of COVID-19. In Chapter 2, *Eric W. Layman* and *Lev Nachman* present the case of Taiwan as an exemplary model for how HEIs can operate within a society organized overall to plan and execute in a predictable and stable manner despite COVID-19, and suggest that significant soft power advantages flow from this position in general, and for Taiwan in particular given its location, cultural traditions, and at this moment in history. In Chapter 3, *Kelber Tozini, Claudia Schiedeck Soares de Souza, Fernanda Leal,* and *Bernardo Sfredo Miorando* discuss the important societal role universities play in Brazil, in addition to traditional academic roles, and how COVID-19 altered the social fabric thereby highlighting both the recent political challenges universities face as well as the importance of outreach and service to the communities where they are located. In Chapter 4, *Li Wang* portrays the delicate and purposeful roles that universities in China have towards developing both intellectual talent and social cohesion, and how this was able to be harnessed productively during the pandemic in ways that represent both the traditions of Chinese higher education and also the values embedded in how a large nation approached this great challenge. In Chapter 5, *Joshua S. McKeown* analyzes the complex and enduring academic relationship between China and the United States that was under strain before COVID-19 and worsened during the pandemic; ways forward are discussed to preserve what is essential about the international academic exchange between the world's two largest economies while encouraging sustainable and realistic approaches to avoid an unnecessary "new Cold War" of academic decoupling.

In the **second part**, the contributors look into what became existential threats to particular higher education sectors resulting from the COVID-19 pandemic, with an emphasis on the Global South (lower-income countries). National policies impacting global higher education reveal great disparities around the world due to inequities in state funding for public institutions, the inability for private institutions to withstand COVID-induced tuition volatility, and the necessary innovations required by some HEIs in the face of the unprecedented challenge. In Chapter 6, *Caroline S. Wekullo, John O. Shiundu, James B. Ouda,* and *Anthony Mutevane* discuss how Kenya had demonstrated respectable economic growth and improvements in overall quality of life prior to COVID-19; however, the pandemic revealed an incomplete and unequal path in the development of Kenyan higher education; universities' lack of distance learning and other pedagogical resources were made apparent requiring considerable investment in and development of the higher education sector going forward. In Chapter 7, *Benny Lim* analyzes the private university sector in Malaysia that, as in many developing countries, has a vital role in expanding higher education opportunities in a growing and diverse nation, but that is uniquely susceptible to tuition-driven crises as the economy faltered during the pandemic, amplifying ethnic inequalities in higher education access there. In Chapter 8, *Samuel Adeyanju, Oluwatoyin Ajilore, Oluwafemi Ogunlalu, Alex Onatunji*, and *Emmanuel Mogaji* outline the existential threat to many Nigerian universities as a result of COVID-19, particularly due to severe deficits in funding and capacity revealed during the outbreak's aftermath; to face this challenge, impressive innovations to lessen the worst of these hardships point to new directions for HEIs in Nigeria.

The **third part** of the book includes four chapters where contributors examine institutional policies, resources, technology priorities, and critical examinations of campus racial climate for international students moving forward in the post-pandemic world. In Chapter 9, *David Edens* and *Emily Kiresich* examined the abrupt transition to remote learning in the United States as the COVID-19 pandemic hit; faculty-student engagement was key to student satisfaction and success in the new technology-mediated environment, but the slow pace of decision-making and other cultural aspects typical of U.S. campuses hindered an optimal transition. In Chapter 10, *Xi Lin, Mingyu Huang*, and *Qingchuan Zhang* examine the considerable risks and uncertainties associated with implementing LMS for distance learning, and the importance of building community and support structures for students with differing abilities and comfort level with new technology. In Chapter 11, *Kim Manturuk* and *Grey Reavis* highlight implications for policy and practice that improve student learning outcomes and support more flexible pedagogy, with the goal to create more resilient learning environments in the future as faculty and students interact through new technologies. Finally, in Chapter 12, *Wu Xie* and *Musbah Shaheen* remind us that the COVID-19 pandemic did not impact all students and scholars equally and that while it may not have created campus and national problems of race and division, it tended to exacerbate and intensify those problems particularly on issues of perceived "foreignness" of some and not others.

Moving Forward

International student mobility is at the center of a growing and diversifying global higher education discourse, particularly its directions in the post-pandemic world. National and institutional leaders are worried about physical mobility since COVID-19 paused the entire world for so long, and came immediately after a period of declining growth in international education, declining support for international trade and institutions, and in general a less liberal, more nationalistic mindset in many parts of the world. Meanwhile, the pandemic has taught great lessons to educators and students that point global higher education towards new directions in areas of policy, societal impact, and technology, as well as fair, equitable, and sustainable ways to deliver higher education that may have existed pre-pandemic but have become catalyzed as essential during it and beyond.

It is time to focus on those collaborative responses to the COVID-19 pandemic that improve new environments and initiatives for global learning; the time to focus on internationalization at home; the time to expand inclusive and equitable study abroad; the time to empower and incentivize both faculty and students in designing new international initiatives; and the time to create a humane world that focuses on diversity, equity, and inclusion, one that embraces the voices of underrepresented students and scholars for sustainable excellence and growth for all.

In response to the disruptions caused by COVID-19, the editors and contributors in this book have identified examples from around the world that are worthy of collective reflection on best practices, brought forward a thought-provoking discussion of perspectives and initiatives for scholars and policymakers, and provided university administrators new tools and approaches that can be adopted to improve and enhance global higher education. In this book, the contributors have made an attempt to offer clarity and a new direction for the field. It is anticipated that the insights resulting from this volume will engage scholars, researchers, teachers, policymakers, and practitioners in a discussion reimagining the opportunities and frameworks to facilitate global learning, intercultural communication, and innovative international initiatives during and following COVID-19. The ultimate goal of this book is to provide a critical reflection on the opportunities and challenges for internationalization, and how HEIs and tertiary education systems around the world learn from each other to address the new challenges brought on, but not necessarily created by, COVID-19. A more critical and purposeful conversation around the discourse of global higher education is urgently needed now, and this volume seeks to make an important contribution.

References

Chan, R. Y., Bista, K., & Allen, R. M. (2021). *Online teaching and learning in higher education during COVID-19: International perspectives and experiences.* Routledge.

Glass, R. C., Godwin, K. A., & Helms, R. M. (2021). *Toward greater inclusion and success: A new compact for international students.* American Council on Education.

World Health Organization (WHO). https://covid19.who.int/

Bios

Joshua S. McKeown, Ph.D. is Associate Provost for International Education & Programs at SUNY Oswego and International Education Leadership Fellow at the State University of New York (SUNY) at Albany.

Under his leadership SUNY Oswego has earned awards for international education from the American Association of State Colleges & Universities (AASCU), the Institute of International Education (IIE), Diversity Abroad, the Chinese Service Center for Scholarly Exchange (CSCSE), and achieved top rankings in the annual Open Doors survey for education abroad enrollment and for student Fulbright awards. McKeown is a scholar-practitioner who authored *The First Time Effect: The Impact of Study Abroad on College Student Intellectual Development* (SUNY Press, 2009), several book chapters including in *Education Abroad: Bridging Scholarship and Practice* (Routledge, 2021) and NAFSA's *Guide to Education Abroad* (NAFSA, 2014), and numerous articles and presentations worldwide including in the *Journal of Contemporary China*. E-mail: joshua.mckeown@oswego.edu

Krishna Bista, Ed.D. is Professor of Higher Education in the Department of Advanced Studies, Leadership and Policy at Morgan State University, Maryland. Dr. Bista is the founding editor of the *Journal of International Students*, a quarterly publication in international education. His latest books include *Higher Education in Nepal* (Routledge, 2020), and *Global Perspectives on International Experiences in Higher Education: Tensions and Issues* (Routledge, 2019). He holds a master's degree from Troy University, a doctoral degree in educational leadership/higher education, and a specialist degree in community college teaching and administration from Arkansas State University. E-mail: krishna.bista@morgan.edu

Roy Y. Chan, Ph.D. is Assistant Professor of Education and Director of the Doctor of Education (Ed.D.) program in Leadership and Professional Practice in the Helen DeVos College of Education at Lee University, Tennessee. Previously, he served as the Director of TRIO Student Support Services (SSS). His latest books include *Online Teaching and Learning in Higher Education during COVID-19: International Perspectives and Experiences* (Routledge, 2021), *The Future of Accessibility in International Higher Education* (IGI Global, 2017), and *Higher Education: A Worldwide Inventory of Research Centers, Academic Programs, Journals and Publications* (Lemmens Media, 2014). Dr. Chan holds a Ph.D. in History, Philosophy, and Policy in Education from Indiana University Bloomington, an M.A. in Higher Education Administration from Boston College, an M.Ed. in Comparative Higher Education from The University of Hong Kong, and a B.A. from the University of California, Irvine. E-mail: rchan@leeuniversity.edu

Part I

Roles of Higher Education Institutions in Societies

2 Taiwan's COVID-19 Success

A Lifeline for Its Higher Education Sector?

Eric W. Layman and Lev Nachman

Abstract

Taiwan's success in preventing and containing the COVID-19 outbreak within its borders has drawn unprecedented international attention and recognition. This achievement presents many important prospects for Taiwan to counter escalating diplomatic isolation from the increasingly hardline governance of China's Xi Jinping. Taiwan's feat in crisis management also opens a critical window of opportunity to increase mutual cooperation with the international community. Particularly with regard to Taiwan's higher education sector, this is a moment not to be missed. Taiwan's universities are facing seemingly insurmountable obstacles in the coming decade as university student populations are expected to drop by 40%, due in part to Taiwan's declining birth rate. This chapter explores the potential for Taiwan to capitalize on its COVID-19 success by attracting students internationally to strengthen its higher education sector and thereby further bolster its reputation and prestige in the global community.

Keywords

COVID-19, Taiwan, Higher Education Sector, Soft Power

Introduction

Taiwan's university sector is in a crisis. Registration across the country is plummeting, partially due to low birth rates and smaller cohorts (Green, 2020), and because university degrees are overabundant and therefore becoming less valuable. Even as this downward trend seems to continue, a potential reversal has begun to show. One of the most unexpected side effects of the COVID-19 pandemic is the renewed position of Taiwan's education system within East Asia and beyond. Taiwan is one of the only places in the world to successfully manage COVID-19 due to a combination of robust institutions, historic learning from earlier pandemics, and a civil society that cooperated with government mandates (Aspinwall, 2020). Taiwan has boasted such success with fighting COVID-19 that it has begun to export its assistance programs around the world, donating millions of masks and policy strategies to countries in need (Woods, 2020). Most importantly, Taiwan's education system remains intact and is one of the only systems to have fully in-person classes in 2020, both with regard to K-12 education and in the higher education sector (Taylor et al., 2020). Increasing tensions between Washington and Beijing have also further solidified Taiwan's position as a Mandarin education hub (Lim, 2020). Contentious attitudes between the U.S. and the People's Republic of China (PRC) have made Taiwan a more attractive and feasible option for Mandarin language learners instead of going to China. COVID-19 has unexpectedly given Taiwan a strong soft power boost that carries a number of important implications for both its education system at home and abroad (Hernandez & Horton, 2020). Could this COVID-19 success story serve as a much-needed boost for Taiwan's institutions of higher education that are suffering at a tragic nexus point of decades of over-expansion coupled with one of the lowest birthrates in the world? This chapter will explore how Taiwan managed to fight against COVID-19 successfully, and the potential it has to help its hurting higher education sector if capitalized upon in due fashion.

Taiwan's Imperiled Higher Education Sector

Taiwan's higher education sector has not always been a source of concern, but two decades of policy missteps at the confluence of a number of growing forces have given rise to an impending alarm that current trends are unsustainable and will result in the closure of many institutions, departments, and programs. Historically, Taiwan's higher education sector has been an invaluable asset in furthering economic growth and aiding vast portions of Taiwan's populace to contribute to its world-class technological sector (Lin, 2004; Liu & Armer, 1993). Taiwan's near-total enrollment rate in higher education is one of the highest in the world, perhaps only rivaled by South Korea (Chou, 2014). However, this nearly universal level of post-secondary school attendance has not resulted in universal benefit for Taiwan's society, and the high level of enrollment has mostly favored the already privileged groups (Chou & Wang, 2012). The benefits of a university degree are relegated primarily to more prestigious university placements (Cheng & Jacob, 2012; Pretzer-Lin, 2015). As such, the expansion of access to higher education has also resulted in an expansion of social inequality (Smith et al., 2016) and decreased social mobility (Lin, 2020). The overabundance of university degrees has unsurprisingly led to inflation in the value of university credentials thereby decreasing their worth (Chan & Lin, 2015). Therefore, the crisis faced by the higher education sector is not one that can be blamed simply on Taiwanese families' lack of progeny but is an inevitable result of growth that was overextended, to begin with.

There were contextual factors that contributed to this misguided policy trajectory. Taiwan's rapid expansion of universities in the 1990s was arguably a reaction to the heavily centralized control of Taiwan's higher education sector over many decades of the Chinese Nationalist Party, *Kuomintang* (KMT) rule (Wu et al., 1989). Taiwan's birth rate began declining alongside government policies to rapidly expand university placements. (Huang et al., 2018). Between 1994 and 2004, there was a 44% increase in the number of universities, growing from 67 to 151 (Tsai, 2015). In 2006, the number of universities peaked at 163 (Chen, 2015). Enrollment peaked in 2012 at approximately 1.35 million university students, numbers have been in consistent decline with 2018 numbers at 1.24 million (MOE Taiwan, 2019). Taiwan's hunger for democratization and equity of opportunity therefore fed into the assumptions that higher education credentials were the sole means of individual and collective prosperity. A newly formed, democratically accountable government simply had no choice but to acquiesce to this popular and, at face value, entirely reasonable demand.

However, the myth of universal higher education leading to universal benefit was soon exposed. Taiwan's rapid massification of university placements occurred mainly in the private sector (Chou & Ho, 2007), and now the government is looking at ways to systematically shut down excess private universities (Maxon, 2018). Course cancelations among private universities have been especially severe in the technical and vocational training colleges (Drillsma, 2018). The overall population of college age students is expected to drop by 40% by 2028 due to the declining birth rate, and plans are in place to help close failing institutions of education as well as help students transition from those institutions (The Straits Times, 2017). Therefore, those who have benefitted the most from access to higher education are those who have been able to secure placements in public institutions of higher learning, while those who were forced to pay more for inferior private higher education slots are now the ones also most threatened as the higher education crisis begins to crescendo.

Although Taiwan's higher education has been on a continual quest to bring its universities to world-class status (Zhou & Ching, 2012), there have been additional factors complicating their ambitious goals. The problems due to the declining birthrate are exacerbated by the increased flow of students to universities in China (Fulco, 2018b). China has introduced attractive incentives for both students and academics to migrate to China's higher education sector, while conversely Taiwan and China have *both* instituted measures to restrict those able to come to Taiwan *from* China (Hsueh, 2018). Taiwan's university students are not only headed to China but many other places as well. In 2018, more than 40,000 students were studying at universities overseas, with the United States as the top destination attracting nearly a third of all Taiwanese students heading abroad (Li, 2020). Therefore, Taiwan's higher education sector has not only been drained by overexpansion and declining population but also through a plethora of enticements abroad that have given their own students many incentives to pursue higher education elsewhere.

Taiwan's COVID-19 Success

Taiwan's shortcomings in higher education policy stand in sharp contrast to its policy victories in containing the COVID-19 epidemic within its borders.

At the height of the pandemic elsewhere in July 2020, Taiwan had seen a total of only 449 cases, with only seven deaths and the majority of cases imported from Taiwanese returning after traveling abroad (Rowen, 2020). While there was some alarm in January 2020, daily life returned to normal as early as late February, with only a few alterations, such as required mask use on public transportation. By the *end* of 2020, Taiwan *still* had less than 800 reported cases totally since the pandemic's onset, *still* only seven deaths, and had reached over *200* days without a single local infection. Taiwan's ability to swiftly and effectively mitigate harms from COVID-19 can be attributed to a number of important factors, but three key variables are its robust public healthcare system, historic memory of the 2003 SARS pandemic, and good governance.

Taiwan's strong public healthcare system is an indispensable factor in considering its COVID-19 success. Taiwan has a population comparable to Australia and stands 23rd among the highest GDP growth rate countries in the world (Horton, 2018). Taiwan is one of the most progressive democracies in East Asia despite constant threats by the PRC. One of the key features of Taiwan's democratic development has been its comprehensive and advanced healthcare system. Established in 1995, it is a government-administered insurance-based healthcare system. It gives every Taiwanese citizen and residency cardholder access to healthcare. Individual costs are low, access is high, and coverage is widespread. This system is not cheap, and it is one of the biggest challenges that Taiwan faces with its healthcare professionals being overburdened coupled with high taxes (Leong, 2018). Yet despite these weaknesses, Taiwan was ranked as the number one healthcare system in the world for two years consecutively by the Health Care Index (Yeh, 2020).

Taiwan's healthcare system and governmental capacity were put under a stress test during the 2003 SARS crisis. In Taiwan, SARS had a far higher mortality rate than COVID-19 and resulted in 73 deaths. Some of the strategies Taiwan used in 2002 were demonstrated in their 2019 response to COVID-19. For example, in 2002 the government ordered an immediate ban on mask exports in order to ensure enough domestic supply, a tactic that was repeated again in 2019. Of course, not all of the government's handling in 2002 was laudable, and many hard lessons related to hospital management and isolation control were partially responsible for the relatively higher mortality rate (Chen et al., 2005). However, not only did SARS give Taiwan an established pandemic response policy but also the man who designed the policy, Chen Chien-Jen, who was Taiwan's Vice President during the time of the COVID-19 outbreak. Chen, a Johns Hopkins trained epidemiologist, served as one of the health officials in charge of the SARS response. After SARS, he was responsible for pushing reforms to prepare Taiwan for its next pandemic. Despite a relatively quiet career as Vice President, his last six months in office put his expertise to use, cementing his name as a politician who helped navigate Taiwan through two perilous pandemics.

The good governance practices developed by politicians such as Chen extend far beyond just mask regulation. As soon as Taiwan got a whiff of a potential quick-spreading virus in Wuhan, China, the current administration began to take drastic actions to minimize domestic exposure. On January 20th, 2020 Taiwan established a Central Epidemic Command Center (CECC). Flights from hard-hit countries were quickly banned, including China and soon after Japan and Hong Kong. Mandatory two-week isolations became required for *all* persons entering Taiwan, without exception. Taiwan required those in quarantine to regularly monitor and record their temperature and used cell phone towers to keep track of locations to ensure they stuck to quarantine. The Taiwanese government also sent care packages to everyone in quarantine, including practical items such as food and free Netflix passes. For those outside of quarantine, masks became required in public transportation. Most public businesses and restaurants were sent wireless thermometers to take everyone's temperature upon entry and identify anyone with a potential fever. Early on, mask and sanitizing alcohol productions were vastly expanded. Although the Taiwanese government regulated mask distribution at the outset in order to ensure a safe quantity, its boost in mask production soon became strong enough that mask control was lessened. In early January, Taiwan was already making 1.9 million masks a day, and by April it was making 15 million masks per day. By the end of March, these good governance approaches led to public approval for the CECC at almost 80% and approval for the president at 75% (Rowen, 2020).

Despite not being formally recognized as a country, Taiwan handled its response to COVID-19 arguably on par with, if not better than, the world's most developed sovereign states. The statistics speak for themselves; no other country can boast of the kind of low exposure or effective governmental response. Taiwan's success has not gone unnoticed. For the first time in decades, Taiwan began to pop up in media headlines as a COVID-19 success story, a positive, non-militarized framing of Taiwan rarely seen. The Taiwanese government has tried its best to capitalize on the good publicity to further Taiwan's normalization within the global order. "Mask Diplomacy" was a program started by the Taiwan government to send millions of masks abroad and resulted in dozens of countries making formal statements thanking Taiwan for their assistance (Woods, 2020). Countries have begun to see Taiwan in a new light, not as a military flashpoint, but as a contributing member to an imperiled global community that needs help fighting a horrible disease.

COVID-19 Success and Possibilities for Aiding Higher Education Sector

Taiwan was looking abroad for help with its higher education woes long before the COVID-19 pandemic. International integration and fostering of global consciousness have been primary drivers for higher education reform in Taiwan for many years (Law, 2004). The "internationalization" of Taiwan's university campuses has already been a chief goal of the Department of Higher Education (MOE Taiwan, 2012). In 2007, there were only about 18,000 international students enrolled in Taiwan universities (Chou, 2015). There have been attractive subsidies to encourage the enrollment of international students (MOE Taiwan, 2013) and a goal for 2020 to have 150,000 international students (Magaziner, 2016). Taiwan universities have been actively recruiting from the Philippines (NSYSU, 2018), and other Southeast Asian nations (DeAeth, 2019), as part of its "Southbound Policy," which seeks to offset Taiwan's bipolar reliance on either China or the US (MOFA, 2016). This policy has not been without incident, as there was an accusation of racism when students from these countries were touted as ideal for undesirable manual labor (Green, 2020). Despite this minor setback, a survey at the end of the 2020 school year indicated that 83.6% of departing international students wished to remain in Taiwan if given the opportunity, a figure up more than 10% from when the survey was conducted two years ago. More than 130,000 international students were registered in institutions of higher learning in Taiwan during the 2019–2020 school year and they indicated that the biggest factors influencing their desire to continue in Taiwan were the "safe and free environment" and the high standards of healthcare (Chen & Chiang, 2020a).

Taiwan's success in handling COVID has already begun to be marketed as a reason to make it a destination for study (Study in Taiwan, 2020). The United States, the most popular destination for Taiwanese university students (Li, 2020), will see a decline in foreign student numbers (Anderson, 2020) due in part to COVID difficulties and also capricious government policies threatening the visa status of international students (Joung & Rosenthal, 2020; Treisman, 2020). Attracting and enrolling international students in most countries during the COVID-19 pandemic is arguably and fundamentally an unethical endeavor (Mason, 2020), but one that Taiwan can face with confidence and a clear conscience knowing that its universities are housed within a public health infrastructure that is capable of protecting visitors, as well as its population. In recognition of Taiwan's unmatched success, Antipodean nations are considering a mutual COVID-19 "travel bubble" (Brady, 2020; Smith, 2020) despite concerns that lauding Taiwan's success may incur the disapprobation of Beijing (Reuters, 2020). Similar preferential treatment could become normalized in the near future from countries wanting their students to have an international experience while simultaneously ensuring their access to quality healthcare.

Nye (2004) has written on the importance of "soft power" as the ability of a nation to achieve influence through "attraction" rather than coercion, and he and others have since argued that soft power and international exchange through higher education are interlinked (Li, 2018; Nye, n.d.) Taiwan would do well to consider joining other East Asian nations such as Japan (Sawahel, 2018), Singapore (Sheng-Kai, 2015), and China (Hartig, 2016; Luqiu &

McCarthy, 2019) who are looking to increase soft power initiatives through higher educational exchange. More soft power resources should be utilized rather than strictly relying on hard power military options (Lee, 2005), particularly as its soft power diplomacy is sorely underfunded (Cole, 2018). President Tsai's administration is beginning to focus more on its cultural soft power resources rather than fixating on political limitations (Rawnsley, 2014), as shown in its Southbound Policy and diversification of international alliances (Manantan, 2019). However, the possibility of higher education being used as a tool of government legitimization may be fraught as the relationship between the government and universities in Taiwan has been a complicated one, with universities gradually asserting their independence from state control over many decades of reforms (Law, 1995). Moreover, some question the efficacy of higher education as a tool for soft power, stating that students who travel to another country for study don't necessarily develop a higher opinion of their host country and, even if they do, they may not necessarily be in a position of power to influence the policies of their home country towards their host country regardless (Lomer, 2016). Admittedly, although culture and higher education may be the entry point for soft power influence, ultimately they need to result in political influence to be useful (Wang & Lu, 2008). However, by focusing on culture, Taiwan could usurp some of China's tremendous investment in public diplomacy, by arguing that Taiwan has all the admirable qualities of Chinese culture, without the problematic baggage of authoritarianism and human rights abuses (Tiezzi, 2016).

Although Taiwan's soft power influence on China is ultimately muted *in* China by extensive counter campaigns (Tsang, 2017), Taiwan could gain a much-needed victory in the realm of public relations with respect to other nations. China's very expensive investments in soft power initiatives are obviously not achieving their intended outcomes, as indicated by the need to completely rebrand their signature Confucius Institutes due to suspicion and expulsion from higher education institutions across the globe (Volodzko, 2015; Zhuang, 2020). Healthcare was already helping Taiwan to achieve soft power prominence (Lin, 2019), as even before its success in preventing the outbreak of COVID-19, Taiwan was already asserting its status in biomedical advancement and technology (Fulco, 2018a). Taiwan's success in COVID-19 has already spared the economy from much of the damage faced by other locations (Hille, 2020). Their success should be further leveraged to reap similar dividends in sparing their higher education sector from the impending COVID-19 devastation faced by many higher education systems (Adams, 2020; Murakami, 2020; Price, 2020).

Taiwan has successfully incorporated higher education into its COVID recovery plan. The possibility of Taiwan as one of the only countries in the world able to confidently offer face-to-face higher education classes during the pandemic offers an additional soft power asset for the island. Initially, in March, international students were not allowed back into Taiwan out of concern for potential pandemic spread. By August, however,

Taiwan's quarantine protocol had shown to be effective, and the ministry of education slowly began to let more students back into Taiwan. For the Fall 2020 term, international students were allowed back into Taiwan (Chen & Chiang, 2020b). This reflects not only Taiwan's confidence in its ability to trace and prevent COVID spread but its ability to push its international image as one of the only places where international students can study in person, not online. Students from China, however, were not allowed back in for the Fall term. The ministry was unclear about whether limiting Chinese students was from COVID spread-related concerns or geopolitical considerations. Despite this shortcoming, Taiwan still celebrated a higher education win by not only allowing in-person classes but also by including international students within their equation. Moreover, another way that President Tsai's administration indicated that it will leverage its COVID-19 soft power success, and the concurrent COVID-19 soft power disaster for China, with respect to higher education is through its commitment and investment in the U.S. sponsored Fulbright program. In response to the Trump administration's controversial decision to halt this important avenue of scholarly exchange (Redden, 2020), Taiwan has now pledged more than $350,000 USD to increase the Taiwan Fulbright program, partly as a way to redirect and absorb some of the higher educational exchange that was originally intended for China (林, 2020). Even with the late-2020 joyous news of imminent and numerous vaccines on the way, and the possibilities for in-person learning to resume globally as early as 2021, Taiwan's COVID-19 success has nonetheless left an indelible mark on global consciousness. The COVID-19 pandemic has brought to the forefront neglected areas of public infrastructure worldwide, and Taiwan has positioned itself as a global leader in advancing knowledge and strategies of how to safeguard vulnerable populations from contagious disease. Taiwan's higher education sector should be placed in lockstep with this global recognition, both as a means for alleviation of domestic education policy failures, but also to ensure increased international interconnectivity.

Conclusion

Taiwan's COVID-19 success offers its higher education sector a unique and necessary opportunity to increase enrollment and funding by reaching out internationally. Moreover, Taiwan's diplomatic isolation could experience a much-needed reprieve by capitalizing on the soft power credibility established through successfully navigating the perils of a potential public health disaster encountered by many other nations of otherwise stronger international standing. Taiwan's example and experiences in dealing with the infectious disease have much to offer the world. Therefore, its precarious higher education sector should be brought into consideration both to receive additional investment and extend the benefit to others. Taiwan can and should do this in a number of ways. First, Taiwan should continue to diversify its international student portfolio by not only attracting students from the "South," but also from wealthier nations from the global "North." Taiwan's commitment to bolster its capacity to foster Mandarin language education and increased investment in the Fulbright program is a step in the right direction with regard to its U.S. relationship, but the government should also consider similar such measures with other wealthier nations as well. Second, Taiwan should position itself as a gateway and regional hub for access to not only China but also to Southeast Asia and the wider Pacific region. Their COVID-19 success should be used as a way to market their expertise in the advancement of biotechnological and public health knowledge, and not solely as a place to study Mandarin. Third, Taiwan should use this opportunity to increase investment in and placements at *public* higher education institutions. The massification of privatized universities was a policy fraught, to begin with, and any advantages brought by current successes should not be misdirected towards these inherently problematic institutions. Taiwan has the opportunity now to revive and propel its public universities to avenues of international success and recognition that have long been the explicitly sought after, yet under-achieved, policy goals.

References

Adams, R. (2020, July 6). UK universities facing possible financial disaster, research says. *The Guardian*. https://www.theguardian.com/education/2020/jul/06/uk-universities-facing-possible-financial-disaster-research-says

Anderson, S. (2020, July 13). New international students to U.S. May hit post-WW2 low. *Forbes*. https://www.forbes.com/sites/stuartanderson/2020/07/13/new-international-students-to-us-may-hit-post-ww2-low/#7acc74c8267f

Aspinwall, N. (2020, July 14). How Taiwan beat COVID-19 with transparency and trust. *Medium*. https://medium.com/@nickaspinwall/how-taiwan-beat-covid-19-with-transparency-and-trust-6838e2b131b

Brady, A.-M. (2020, April 20). Coronavirus: Could an alliance with Taiwan help NZ survive the coronavirus cataclysm? *Stuff*. https://www.stuff.co.nz/national/politics/opinion/121113908/coronavirus-could-an-alliance-with-taiwan-help-nz-survive-the-coronavirus-cataclysm

Chan, S.-J., & Lin, L.-W. (2015). Massification of higher education in Taiwan: Shifting pressure from admission to employment. *Higher Education Policy, 28*(1), 17–33. https://doi.org/10.1057/hep.2014.33

Chen, K.-T., Twu, S.-J., Chang, H.-L., Wu, Y.-C., Chen, C.-T., Lin, T.-H., Olsen, S. J., Dowell, S. F., Su, I.-J., & Taiwan SARS Response Team. (2005). SARS in Taiwan: An overview and lessons learned. *International Journal of Infectious Diseases, 9* (2), 77–85.

Chen, C., & Chiang, Y. (2020a, June 25). Most international students want to stay in Taiwan after graduation: Survey. *Focus Taiwan CNA English News*. https://focustaiwan.tw/society/202006250006

Chen, C., & Chiang, Y. (2020b, August 5). Taiwan allows return of foreign students, excluding those from China. *Focus Taiwan CNA English News*. https://focustaiwan.tw/society/202008050024

Chen, R. J. (2015). *Public and Private Universities in Taiwan: To compete or not to compete?* (No. 23; RIHE International Seminar Reports, pp. 101–118). National Chengchi University Taiwan. https://files.eric.ed.gov/fulltext/ED574207.pdf

Cheng, S. Y., & Jacob, W. J. (2012). Expansion and stratification of higher educational opportunity in Taiwan. *Chinese Education and Society, 45*(5–6), 112–133. https://doi.org/10.2753/CED1061-1932450509

Chou, C. P. (2014, November 12). Education in Taiwan: Taiwan's colleges and universities. *Brookings Institute.* https://www.brookings.edu/opinions/education-in-taiwan-taiwans-colleges-and-universities/

Chou, C. P. (2015). Higher education development in Taiwan. In J. Cheol Shin, G. A. Postiglione, & F. Huang (Eds.), *Mass higher education development in East Asia: Strategy, quality, and challenges* (pp. 89–103). Springer. http://www3.nccu.edu.tw/~iaezcpc/publications/C_publications/Journals/Ch5._Prudence_Higher_Education_Development_final.pdf

Chou, C. P., & Ho, A.-H. (2007). Schooling in Taiwan. In G. A. Postiglione & J. Tan (Eds.), *Going to school in East Asia* (pp. 344–377). Greenwood Press.

Chou, C. P., & Wang, L.-T. (2012). Who benefits from the massification of higher education in Taiwan? (M. LeSourd, Trans.). *Chinese Education and Society, 45*(5–6), 8–20.

Cole, J. M. (2018, October 4). Taiwan's 'soft power' is severely underfunded—And China is partly responsible. *Taiwan Sentinel.* https://sentinel.tw/taiwans-soft-power-severely-underfunded/

DeAeth, D. (2019, February 3). Foreign students in Taiwan 10% of total university and college students in 2018. *Taiwan News.* https://www.taiwannews.com.tw/en/news/3631340

Drillsma, R. (2018, December 5). MoE: Taiwan University and college departments closing due to declining birth rates. *Taiwan News.* https://www.taiwannews.com.tw/en/news/3590293

Fulco, M. (2018a, September 6). Can Taiwan become a regional biomedical powerhouse? *The News Lens.* https://international.thenewslens.com/article/103492

Fulco, M. (2018b, November 14). Falling population squeezes Taiwan's universities. *Taiwan Business TOPICS.* https://topics.amcham.com.tw/2018/11/falling-population-squeezes-taiwans-universities/

Green, B. (2020, January 30). Taiwan's universities are fighting for their lives as birth rates plummet. *Ketagalan Media.* https://ketagalanmedia.com/2020/01/30/taiwans-universities-are-fighting-for-their-lives-as-birth-rates-plummet/

Hartig, F. (2016). *Chinese public diplomacy: The rise of the Confucius Institute.* Routledge.

Hernandez, J. C., & Horton, C. (2020, April 23). Coronavirus crisis offers Taiwan a chance to push back against China. *The New York Times.* https://www.nytimes.com/2020/04/22/world/asia/coronavirus-china-taiwan.html

Hille, K. (2020, April 21). Taiwan's early success against coronavirus cushions economy. *Financial Times.* https://www.ft.com/content/b59c238c-d004-44a2-bd9f-c5b1e7a5bc8a

Horton, C. (2018, July 25). How Beijing enlists global companies to pressure Taiwan. *Nikkei Asian Review.* asia.nikkei.com/Spotlight/The-Big-Story/How-Beijing-enlists-global-companies-to-pressure-Taiwan

Hsueh, C.-M. (2018, October 3). Taiwan's higher education threatened by low birthrate, "China Factor." *Taiwan Insight: The News Lens.* https://international. thenewslens.com/amparticle/105336

Huang, Y.-L., Chang, D.-F., & Liu, C.-W. (2018). Higher education in Taiwan: An analysis of trends using the theory of punctuated equilibrium. *Journal of Literature and Art Studies, 8*(1), 169–180. https://doi.org/10.17265/2159-5836/2018.01.018

Joung, M., & Rosenthal, R. (2020, July 6). Drastic declines expected in foreign students in US. *Voice of America.* https://www.voanews.com/student-union/ drastic-declines-expected-foreign-students-us

Law, W.-W. (1995). The role of the state in higher education reform: Mainland China and Taiwan. *Comparative Education Review, 3*, 322.

Law, W.-W. (2004). Globalization and citizenship education in Hong Kong and Taiwan. *Comparative Education Review, 48*(3), 253–273.

Lee, S. (2005). A new interpretation of "soft power" for Taiwan. 台灣國際研究季刊 *Taiwan International Studies Quarterly, 1*(2), 1–23.

Leong, S. H. (2018, November 13). Health care for all: The good & not-so-great of Taiwan's universal coverage. *The News Lens.* https://international.thenewslens. com/article/108032

Li, H. T. (2020, January 12). Has educational reform succeeded in Taiwan? 4500-percent rise in cram schools over past 30 years. *Commonwealth Magazine, 689.* https://english.cw.com.tw/article/article.action?id=2639

Li, J. (2018). *Conceptualizing soft power of higher education.* Springer.

Lim, E. (2020, December 3). Taiwan, U.S. launch language education initiative. *Focus Taiwan CNA English News.* https://focustaiwan.tw/politics/202012030022

Lin, C. (2019, October 7). Healthcare is Taiwan's most useful soft power. *Taipei Times.* http://www.taipeitimes.com/News/editorials/archives/2019/ 10/07/2003723500

Lin, T.-C. (2004). The role of higher education in economic development: An empirical study of Taiwan case. *Journal of Asian Economics, 15*(1), 355–371. https://doi.org/10.1016/j.asieco.2004.02.006

Lin, Y.-L. (2020). Stagnation generation: Evaluating the impact of higher education expansion on social mobility from the perspective of Taiwan. *Panoeconomicus, 67*(2), 167–185.

Liu, C., & Armer, J. M. (1993). Education's effect on economic growth in Taiwan. *Comparative Education Review, 37*(3), 304–321.

Lomer, S. (2016). Soft power as a policy rationale for international education in the UK: A critical analysis. *Higher Education, 74*(1), 581–598. https://doi. org/10.1007/s10734-016-0060-6

Luqiu, L. R., & McCarthy, J. D. (2019). Confucius Institutes: The successful stealth "soft power" penetration of American universities. *The Journal of Higher Education, 90*(4), 620–643. https://doi.org/10.1080/00221546.2018.1541433

Magaziner, J. (2016, June 7). Education in Taiwan. *World Education News + Reviews.* https://wenr.wes.org/2016/06/education-in-taiwan

Manantan, M. (2019, March 4). How Taiwan stands up to China through soft power. *The Philippine Star.* https://www.philstar.com/other-sections/news-feature/2019/03/04/1898588/commentary-how-taiwan-stands-china-through-soft-power

Mason, T. (2020, May 14). Is it ethical to take in foreign students mid-crisis? *University World News*. https://www.universityworldnews.com/post.php?story=202005141501467

Maxon, A. (2018, January 12). Colleges' enrollment not only criterion for school closure: MOE. *Taipei Times*. https://www.taipeitimes.com/News/taiwan/archives/2018/01/12/2003685637

MOE Taiwan. (2012, December 20). Department of higher education. *Ministry of Education Taiwan ROC*. https://english.moe.gov.tw/fp-4-15155-8F594-1.html

MOE Taiwan. (2013). *Higher education in Taiwan*. Ministry of Education Taiwan. https://ws.moe.edu.tw/

MOE Taiwan. (2019). *Table 15. Higher education*. Ⅰ. *Summary of universities, colleges and junior colleges* [Statistical Yearbook of the Republic of China]. National Statistics Republic of China (Taiwan). https://eng.stat.gov.tw/public/data/dgbas03/bs2/yearbook_eng/y015.pdf

MOFA. (2016). *New Southbound Policy Portal*. Ministry of Foreign Affairs Taiwan ROC. https://nspp.mofa.gov.tw/nsppe/index.php

Murakami, K. (2020, April 13). The next financial blow. *Inside Higher Ed*. https://www.insidehighered.com/news/2020/04/13/public-colleges-face-looming-financial-blow-state-budget-cuts

NSYSU. (2018). Southbound talent exchange picks up speed as Taiwan launches higher education fair in the Philippines. *National Sun Yat-Sen University*. https://www.nsysu.edu.tw/p/406-1000-193697,r3244.php?Lang=en

Nye, J. S. (n.d.). Soft power and higher education. *Forum for the Future of Higher Education*. http://forum.mit.edu/articles/soft-power-and-higher-education/

Nye, J. S. (2004). *Soft power: The means to success in world politics* (1st ed.). Public Affairs.

Pretzer-Lin, N. (2015, July). A public policy perspective on the privatization of HEIs in Taiwan. *Higher Education Policy in Asia: Reform, Outcomes, Equity and Access*. International Conference on Public Policy, Milan. https://www.ippapublicpolicy.org/file/paper/1435817399.pdf

Price, J. (2020, September 22). Australian universities cower as disaster looms. *Sydney Morning Herald*. https://www.smh.com.au/national/australian-universities-cower-as-disaster-looms-20200920-p55xh6.html

Rawnsley, G. (2014). Taiwan's soft power and public diplomacy. *Journal of Current Chinese Affairs, 43*(3), 161–174. https://journals.sub.uni-hamburg.de/giga/jcca/article/download/772/772-797-1-PB.pdf

Redden, E. (2020, July 16). Trump targets Fulbright in China, Hong Kong. *Inside Higher Ed*. https://www.insidehighered.com/news/2020/07/16/trump-targets-fulbright-china-hong-kong

Reuters. (2020, May 12). New Zealand backs Taiwan joining the WHO despite China rebuke. *The Guardian*. https://www.theguardian.com/world/2020/may/12/new-zealand-backs-taiwan-joining-the-who-despite-china-rebuke

Rowen, I. (2020). Crafting the Taiwan model for COVID-19: An exceptional state in pandemic territory. *The Asia-Pacific Journal, 18*(14). https://apjjf.org/2020/14/Rowen.html

Sawahel, W. (2018, November 9). Enhancing university partnerships in soft power drive. *University World News*. https://www.universityworldnews.com/post.php?story=20181108100611418

Sheng-Kai, C. C. (2015). *Higher education scholarships as a soft power tool: An analysis of its role in the EU and Singapore* (Working Paper No. 23). EU Centre in Singapore.

Smith, M., Tsai, S.-L., Mateju, P., & Huang, M.-H. (2016). Educational expansion and inequality in Taiwan and the Czech Republic. *Comparative Education Review, 60*(2), 339–374.

Smith, N. (2020, April 25). How "safe" countries could start forming regional alliances to keep trade and tourism going. *The Telegraph.* https://www.telegraph.co.uk/news/2020/04/25/safe-countries-could-start-forming-regional-alliances-keep-trade/

Study in Taiwan. (2020, June 3). Post COVID-19 Era—Let's study in Taiwan. *Study in Taiwan.* https://www.studyintaiwan.org/news/content/86

Taylor, C., Kampf, S., Grundig, T., & Common, D. (2020, March 21). Inside Taiwan during COVID-19: How the country kept schools and businesses open throughout pandemic. *Canadian Broadcasting Corporation.* https://www.cbc.ca/news/business/taiwan-covid-19-lessons-1.5505031

The Straits Times. (2017, March 30). Low birth rate spells trouble for Taiwan's universities: The China Post. *The Straits Times.* https://www.straitstimes.com/asia/east-asia/low-birth-rate-spells-trouble-for-taiwans-universities-the-china-post

Tiezzi, S. (2016, August 18). 'Lovable' Taiwan and its soft power quest. *The Diplomat.* https://thediplomat.com/2016/08/lovable-taiwan-and-its-soft-power-quest/

Treisman, R. (2020, July 14). ICE agrees to rescind policy barring foreign students from online study in the U.S. *National Public Radio.* https://www.npr.org/sections/coronavirus-live-updates/2020/07/14/891125619/ice-agrees-to-rescind-policy-barring-foreign-students-from-online-study-in-the-u

Tsai, C.-C. (2015). A review of Taiwan's current higher education development and challenges. *Journal of Education & Social Policy, 2*(3), 89–92.

Tsang, S. (Ed.). (2017). *Taiwan's impact on China why soft power matters more than economic or political inputs.* Springer.

Volodzko, D. (2015, July 8). China's Confucius Institutes and the soft war. *The Diplomat.* http://thediplomat.com/2015/07/chinas-confucius-institutes-and-the-soft-war/

Wang, H., & Lu, Y.-C. (2008). The conception of soft power and its policy implications: A comparative study of China and Taiwan. *Journal of Contemporary China, 17*(56), 425–447. https://doi.org/10.1080/10670560802000191

Woods, N. (2020, June 25). Taiwan's mask diplomacy and the international responses. *Taiwan Insight.* https://taiwaninsight.org/2020/06/25/taiwans-mask-diplomacy-and-the-international-responses/

Wu, W.-H., Chen, S.-F., & Wu, C.-T. (1989). The development of higher education in Taiwan. *Higher Education, 18*(1), 117–136.

Yeh, J. (2020, February 9). Taiwan's health care system ranks number 1 in online survey. *Focus Taiwan CNA English News.* https://focustaiwan.tw/society/202002090006

Zhou, Z., & Ching, G. S. (2012). *Taiwan education at the crossroad: When globalization meets localization* (1st ed.). Palgrave Macmillan.

Zhuang, P. (2020, July 4). China's Confucius Institutes rebrand after overseas propaganda rows. *South China Morning Post.* https://www.scmp.com/print/news/china/diplomacy/article/3091837/chinas-confucius-institutes-rebrand-after-overseas-propaganda

林興盟. (2020, November 25). 傅爾布萊特計畫自中港移轉台灣 外交部增預算支應 (Fulbright plans to transfer from China and Hong Kong to Taiwan's Ministry of Foreign Affairs to increase budget support). *CNA News.* https://www.cna.com.tw/news/aipl/202011250224.aspx

Bios

Eric W. Layman, is a Ph.D. Candidate with Indiana University-Bloomington pursuing a dual major in Education Policy Studies and Qualitative Inquiry Methodology. He is a Fulbright-Hays Scholar and his dissertation research explores Indigenous education reform in Taiwan. E-mail: ewlayman@indiana.edu

Lev Nachman, is a Ph.D. Candidate with University of California-Irvine in Political Science. He is a Fulbright Scholar and his dissertation research investigates novel political party formation in Taiwan. E-mail: lnachman@uci.edu

3 Public Higher Education Response to COVID-19

The Case of Federal Institutions in Southern Brazil

Kelber Tozini, Claudia Schiedeck Soares de Souza, Fernanda Leal, and Bernardo Sfredo Miorando

Abstract

The COVID-19 pandemic has affected higher education around the world in unprecedented ways. Given the historical centrality of federal higher education institutions (HEIs) for Brazil's development, the purpose of this chapter is to discuss the initial response of Southern Brazilian public federal HEIs to COVID-19 regarding their social role. We characterize the actions performed in these institutions to mitigate the effects of the pandemic as described in their institutional websites. Results highlight the importance of extension activities and the need for federal public HEIs' autonomy, assuring them the possibility to construct human development capabilities for the public good.

Keywords

COVID-19, public higher education, Brazil, autonomy, extension

Introduction

To repeat, the purpose of researching higher education is not just to make higher education "better"—although hopefully it will also do that—but to enhance our understanding of contemporary societies and the futures that are available to them. (Brennan, 2008, p. 392)

In March 2020, the realities of higher education (HE) in the world were changed dramatically by COVID-19. Following the World Health Organization's social isolation guidelines, public and private institutions around the world suspended their face-to-face activities. At this first moment, the research produced on HE and COVID-19 tended to focus on the learning shifts that the pandemic brought to the institutions' educational environment (Peters et al., 2020). This work argues that the impact on HE goes beyond learning methodologies or hybrid learning. It is also linked with society's well-being or the local community's needs in which the institutions are inserted. If there is learning from this moment of crisis, we may see a new approach to the social role of the higher education institutions (HEIs) towards human development (Boni & Walker, 2016).

The focus of this study is on the case of Brazil. The question that guided our initial study was how federal public HEIs initially responded to the effects of COVID-19. We analyzed articles from universities and federal institutes located in the Southern Region of the country, considering the evolution and transmission of COVID-19 at the time and also the institutions' relevance in the Brazilian educational scenario. This study is imperative as it demonstrates that public HEIs continued to perform an important role for the public of their local communities that goes beyond campus borders despite having their classes suspended.

Literature Review

Over centuries, the university has been one of the most permanent social institutions in the Western world, ensuring the tradition of its structures and being permeable to the demands of a new global society. Much of the high-level knowledge that society currently holds has been generated at university through teaching, research, and extension (Karlsen, 2005; Sobrinho, 2005). The role of HE in social transformation and its relationship with social justice has furthered vast, complex, and paradigmatic debates. From a critical perspective, we may question HE's role in producing and reproducing social inequalities, especially concerning the access to knowledge, i.e., who produces and for whom it is produced (Brennan, 2008; Castells, 2016).

According to Marginson (2011), the central question is about where HE lies in different concepts of the public good. For the author, these assumptions may involve ambiguity; the concept of the public good closest to university institutions is associated with transparency, the common and collective good, bringing to the HE arena the vision of the agency and human development (Boni & Walker, 2016). Walker (2019) argues that it is central to HE to involve public good students' capabilities, recognizing the need for social inclusion, mutual acceptance, access to different knowledge, development of a critical reason, as well as sufficient access to funding for educational wellbeing. So, we address HE from a perspective that recognizes these dimensions of human development. We convey that HEIs are always challenged to have better results, especially regarding economic and social development. Although we have to incorporate the assumption that postsecondary institutions may not do everything to eradicate inequality and social injustice, they can do something to minimize these conditions, engaging the academic community with local and global issues (Boni & Walker, 2016).

In early 2020, the COVID-19 pandemic hit the world, putting 43% of the global population in lockdown, affecting approximately 90% of all students enrolled in HE and causing more than 70% of institutions to migrate online teaching activities (Marinoni et al., 2020). However, De Sousa Santos (2020) points out that the pandemic aggravated the world crisis. The author argues that this moment will be most challenging for social groups already invisible by the Global North (seen as a political, social, and cultural use of capitalist exploitation established over hundreds of years). Women, self-employed or precarious workers, street populations, residents of peripheries or slums, refugees, disabled and elderly are more susceptible to the perverse effects of the virus because they tend to be even less visible by the society in panic and whose social inequality was naturalized by calling it "meritocracy."

Brazil, from 2004 to 2014, through the action of a government committed to the social inequality causes, reduced hunger, and poverty, promoting the most extensive social mobility of the country through its history (Kingstone & Power, 2017). Even in the midst of a global neoliberal context, Presidents Luis Inácio Lula da Silva and Dilma Rousseff highly invested in health, education, income, and employment programs. However, from 2016, and with the rise of a president recognized internationally as a far-right and defender of extreme liberalism, all social welfare programs were attacked, reducing budgets, putting relevant agendas into invisibility (including environmental, social, and racial) and rigging of state enterprises by political leaders committed to this new agenda. Brazilian Federal Higher Education, funded exclusively with governmental resources, has been one of the most impacted spheres by the current government's actions, whether by cutting resources, intervention in institutional autonomy, or denying institutions' importance for developing the country (Neto & Pimenta, 2020).

Overview of Brazilian Federal Higher Education

The Brazilian education model is complex, anchored in a postcolonial political culture, and grounded on federal tripartite relations (i.e., power shared over federal government, states, and municipalities). The coordination between the spheres is influenced by politics and intervention, accentuating its historical, social, and regional inequalities. In this way, the country's HE system has been historically submitted to the Federal Government's interests through policy, funding, and regulation (Prolo et al., 2019; Verhine & Vinhaes, 2018), aligned to the international neoliberal education flow on managerialism and accountability (Ball, 2012; De Sousa Santos, 2016).

The first Brazilian university came only in 1920 and was located in Rio de Janeiro (Schwartzman et al., 2015). After World War II, anchored in the demand for social mobility (Cantwell et al., 2018) and the action of international organizations in promoting economic and social development mainly in peripheral countries (Ball, 2012; Boni & Walker, 2016), Brazil also expanded its HE system, mainly through the formation and expansion of its private system (McCowan, 2004; Miranda & de Azevedo, 2020; Verhine & Vinhaes, 2018).

From 2004, through government policies such as the Program for the Support of Restructuring and Expansion Plan of Federal Universities (REUNI) and the creation of Federal Institutes, which nowadays offer higher vocational education and training (VET), Brazilian public and free HE expanded its programs and vacancies. However, it encompasses only 11.8%

out of 2,537 HEIs. Nevertheless, these federal HEIs are, in many ways, central to the development of the country mainly because they have become research reference centers and by the inland expansion movement serving communities that previously did not have access to federal education (Knobel & Leal, 2019; Ristoff, 2013, 2019).

Brazilian Federal HE is funded by the Union and offers free programs for all students enrolled. It comprises 68 universities and 38 federal institutes—with hundreds of campuses, two Centers of Technological Education, and one Technological University, besides secondary technical schools linked to the universities (Brasil, 2008, 2020a). Although these institutions have expanded their campuses, in 2019, they hold 24.2% of undergraduate and graduate enrollments with 1.99 million students (Brasil, 2020a). Additionally, these universities consist of 40 public hospitals, which form the most comprehensive public health network in Brazil, providing around 7 million free consultations, 16 million free examinations to Brazilians per year, and more than 165 thousand free annual surgeries (Brasil, 2020b).

Like other countries, Brazilian Public HEIs are grounded in three institutional missions: teaching, research, and extension. In terms of research outputs, they are responsible for 95% of national R&D performance, and 60% of all this production is restricted to 15 federal universities (Brasil, 2019).

On February 26, the Brazilian government registered the first confirmed case of Coronavirus in the country and, on March 17, the first death. The first states most affected by the COVID-19 were Amazonas, São Paulo, and Rio de Janeiro. By the end of March, all federal universities had already suspended face-to-face teaching, research, and extension activities. After much contemplation, some public HEIs have transitioned to remote learning.

Methods

The development of scientific research from the end of the 19th century has reflected the moment of global transition. In the last 50 years, the field literature pointed to the methodological diversity and the need for inter-, trans- and multidisciplinary research, incorporating new approaches to performing an inquiry (Clarke et al., 2018; De Sousa Santos, 2016; Denzin & Lincoln, 2017). This study lies in a qualitative and exploratory research tradition, aiming at analyzing data emerging from the empirical field, seeking to explain the role of Federal HEIs in Brazil in a moment of crisis.

We focused the data collection on a single region of the country, the South, comprised of three states—Paraná, Rio Grande do Sul, and Santa Catarina. Initially, these were not the most affected Brazilian regions by COVID-19. However, the South of the country has very close characteristics to European countries such as Italy and Spain, which were strongly impacted by the virus: the highest elderly population, aging rate of 86% (Alves, 2020; Souza et al., 2020), and a very similar climate, with harsh winters. Besides, the country's

Southern Region is cut off by two of the longest country's highways and is likely to promote national and regional mobility (Emer et al., 2020; Lopes et al., 2020). In March, the Southern Region was preparing for winter, and it reached the country's highest peaks of Acute Severe Respiratory Syndrome. So, although the national broadcast media described how COVID-19 evolved critically in other states and regions at the beginning, the society's eyes naturally turned to Southern Brazil, where the structure of the health sector is better than in other states, but still precarious, but could still prepare such a structure to absorb the effect of the virus (Emer et al., 2020; Souza et al., 2020). If the Southern Region has weaknesses in the public health sector, paradoxically, it also has some of the country's best HEIs, as pointed out by the National System of Evaluation of Higher Education (Brasil, 2015).

For this initial analysis, we collected data from articles about Coronavirus published by the federal HEIs located in Southern Brazil from March to May 2020 since the purpose of this work was to verify the immediate response of institutions from the declaration of the pandemic state in the country. All articles came from their institutional websites. The database comprises 11 Federal Universities and 6 Federal Institutes. They account for 17.1% of the total student population in federal HEIs in the country. Besides, all members of the research team studied, held administrative positions, and/or taught in institutions in two of the three states and are familiar with the region's particularities, which was relevant for data collection and analysis (Charmaz, 2006). Table 3.1 presents the HEIs covered by the study and the number of articles identified in each institution.

The analysis began during data collection, as authors made notes on the news' remarkable aspects. Simultaneous data collection and analysis are preferred in qualitative studies as the final product is shaped by the data being collected and the analysis that accompanies the entire process (Merriam & Tisdell, 2015). The articles were then organized by institution and month, classified, and coded under nodes related to the topic. According to Charmaz (2006), the coding process requires a continuous evaluation of the data, moving from the initial phase to the focused one, where the categories are refined, allowing at the end to build the story to be told. During the data collection phase, the researchers identified commonalities throughout the articles and established three broad categories to characterize HEIs' initiatives' main aspects to mitigate the impact of COVID-19: (a) agents, (b) beneficiaries, and (c) actions. The articles were classified according to their primary focus. We defined subcategories within each broad category, through a constant comparative approach: by reviewing articles' details, we clustered the agents, beneficiaries, and scopes of the actions according to their characteristics, whose definitions were enhanced as the information saturated the coding process. When necessary, new codes were created by the group. This abductive approach favored an overview of what the institutions have been doing since the beginning of the Pandemic.

Table 3.1 Federal institutions' overview and data collected to be continued

State	HEI	Campuses	Students	Status	Articles
Paraná	Universidade Federal do Paraná (UFPR)	7	27,995	Remote	196
	Universidade Tecnológica Federal do Paraná (UTFPR)	13	29,935	Suspended	79
	Universidade Federal da Integração Latino-Americana (UNILA)	1	3,629	Suspended	34
	Instituto Federal do Paraná (IFPR)	26	30,228	Remote	33
Santa Catarina	Universidade Federal de Santa Catarina (UFSC)	5	29,303	Suspended	237
	Universidade Federal da Fronteira Sul (UFFS)[a]	6	7,826	Partial operations	93
	Instituto Federal de Santa Catarina (IFSC)	22	50,335	Remote	39
	Instituto Federal Catarinense (IFC)	15	17,528	Remote	27
Rio Grande do Sul	Universidade Federal do Rio Grande do Sul (UFRGS)	3	30,105	Remote	210
	Universidade Federal de Pelotas (UFPEL)	3	17,419	Suspended	214
	Universidade Federal de Rio Grande (FURG)	4	9,422	Suspended	123
	Universidade Federal de Santa Maria (UFSM)	4	20,446	Remote	116
Rio Grande do Sul	Universidade Federal do Pampa (UNIPAMPA)	10	11,201	Suspended	74
	Universidade Federal de Ciências da Saúde de Porto Alegre (UFCSPA)	1	2,523	Remote	58
	Instituto Federal do Rio Grande do Sul (IFRS)	17	27,366	Suspended	66
	Instituto Federal Farroupilha (IFF)	11	14,859	Suspended	38
	Instituto Federal de Educação, Ciência e Tecnologia Sul-riograndense (IFSUL)	15	24,369	Suspended	37
Total		163	354,489		1,674

Source: Elaborated with data collected from the Ministry of Education's Coronavirus portal and HEI's websites (2020).

a UFFS's Rector's Office is seated in Santa Catarina, but it has campuses in Paraná and Rio Grande do Sul.

Limitations

The first limitation refers to the data used in the study. The research team collected data from each institution's official website because federal educational institutions are not allowed by law to make advertisements in traditional media, being the website the unique source available. We highlight that the period covered by the data only focuses on the institutions' immediate response. Another limitation of this study is that the pandemic impacted each region at a time and differently, and due to the geographical characterization and the evolution of COVID-19, other federal HEIs may have responded differently. Lastly, we collected the news articles from each institution's main website which often includes news from their satellite campuses. It is possible, however, that their satellite campuses may have published other articles on their own campus' websites, but these were not included in the study.

Findings and Discussion

The coding process in qualitative research is not linear. On the contrary, from insights or questions raised throughout the work, the researcher refines and includes new categories or subcategories (Charmaz, 2006). This way, while coding, we identified a distinctive pattern of how HEIs communicate regarding COVID-19. Some institutions created news tabs on their websites to convey institutional actions, while others chose to keep information related to pandemic into their leading portals. Besides, some institutions were not clear about what agents performed the actions. For instance, UFSC and UFPR reported the initiatives directly to individual faculty or students and rarely reported them to the schools, the departments, or the research/extension groups. On the other hand, IFRS, UFRGS, and UFPEL often connected actions to established academic groups. This discrepancy may indicate that the institutions organize internally and also relate institutionally to society in different ways. An analysis of this specific feature can further research the organization identity field (Weerts et al., 2014) or the workplace's multiple commitments (Cohen, 2003).

There was some difficulty in identifying the articles's main feature, revealing that institutions are in distinctive stances in terms of communication capacity, which might be linked to their time of existence or even the absence of understanding of organizational knowledge (Canary & McPhee, 2010) since ten of these 17 institutions were recently founded.

In March, the articles were mostly characterized by shifts in institutions' operations, informing how COVID-19 impacts students, faculty, and staff. Between April and May, there was a significant increase in the institutional news about the virus (March—475, April—673, and May—554), and the publications migrated from the administrative guidelines to health information about COVID-19 and also research and extension projects reports. In other words, HEIs began to care more about the external audience, seeking to engage in society's daily agenda. In a way, this shows that universities and university-related institutions face external demands and pressures for quick responses and flexible solutions to problems for the public good (Boni & Walker, 2016; Brennan, 2008; Castells, 2016).

We also noticed a multiplicity of actors involved in HEIs' response to COVID-19. They were categorized by an individual (such as faculty) and collective participation (such as unions, associations, or teams). Likewise, the institutions' efforts through the formal channels of central and formal administration (such as the provosts or the departments) became evident in the articles, putting the administrative agents' role as central in the initiatives linked to COVID-19. Seven hundred and sixty out of the published institutional news involved directors, secretariats, provosts, or other HEI units, although the proactivity of recognized research groups in the Brazilian HE scenario can also be a distinctive action pattern. We highlight that 16 institutions have used a collaborative management strategy from the beginning of the sanitary crisis: creating a crisis committee involving academic, medical, and community sectors. According to Marginson (2018), the presence of this kind of alliance inside the institutional arena can characterize HEIs as essential players of the national public sphere, where civil society actors seek solutions to societal challenges. Thus, they can bring the public good conception within the institutions beyond the state-related characteristic or the public/private division, advancing to issues related to societal needs or civil society engagement (Jongbloed et al., 2008).

Agency is central in a human development approach for social justice because it challenges the HE environment (students, scholarship, and managers) to face daily issues embedded in its functions (Boni & Walker, 2016). During the coding process, the institutional or individual actions gained our full attention. We found them to be directed towards a set of beneficiaries, individuals, or groups targeted to receive different support types to cope with the diverse effects of the pandemic. The scopes of the actions ranged through a multitude of knowledge and application areas. We established six subcategories within the broad category of performed actions, also coding the articles according to internal particularities to such subcategories. We highlight that four actions could not be coded under these categories, mainly because the news was unclear about what, where, or who did it. The subcategories are explained and exemplified below.

- **Contingency measures (551 entries):** The shifts in operation and support for the internal community whose administrative measures were enacted to allow the academic activities, even in remote mode, while also contributing to local government and society at large. For instance, communications to state governments to make institutional buildings available for treating patients infected with the virus, allocation of own budgets to fund extension projects and research studies on the pandemic, and anticipation of student's graduation in health programs so that the country could increase professionals' capacity in public health.

- **Research on COVID-19 (215 entries):** The Federal HEIs engaged in clinical and social research, raising funding from specific public calls, conducting studies on the virus and its impact on the local economy, developing equipment for hospitals, and using artificial intelligence to reach faster results to detect the coronavirus. The most prominent participation in coronavirus research was from a traditional university, which coordinated large-scale testing research on COVID-19 detection in the whole country.
- **General information initiatives (309 entries):** The production of informational materials (videos, charts, websites, and manuals), policy guidelines, and manifestos were among the most significant kinds of HEIs actions. Local broadcast partnerships, production of own media, videos and debates on COVID-19, physical and mental health instructions, and medical teleassistance on coronavirus symptoms are examples.
- **Services (388 entries):** All kinds of services were developed by HEIs for local communities, ranging from capacity building to health and nutrition care, from psychological support to lectures with experts, from cultural activities, art repositories to entrepreneurship support, from domestic violence awareness to partnerships for providing clinical treatment solutions (social and technological incubators).
- **Solidarity actions (229 entries):** Due to the enormous socio-economic impact of COVID-19 on local communities, the internal community's massive effort was to support vulnerable groups. Among the initiatives, we found health article production, including face masks, hand sanitizers, and donation campaigns for essential items such as food, medicines, and hygiene materials, especially food donation for communities at risk.

This categorization lines up with what De Sousa Santos (2020) calls the virus's cruel pedagogy. COVID-19 put social inequality on stage, pushing HEIs to face the need of being next to the most vulnerable social groups. The analyzed articles also reveal that, even when teaching is suspended at federal public HEIs, both research and extension activities continue to occur and contribute significantly to Brazilian society, especially to the local communities these institutions are settled.

These assumptions contradict the traditional notion of HE as a site of teaching and research only (Castells, 2016; Meyer & Sporn, 2018; Rowan et al., 2019). Suppose we observed at least three of these categories (general information initiatives, services, and solidarity actions). In that case, we can say that the Brazilian Federal HEIs engaged in the local communities' everyday lives, searching for ways to provide them with the knowledge they produce. Boni and Walker (2016) framework for a human development university helped us with some of the features presented in this analysis. These activities are linked to a sense of participation and empowerment, which involves agency and social transformation through participation. Besides, they are embedded into a holistic perspective that allows students, faculty, and staff to absorb from community-based learning and use the knowledge produced through this learning for what Marginson (2011) defines as a public good.

Although it is not the objective of this work to analyze these actions' beneficiaries, it is essential to highlight some aspects. Two large groups of beneficiaries stand out from the news: students (670 articles) and society at large (600 articles). The first group prominently indicates institutional concern in maintaining bonds with students during the pandemic since they are vital for institutional survival. However, it also draws attention to the relationship established by institutions with society at large. The collected news is mostly related to people in general, with lots of information and guidance about physical and mental health during the quarantine. There was also a significant concern to the deaf community (60 articles). The majority of the federal HEIs created groups to work in translating videos and news for the deaf. This brief analysis points to the importance of the extension (or third mission) of HE, aligning to the literature emphasizing that universities need to be inserted in local communities not only to account for what they do in their institutions but also as a way to bring real-life into the pedagogical environment (Boni & Walker, 2016; Walker, 2012). The idea of extension as social work (Melo Neto, 2002) makes sense as it highlights the role of the different society members in developing activities to fight against the virus and its effects on well-being. Thus, in the context of the coronavirus crisis, the extension (articulated with teaching and research) might serve as an opportunity to strengthen the relationship between federal HEIs and society.

Conclusions

This chapter aimed to discuss the Southern Brazilian federal universities and institutes' initial response to the COVID-19 sanitary emergency and analyze it through HE's social role.

Results have led to the conclusion that these institutions have played an essential role during this global crisis. Several individual actions and institutional initiatives show that the HEIs have made serious efforts to reduce the pandemic impact on society, such as general clarification and instructions for local communities about the virus, conduction of studies and reports on the socio-economic effects of the pandemic on vulnerable Brazilian groups, and promotion of on-line activities to cope with the effects of social isolation.

This first analysis emphasized at least two essential features of these institutions at the moment:

- extension as a fundamental mission for Brazilian HE: Although extension activities were enacted in an impromptu fashion, they have served as the "visible face" of the university for local communities and society at large in a time when classes are suspended: and,
- the relevance of administrative, pedagogical, and financial autonomy for both federal universities and institutes, even when facing an unstable

scenario in Brazil due to the budget-cutting and constant threats to their legitimacy made by the government. These institutions took a proactive role concerning the most vulnerable.

In a way, the global health crisis has placed the social role of HE on the stage, since from the physical emptying of institutions and, therefore, without being able to exercise teaching in its traditional form, teachers, technicians, students, and management had to recreate the pedagogical locus. In teaching, there was migration to remote education. However, in research and extension, daily social life became a living laboratory, where the academic community had to insert, participate, listen, and discuss economic solutions and death or life issues. Thus, we can say that the curriculum, projects, and learning drifted to developing human capabilities for better living. Boni and Walker (2016) argue that this is the expected role of HEIs: human development that seeks social transformation through freedom and the collective good. De Sousa Santos (2020) proposes a new articulation between political and civilizing processes to think holistically, through epistemological, cultural, and social assumptions, the human life's dignified survival.

This chapter focused on the initial actions that have been performed by federal HEIs in Southern Brazil. Given the focus on this region, empirical studies could look into how institutions in other regions have responded to the crisis. Future studies need to further on questions that can answer the extent to which HEIs, a prime source of knowledge produced globally, have incorporated the pedagogy of this tremendous global crisis. Future research should also develop new approaches to HE, surpassing models that point only to research and teaching as the first functions of HEIs. Perhaps this way, we can understand and discuss whether the thousands of deaths resulting from the first major pandemic of the 21st century were enough to alter the world's educational paradigm.

References

Alves, J. E. D. (2020, July/August/September). A Pandemia da COVID-19 e o envelhecimento populacional no Brasil. *Revista Longeviver, Ano II, n.7,* 13–18.

Ball, S. J. (2012). *Global Education Inc.: New policy networks and the neoliberal imaginary.* Routledge.

Boni, A., & Walker, M. (2016). *Universities and global human development: Theoretical and empirical insights for social change.* Routledge.

Brasil. (2008). Lei nº 11.892, de 29 de dezembro de 2008. Institui a Rede Federal de Educação Profissional, Científica e Tecnológica, cria os Institutos Federais de Educação, Ciência e Tecnologia, e dá outras providências. *Diário Oficial da União.*

Brasil. (2015). *Projeto CNE/UNESCO 914BRZ1144.3- Sistema Nacional de Educação Superior.*

Brasil. (2019). *A Pesquisa no Brasil: Promovendo a excelência.*

Brasil. (2020a). *Notas Estatísticas: Censo da Educação Superior 2019.*

Brasil. (2020b). *Relatório Integrado 2019*. https://www.gov.br/ebserh/pt-br/acesso-a-informacao/auditorias/processos-de-contas-anuais/2019/relatorio-integrado-2019.pdf

Brennan, J. (2008). Higher education and social change. *Higher Education, 56*(3), 381–393.

Canary, H. E., & McPhee, R. D. (Eds.). (2010). *Communication and organizational knowledge: Contemporary issues for theory and practice*. Routledge.

Cantwell, B., Marginson, S., & Smolentseva, A. (2018). *High participation systems of higher education* (1st ed.). Oxford University Press.

Castells, M. (2016). Universities as dynamic systems of contradictory functions. In J. Muller, N. Cloete, F. van Schalkwyk, & M. Castells (Eds.), *Castells in Africa: Universities and development* (pp. 35–55). African Minds.

Charmaz, K. (2006). *Constructing grounded theory: A practical guide through qualitative analysis*. SAGE Publications.

Clarke, A. E., Washburn, R., & Friese, C. (2018). *Situational analysis: Grounded theory after the interpretive turn* (2nd ed.). SAGE Publications.

Cohen, A. (2003). *Multiple commitments in the workplace: An integrative approach*. Psychology Press.

De Sousa Santos, B. (2016). *Epistemologies of the South: Justice against epistemicide*. Routledge.

De Sousa Santos, B. (2020). *La cruel pedagogía del virus*. Ediciones AKAL.

Denzin, N. K., & Lincoln, Y. S. (2017). *The Sage handbook of qualitative research* (5th ed.). SAGE Publications.

Emer, C., Maia, K. P., Santana, P. C., Santana, E. M., da Silva, D. G., Cosmo, L. G., Assis, A. P., Burin, G., Cantor, M., & Lemos-Costa, P. (2020). Vulnerabilidade das microrregiões da Região Sul do Brasil à pandemia do novo coronavírus (SARS-CoV-2).

Jongbloed, B., Enders, J., & Salerno, C. (2008). Higher education and its communities: Interconnections, interdependencies and a research agenda. *Higher Education, 56*(3), 303–324.

Karlsen, J. (2005). When regional development becomes an institutional responsibility for universities: The need for a discussion about knowledge construction in relation to universities' third role. *AI & SOCIETY, 19*(4), 500–510.

Kingstone, P., & Power, T. J. (2017). *Democratic Brazil divided*. University of Pittsburgh Press.

Knobel, M., & Leal, F. (2019). Higher education and science in Brazil: A Walk toward the Cliff? *International Higher Education, 99*, 2–4.

Lopes, L. F. D., de Faria, R. M., Lima, M. P., Kirchhof, R. S., de Almeida, D. M., & de Moura, G. L. (2020). Descrição do perfil epidemiológico da COVID19 na Região Sul do Brasil. *Hygeia-Revista Brasileira de Geografia Médica e da Saúde, 16*, 188–198.

Marginson, S. (2011). Higher education and public good. *Higher Education Quarterly, 65*(4), 411–433.

Marginson, S. (2018). Public/private in higher education: A synthesis of economic and political approaches. *Studies in Higher Education, 43*(2), 322–337.

Marinoni, G., Van't Land, H., & Jensen, T. (2020). The impact of COVID-19 on higher education around the world. *IAU Global Survey Report*.

McCowan, T. (2004). The growth of private higher education in Brazil: Implications for equity and quality. *Journal of Education Policy, 19*(4), 453–472.

Melo Neto, J. F. (2002). Extensão Universitária: bases ontológicas. Extensão universitária: diálogos populares, 13.

Merriam, S. B., & Tisdell, E. J. (2015). *Qualitative research: A guide to design and implementation* (4th ed.). John Wiley & Sons.

Meyer, M., & Sporn, B. (2018). Leaving the ivory tower: Universities' third mission and the search for legitimacy. *Zeitschrift für Hochschulentwicklung, 13*(2), 41–60.

Miranda, P. R., & de Azevedo, M. L. N. (2020). Fies e Prouni na expansão da educação superior brasileira: políticas de democratização do acesso e/ou de promoção do setor privado-mercantil? *Educação & Formação, 5*(3), e1421–e1421.

Neto, O. A., & Pimenta, G. A. (2020). The first year of Bolsonaro in office: Same old story, same old song? *Revista de Ciencia Politica, 40*(2), 187–213.

Peters, M. A., Rizvi, F., McCulloch, G., Gibbs, P., Gorur, R., Hong, M., et al. (2020). Reimagining the new pedagogical possibilities for universities post-COVID-19: An EPAT Collective Project. *Educational Philosophy and Theory*, 1–44. https://www.tandfonline.com/doi/pdf/10.1080/00131857.2020.1777655?needAccess=true

Prolo, I., Vieira, R., Lima, M., & Leal, F. (2019). Internacionalização das universidades brasileiras: contribuições do Programa Ciência sem Fronteiras. *Administração: Ensino e Pesquisa, 20*(2), 319–361.

Ristoff, D. (2013). Vinte e um anos de educação superior: expansão e democratização. *Cadernos do GEA, 3*, 1–59.

Ristoff, D. (2019). Os desafios da avaliação em contexto de expansão e inclusão. *Revista Espaço Pedagógico, 26*(1), 9–32.

Rowan, L., Rowan, L., & Christie. (2019). *Higher education and social justice.* Springer.

Schwartzman, S., Pinheiro, R., & Pillay, P. (2015). *Higher education in the BRICS countries: Investigating the pact between higher education and society* (Vol. 44). Springer.

Sobrinho, J. D. (2005). *Dilemas da educacao superior no mundo globalizado: Sociedade do conhecimento ou economia do conhecimento?* Casa do Psicólogo.

Souza, C. D. F. d., Paiva, J. P. S. d., Leal, T. C., Silva, L. F. d., & Santos, L. G. (2020). Evolução espaçotemporal da letalidade por COVID-19 no Brasil, 2020. *Jornal Brasileiro de Pneumologia, 46*(4), 1–3.

Verhine, R., & Vinhaes, L. (2018). Brazil: Problematics of the tripartite federal framework. In M. Carnoy, I. Froumin, I. Leshukov, & S. Marginson (Eds.), *Higher education in federal countries: A comparative study* (pp. 212–257). SAGE Publications, Inc. https://doi.org/10.4135/9789353280734.n6

Walker, M. (2012). A capital or capabilities education narrative in a world of staggering inequalities? *International Journal of Educational Development, 32*(3), 384–393.

Walker, M. (2019). Why epistemic justice matters in and for education. *Asia Pacific Education Review, 20*(2), 161–170.

Weerts, D. J., Freed, G. H., & Morphew, C. C. (2014). Organizational identity in higher education: Conceptual and empirical perspectives. In M. B. Paulson (Ed.), *Higher education: Handbook of theory and research* (volume 29) (pp. 229–278). Springer.

Bios

Kelber Tozini is an international doctoral student in the Education and Inequality program at The George Washington University where he is also a teaching assistant in the Masters in International Education Program.

He holds an M.A. in International Higher Education from Boston College and an M.S. in Administration from Universidade do Vale do Rio do Sinos (Brazil). His research interests include the internationalization of Brazilian higher education, the international student experience in U.S. colleges and universities, and the role of networks in reducing inequality in international higher education. E-mail: kelber@gwu.edu

Claudia Schiedeck Soares de Souza, Ph.D., is an emeriti professor of Federal Institute of Rio Grande do Sul (IFRS)—Campus Bento Gonçalves, in Bento Gonçalves, Rio Grande do Sul, Brazil. She is also the first Rector of IFRS (2008–2015) and was a visiting scholar at Ontario Institute for Studies in Education—OISE—University of Toronto. She holds a Ph.D. in Education from Universidade do Vale do Rio dos Sinos (UNISINOS). Her research interests are internationalization and comparative studies in vocational education and training. E-mail: claudia.souza@bento.ifrs.edu.br

Fernanda Leal, Ph.D., is an executive assistant at Universidade Federal de Santa Catarina (UFSC), Brazil, and was a visiting scholar at the Center for International Higher Education (CIHE), Boston College, United States, from August 2018 to March 2020. She holds a Ph.D. in Administration from Universidade do Estado de Santa Catarina (UDESC). Her research interests comprise internationalization, South-South relations, and (De)coloniality in higher education. E-mail: fernanda.leal@ufsc.br

Bernardo Sfredo Miorando, Ph.D., is an institutional development fellow at Universidade Federal de Ciências da Saúde de Porto Alegre (UFCSPA), in Porto Alegre, Brazil, and was a visiting scholar at the Finnish Institute for Educational Research (FIER), University of Jyväskylä, Finland. He holds a Ph.D. in Education from Universidade Federal do Rio Grande do Sul (UFRGS). His research interests involve evaluation, innovation, and politics in comparative and international higher education. E-mail: bernardo.sfredo@gmail.com

4 Belonging, Being, and Becoming

Tertiary Students in China in the Battle against COVID-19 Pandemic

Li Wang

Abstract

This chapter provides a critical reflection on a selection of tertiary students' responses in China in the national battle against COVID-19. It explains how tertiary students have responded to the COVID-19 pandemic and why they have responded. Student stories, diaries, and a letter published are reviewed as cases of their response in their national battle against the pandemic. The tertiary students' response to other national events is also retraced through a diary by the author while participating in higher education of China in the 1990s for further exploration. The impact of Chinese education philosophies, policy, system, and practice on the response to COVID-19 by Chinese tertiary students is explored. The belonging, being, and becoming of tertiary students in China is suggested to be the critical factor for the extensive participation and support by the students in the national battle against the COVID-19 pandemic.

Keywords

COVID-19 Pandemic; Education Philosophies; Policy; System and Practice; Students' Belonging, Being, and Becoming; Tertiary Students in China

Introduction

On December 27, 2019, a pneumonia of unknown cause (PUC) was reported to the local authority of Wuhan, China. On December 31, 27 PUC confirmed cases were reported to the World Health Organization (WHO) by Chinese authorities (WHO, 2020a). On January 3, China reported 44 PUC cases to the WHO and started updating it and countries concerned, regions, and organizations about the disease regularly. On January 4, the head of the Chinese Centre for Disease Control and Prevention (Chinese CDC) briefed his US counterpart about the PUC disease for cooperation. From that day, to cooperate, the head of the Chinese CDC briefed the head of the United

States Center for Disease Control (U.S. CDC) multiple times regarding the disease. On January 9, the Chinese Expert Team released information on the pathogen causing the disease and made a preliminary judgment that a novel coronavirus was the cause of the disease. Chinese authorities informed the WHO about the progress. Since January 11, China has been updating the WHO and other parties concerned about the coronavirus on a daily basis (Xinhua, 2020).

On January 16, Wuhan began to screen all patients in the city. On January 17, Beijing sent inspection teams to all provinces to guide the local epidemic prevention and control. During January 18–19, the Chinese National Health Commission (CNHC) sent a national senior medical expert team to Wuhan to study the local response to the epidemic (Xinhua, 2020). Professor Nanshan Zhong, Leader of the Senior Expert Group of CNHC went to investigate the condition of the disease in Wuhan. On January 20, the finding was published that the disease was able to transmit between people (Dong et al., 2020). On the same day, President Xi Jinping gave important instructions on fighting the disease with resolute efforts, emphasizing that people's lives and health must come first and above all else, calling for prompt release of the epidemic information and enhanced international cooperation (Xinhua, 2020). On January 23, Wuhan was under lockdown when 571 Novel Coronavirus Pneumonia (NCP) cases were confirmed in the whole country, including 95 severe cases and 17 deaths (Dong, 2020). All provinces in mainland China then activated Level 1 public health emergency response (Xinhua, 2020).

From January 24, 346 national medical teams composed of 42,600 medical workers and 965 public health professionals across China, and 4,000 medical professionals of the armed forces arrived at Wuhan to join local medical professionals to fight the epidemic (Xinhua, 2020). On the same day, the construction of a two-story Huo Shen Shan Hospital with 1,000 beds was started. It was completed on February 2 and started treating patients on February 3 (GMW.cn., 2020). On January 25, the construction of Lei Shen Shan Hospital with 1,600 beds started. It was completed on February 6 and started admitting patients on February 8 (You & Blanchard, 2020). Meanwhile, 16 makeshift hospitals with 14,000 beds were built up within ten days to accept all mild cases in Wuhan (Xinhua, 2020).

The WHO declared the new coronavirus disease 2019 outbreak on January 30 and announced on February 11 a name for it as coronavirus disease 2019 (COVID-19) (WHO, 2020b). It was the most challenging public health emergency in China since 1949. China launched a "people's war" to fight the epidemic (Xinhua, 2020). On March 6, the daily increase of confirmed cases in Wuhan was reduced to below 100 cases, down from a peak of more than 14,000 in early February (Renminwang, 2020). The 16 makeshift hospitals were closed down in Wuhan on March 10 after more than 12,000 patients accepted were cured with zero death (Zhongxinwang, 2020). On March 11, the daily increased domestic transmitted infections dropped to single digits in mainland China and then further dropped to zero cases on March 18, while the infections imported from overseas jumped to 34 cases (Renminwang, 2020).

Since March 18, China has taken rigorous steps to stop inbound cases to guard the hard-won gains in virus control and resume orderly work and production for its economic and social development. On April 26, Wuhan hospitals cleared all COVID-19 cases. By the end of May, 78,307 of a cumulative 83,017 patients, ranging from the ages of newborn babies to patients that were 108 years old, were cured and discharged from hospitals. This amounted to a cure rate of 94.3%. All COVID-19 patients received free testing and treatment in China. By May 31, a total of 163 million students (from early childhood to the secondary levels) returned to schools or kindergartens for normal classes (Xinhua, 2020). China was among the first countries to resume work and reopen schools and businesses (Xinhua News Agency, 2020).

On May 31, China received letters of support to fight the epidemic from more than 170 countries, 50 international and regional organizations, and more than 300 foreign political parties and organizations. It also received donated emergency medical supplies from 77 countries and 12 international organizations, and donations of materials by local governments, enterprises, non-governmental organizations, and people from 84 countries. Meanwhile, China offered assistance to 150 countries and four international organizations and sent 29 medical expert teams to 27 countries. From March 1st to May 31st, China provided $50 million to the WHO and exported protective equipment to 200 countries and regions to support them in fighting the epidemic. Chinese local governments, enterprises, organizations, and individuals also donated materials to more than 150 countries, regions, and international organizations. China sent the most urgent medical supplies and more medical expert teams and task forces to over 50 African countries and the African Union as well (Xinhua, 2020).

Preliminary statistics show that as of May 31, to fight the pandemic in China, 8.81 million registered volunteers participated in more than 460,000 projects. They volunteered at the front line, standing guard in communities, screening for infection, supporting other residents with their daily needs (Xinhua, 2020). Many volunteers were tertiary students. Universities, research institutes, and businesses across the country also joined forces in developing vaccines and medicines, and treatment. The institutional strengths of 19 provinces were "paired" with 16 cities and prefectures in Hubei to contain the outbreak. Over 42,000 medical workers including academicians and top experts across China joined the local medical professionals to fight the epidemic in Wuhan (Xinhua News Agency, 2020). There were 83 emergency research and development programs initiated. This research and innovation have been fully integrated with pandemic control and clinical treatment, highlighting the use of new technologies including big data and artificial intelligence (Xinhua, 2020). A vaccine developed by them was the first in the world to enter phase-two clinical trials on April 12, 2020. By July 23, 2020, nine enterprises in China started clinical trials of COVID-19 vaccines, and the emergency use of the vaccines has also started. With a decisive achievement in fighting the epidemic, China is now "racing against the clock to win its anti-poverty fight and achieve a moderately prosperous society in all respects" (Xinhua News Agency, 2020). Its economic growth has continued in the third quarter (Morningstar Analysts, 2020).

China has over 0.276 billion students and 16,720,000 teachers on various levels as of 2019. It regards education as the foundation to build up and develop the nation through century-long efforts. (Liang et al., 2019). This chapter is to reflect on the response of tertiary students in China to the pandemic, exploring the student belonging, being, and becoming, in terms of the educational philosophies, policy, system, and practice. After a literature review on the sense of belonging, being, and becoming, cases about the tertiary student response to the pandemic in China will also be reviewed. Based on it, a reflection is provided, including a diary used in retracing the Chinese student response to different events in China in the 1990s, to explore student belonging, being, and becoming, and the relevant education philosophies, policy, system, and practice. A discussion and conclusion are also presented. The limitation of this work includes perspectives of the author; being a participant in higher education in China at different stages and in Australia for the last decades, and personal research and academic experience.

Literature Review

Student belonging, being, and becoming have been increasingly attracted attention and discussion worldwide (Cole et al., 2020; Doroud et al., 2018; Morgan et al., 2012; Robinson et al., 2020; Trieu, 2009) for policy-making and practice in education. Maslow (1943) explained the three concepts in his theory about human needs for motivation. Maslow's theory has been endorsed in Chinese normal (teacher) education since 1949. Although "Maslow's model has been the target of positive and negative criticism over the years since he first suggested it", it has been viewed as an interesting potential "basis" for education research (Raymond, 1992, p. 123). Maslow's (1943) model of five-level human needs included physiological needs of human beings, such as shelter, food, and so on; safety needs for stability and security of physical and spiritual contents, such as safe living and secure job, age, and health system and insurance, and "a safe, orderly, predictable, organized world"; needs for love and belonging; needs for self-esteem and esteem of others; and self-actualization needs (p. 378).

Maslow (1943) mentioned that the five-level human needs were not necessarily in a hierarchical order, while he explained the concept of "belonging" together with "love and affection" at the same level (p. 380). He elaborated that the need for "belonging" was "hunger for affectionate relations with people in general, namely, for a place in his group, and he will strive with great intensity to achieve this goal" (p. 381). He also said that "one thing that must be stressed at this point is that love is not synonymous with sex. Sex may be studied as a purely physiological need…" and "Also not to be overlooked is the fact that the love needs involve both giving and receiving love" (p. 381). Hence, the "love" Maslow (1943) mentioned here can be interpreted as a love for life and love of, or for, people, or the relevant. Furthermore, Maslow (1943) believed that the fulfillment of the belonging needs was connected to "esteem needs", although the order may be changeable. He explained that all people in our society, with a few pathological exceptions, have a need or desire for the "stable, firmly based", and usually high evaluation of themselves, for "self-respect, or self-esteem, and for the esteem of others" (p. 381).

Maslow (1943) refers to the needs for "being" to the "desire for self-fulfillment" in the level for "self-actualization" which can be based on the "esteem needs". Maslow (1943) elaborated, (being is) "What a man can be, he must be" that it refers to "the tendency for him to become actualized in what he is potential" and "This tendency might be phrased as the desire to become more and more what one is, to become everything that one is capable of becoming" (p. 382). Thus, the "being" can be viewed as the temporary or partial fulfillment of a person's potential, while "becoming" can be the actualization of a person's full potential. Furthermore, Maslow (1943) stated,

> Perhaps more important than all these exceptions are the ones that involve ideals, high social standards, high values and the like. With such values people become martyrs; they will give up everything for the sake of a particular ideal, or value. (p. 387)

Maslow (1943) also mentioned, "not all human behavior is determined by the basic needs" and "We might even say that not all behavior is motivated. There are many determinants of behavior other than motives" (p. 390). Those concepts are relevant to the cases being used in this chapter.

Outside of China, although the sense of belonging, being, and becoming can be perceived differently, multiple research reports are viewed as positive for the concepts of belonging, being, and becoming. Matthews et al. (2011) reported that by providing a "space to socialize and relax", students believed that they were "being given the opportunity to form friendships and establish extended social networks with others in their courses" as well as "peers across different year levels" (Matthews et al., 2011, p. 113). He further explained that the students commented on the "shared social space" (even if not a home-like space as the Chinese students enjoyed) as "'familiar,' 'home-like,' 'permanent,' and the 'home-base at uni'" (p. 113). The study further revealed that a "shared social space" helped them to "foster a sense of belonging and community" for students in "broad discipline-based programs," which suggests a "supportive campus environment" and "greater overall satisfaction for student development" (p. 115). Although those research studies were conducted outside of China, it shares sense and values on the needs of student belonging, being, and becoming explored in this work, as addressed by Maslow (1943) as well.

Review of Cases

The Response of the Tertiary Students in China to the Pandemic

The 2020 Chinese New Year break was historically the longest for tertiary students in China due to the pandemic outbreak. While following the national and institutional guidance to protect themselves and their families and study at home, many tertiary students voluntarily participated in the national battle, fighting the epidemic vigorously, being even short of time to sleep, and only able to use their actions to write diaries. The following are partial examples randomly collected from countless published stories, diaries, and letters by Chinese tertiary students, used as part of cases in this work to review their response to the pandemic.

Case 1: *Forming the Wuhan Lei Shen Shan Anti-epidemic Team to Save Lives of People from Pandemic*

At the most critical stage after the epidemic outbreak, Wuhan University Zhongnan Hospital took over the Lei Shen Shan Hospital to treat severe NCP patients. About 286 hospitals across China with 3,202 medical professionals, 13,000 builders, and more than a thousand caring volunteers jointly with the Zhongnan Hospital formed the Lei Shen Shan Anti-Epidemic Team. Many of them were Wuhan University student volunteers. From February 8, on opening the Lei Shen Shan Hospital to April 15 when it was closed, the Team adopted the wartime hospital operation mode, with refined hospital management, homogenization of medical quality, and humanization of medical services, operating in a sincere unity in management, treatment, and scientific research. It carried out bold innovations to ensure the efficiency and highquality of the work. The Team received and treated 2,011 severe NCP patients, with a fully cured rate of 97.67% and zero infection, zero accidents, and zero environmental pollution. The Guidelines for the Prevention and Treatment of NCP by the Team has been adopted by many countries. The Lei Shen Shan teamwork has been acknowledged worldwide as the Chinese miracle. The Wuhan University Zhongnan Hospital won two National First Innovation Awards (Ke & Gao, 2020).

This is one of many examples of the Chinese higher education system's response to the pandemic. Preliminary statistics show that 138 tertiary institutions across China sent 14,000 medical professionals of their 371 affiliated hospitals to Wuhan and Hubei from January 24, being an important force in fighting the epidemic (Education Ministry of the People's Republic of China, 2020). Meanwhile, the Chinese military universities continuously sent medical teams to save and protect people from the epidemic in Wuhan. On January 24, the Chinese New Year Eve, the medical experts of the medical universities from the Army, Navy, and Airforce of China already arrived in Wuhan as the pioneering force (Xinhua, 2020). This case reflects that the graduates and students of Chinese tertiary institutes were fulfilling the full potential of their capacity to protect people's lives. It is not only self-actualization, as being and becoming, but beyond it, a great love and belonging to their big family, China, with ideals, high social standards, high values, and scientific spirits.

Case 2: *Launching Free Online Services to Support People's Psychological and Physical Fitness Needs*

On January 27, Beijing Normal University students, guided by their teachers, voluntarily took the lead in launching the epidemic psychological free support online service for the whole country. By February 9, the program already served nearly 3,000 people. To keep people informed and fit during the epidemic, all the students in the Clinical Medicine Class 2016 of Beijing Concord Medical College also voluntarily worked together to produce authoritative knowledge for NCP prevention and control. It is in simple and plain language, recorded in audio and video, and uploaded to the media platform to inform the public about the epidemic and ways to control spread and prevention. Beijing Sports University students, also guided by their teachers, voluntarily launched a series of "home fitness" programs to guide the whole country's indoor tai chi training for strong lung exercises daily. The first two public programs online were already watched by more than 4 million people/times by February 14 (Shi, 2020).

Again, this activity reflects students' strong sense of belonging and love to fulfill their ideals to keep people fit with their love and energy.

Case 3: *Launching Free Online Service to Help Primary and Secondary School Student Study during the Pandemic*

On February 23, during the epidemic outbreak, nine students from Hunan University, Beijing University, the Capital Medical University, Tsinghua University, the People's University, and other universities voluntarily launched a one-to-one free online learning program to help the primary and secondary school students to study at home in Wuhan. They carefully designed the program according to student needs. Within 24 hours after they issued the first notice, 720 undergraduate and postgraduate students joined them as volunteer tutors. A Chinese student in the United States also joined them via the internet. He said that during the outbreak of SARS, a university student voluntarily helped his brother in his study. Now it is his turn to help others. By April 28, 2,561 students from 346 tertiary institutions joined them as volunteer tutors, including 2,459 tertiary students from mainland China and 102 Chinese students from overseas. From March 4 to April 28, the Team already helped 558 school students with their studies in Wuhan. Among them, 221 were children from the anti-epidemic frontline medical workers' families, or patients' families, or families with difficulties. A total of 6,210 free classes were taught and the online learning resources developed by them were viewed by 40,000 students/times. The program has been greatly praised by learners and their parents. Student volunteer Yihan Liu expressed, "Life has gradually returned to normal. If the epidemic was on, our service will be on." (Xie, 2020)

This case reflects the students' sense of belonging to the country and people, and their being and becoming to fulfill their ideals to keep all the children safe and stable in learning with their deep caring.

Student Diary 1: February 23, 2020: In one-month "lockdown" of the city—My beloved city and campus and I: Wuhan University has protected me as my family and home.

…. Being a student is lucky, being a Wuhan University student is happy. In order to reduce the chance of contact in the epidemic, the School sent meals to the dormitory downstairs, three meals per day with meat, and eggs, etc, and a mask, hand sanitizer, Chinese medicine, and thermometer for each of us, urging us to report our temperature on time every day. If I forgot to do so, I would receive a private letter from my Fudaoyuan (Teacher in student management). Although I was sorry for my memory, I felt very warm in my heart. Wuhan University has been protecting me as my family and home.

On January 29, … I immediately applied for participation as a volunteer. I did not want to be a person only protected by others. As a medical student, I can play my part in the battle, although I am unable to fight in the frontline.

The next day I met a lot of enthusiastic classmates and our work was very interesting, sorting out the goods of support received from all over the world. We need to sort all of the couriers into categories, handling each of them. The goods have been continuously arriving by truck. Each courier was with wholehearted love. Some gifts came with dozens of big boxes and other donations from large companies. Some were small bags of personal gifts. Some gifts were goods attached with letters, written with inspiring words, presenting to us deep loving and warm caring. Great people's will have built up the fortress against the pandemic. Wuhan will win. …. (Fan, 2020, paras. 3–5)

The diary reflects the student's belonging, his love, and pride of his belonging, being, and becoming to fulfill his willingness to contribute his efforts to the country in fighting the pandemic.

Student Diary 2: March 2, 2020: Fighting the epidemic – An "anti-epidemic" diary of a student volunteer born "post-2000" of Nanhua Business and Vocational Institute, Guangdong.

As the pandemic hits China, our college students must respond to it actively. As a college student born "after 2000", I will protect our hometown and keep it clean with my strengths. University students protected us from SARS in 2003. It is our turn to protect others.

On the first day being a volunteer in the anti-pandemic war, I arrived at the inspection post earlier than scheduled. I stood working continuously for more than 7 hours. The feet lost sense, but I persisted on, considering it was worth allowing peers a little more rest. We, youths, should take our responsibility. Being able to guard our hometown and contribute my strengths to society, I feel immensely proud.

.... Life is of paramount importance. The pandemic outbreak is a command. It is our responsibility to prevent and control it. As long as we are determined with confidence, working together, scientifically preventing and controlling the pandemic with precise measures, we will certainly win the anti-epidemic war. (Guo, 2020, paras. 2–8)

The diary reflects the students' belonging and love to the "hometown" with scientific spirits and
    determination to fulfill his being, becoming for ideals to keep people safe and guard the "home".

Student Diary 3: February 15, 2020: An anti-epidemic diary by a college student volunteer.

Today is Saturday, but none of the community staff are resting. My mother and I arrived at the Centre on time at 8:30 a.m. We immediately started volunteering. We are stationed in the Office of Epidemic Prevention and Control, responsible for investigating by phone the situations of the residents who came from and returned to Wuhan, and the Jianhe tourists visiting friends and relatives with close contacts. We are also establishing information accounts and reports for epidemic prevention and control. ... Every day, residents gave me a lot of appreciation, such as, "You've worked hard" and "Thank you" which are great comforts to me. Particularly, we saw 83-year-old academician Professor Nanshan Zhong leading people again in the crucial and dangerous anti-pandemic war. We saw many medical staff working continuously for several days and nights without closing their eyes still willingly persisted in the battle against the epidemic .... We saw those brave heroes protecting people's lives, to guarantee their safety with their great love. They are dedicating their own lives to others, fighting fiercely against the coronavirus, protecting and supporting patients and people .... Seeing those, we feel heartache but deeply moved. It inspired me to be more determined and do better in epidemic prevention and control, and not afraid of any hardship and difficulties.

.... My heart silently shouted, Cheer up, Wuhan! China will win! (Gong, 2020, paras. 3–8)

This diary reflects the student's strong sense of belonging and confidence to her country, and her love, esteem, and pride of her people in fulfilling her being and becoming through her ideals to keep people safe from the pandemic by working hard voluntarily with her mother.

An initiative letter by Hubei University Students Association dated January 26, 2020

Dear Students:

Life is of the utmost value. The epidemic outbreak is a command for our action. Virus prevention and control is our mission. Wuhan, being a "university city" of vibrant and infinite vitality with more than a million tertiary students is the fortress for us to build up our dream and a home for us to grow up. At this moment, most students have returned to their hometowns. .... At the critical stage of the epidemic outbreak, no matter where we are, our hearts are closely related. Let us act promptly to participate in the virus prevention and control, working scientifically and orderly to fight the epidemic with our best resolute efforts for victory. Here we send an initiative to all tertiary students in the University, the City, and this Province: .... (Hubei University Students Association, 2020, January 26, para. 2, as cited in Feng, 2020)

The Hubei University students were one of many tertiary student groups in China who issued an initiative for students to promptly respond to the critical epidemic. It reflects the student "belonging" to the University home, their "being" as students closely related to each other, and they are willing to fulfill their "becoming" by fighting the epidemic vigorously, scientifically, and orderly for victory.

In summary, the cases above reflect the belonging and love of the Chinese tertiary students and graduates to their country, their hometown, university, people, children, and peers; and their being and becoming to fulfill their mission and ideals with high social standards and high values. Facing the death-threatening pandemic, they dedicated themselves to caring, protecting, and saving people from the pandemic. More cases are viewed by the author including the student response to the pandemic in broad areas, such as in translating and preparing materials and equipment for international aid, helping residents with their daily needs, donating protective materials, clothes, blood, and money to people and communities and so on (Shi, 2020). All those demonstrate their belonging, being, and becoming in responding to the pandemic with determination.

Reflection

The Tertiary Students' Belonging, Being, and Becoming

Maslow's (1943) theory on human needs and behavior has been endorsed in Chinese normal (teacher) education as part of the theories for the education policy since 1949. From traditional Chinese cultural perspectives, "belonging" is a sense of belonging to a human being's own family for people to share, care for, and support each other. China is a nation with traditional values of family sense endorsed in education on a deep level. Historically, teachers there were valued in status for worship by students and student families. Contemporarily, the sense of "belonging" in Chinese education has been valued as sharing, caring, and mutual support between students, and teachers, and students. It denotes the connection and relationship among students, students and teachers, and students, teachers and the institutes, as well as the nation. With a collective culture, an individual family is usually addressed as a "small family," while a class collective, school, institute, or the state can be referred to as a "big family". Being is another level of belonging; it can denote each student's role and actions related to university life. Becoming can indicate student actualization of their goals or ideals, including their future roles, employment, and achievements. Thus, Maslow's model has been adopted naturally in Chinese education.

Chinese education policy and the system has paid close attention to cultivating students to develop their sense of belonging, being, and becoming from early childhood to the tertiary and post-tertiary levels. For example, every student has grown up singing their different team songs for children, teenagers, or youths at different stages. Each song clearly expressed their belonging, being, and becoming. Taking the Children's Team Song since 1950 as an example, it sings, "We are children of New China. We are pioneers of new youths. United and inheriting our father and brother, we are not afraid of difficulties and challenges, we are striving for the construction of New China ...." Another song for children titled "I have an ideal" sings, "I have an ideal which is a great ideal. When I grow up, I will become ...."

Chinese Educational Philosophies and Policy

Philosophically, education has been valued as paramount in China for thousands of years except for certain interruptive periods. Chinese education is rooted in love and based on human needs to nurture comprehensively developed human beings. Since 1949, the national higher education policy has been set up to cultivate the students to become the successors and pillars for the national cause, with all-round development in the moral, intellectual, and physical aspects. Aesthetic development has also been required since the 1990s. The Chinese educational policy, supporting the traditional education philosophy, requires education institutions and teachers to fully consider and accommodate student needs. Each curriculum has been requested to be designed according to student differences (yincaishijiao). Furthermore, Chinese tertiary education is not only designed to meet the academic needs of students but also for developing student humanistic ideals which have been included in the curricula for every level. Also, integrating theory closely with reality in practice for innovation has been emphasized in the educational policy of China since 1949. Overall, education is fundamental to develop the nation and it is the cornerstone for Chinese revitalization and its social progress. Chinese value education as the hope for personal growth, the hope of families, and that it is the hope for the development of the nation (Liang et al., 2019).

Chinese Higher Education System and Practice

Chinese higher education system and practice are constructive and consistent with the educational philosophies and policy to address comprehensive needs of tertiary students in ideals, morality, academic achievements, living, health, and so on for personal, social, and professional development. Most Chinese tertiary institutions are in the public education system for Government funding and resources. All the enrolled tertiary students have been guaranteed with stable on-campus dormitories (unless a student chooses to live outside), dining rooms, and a class collective with stable classmates and space till graduation, while students are free to select their academic topics and units.

Every class collective has also a Banzhuren (a teacher in charge of a class) who has been usually an academic teacher for the students' major topic/s, from the beginning of the student enrollment till their graduation. A Banzhuren is responsible to accommodate student comprehensive needs, including each student's academic needs; living needs, including dormitories and dining halls; scholarship, study grants or living assistance grants, and study loans; the physical and health needs; the aesthetic, recreation, and wellbeing needs; and student moral, social, and career development, or employment before their graduation. The system has been reinforced later by increasing one more teacher titled as Fudaoyuan for student management work, such as supervising the students' social practice during holidays. Some universities may also have an Assistant Fudaoyuan for each class, determined by each institute.

Each class has also a student-managed team for the corresponding needs mentioned above, supervised by the Banzhuren/Fudaoyuan. All academic staff in Chinese tertiary institutions have been guaranteed job security, career development, and living stability such as apartments, dining halls, and kindergartens for staff and families. Students and staff have been provided with free medical service via the on-campus clinics or the institutional hospital, gymnastic, recreation, and transportation facilities.

This is an excerpt of a diary entry from 1991 written by the author, while working as a Banzhuren, for a National Higher Education Conference in Student Management in China, regarding student response to other critical events. It can further explain the Chinese higher education system and practices, in terms of the students developing their belonging, being, and becoming.

.... All the 40 students in the class have been sharing, caring and supporting each other through years of studying and living together. For example, after Mr. Liu, a student, fell in the bathroom last week, his classmates voluntarily took turns looking after him until he was fully recovered. Academically, the students have been regularly sharing their learning experiences with classmates and setting up one-to-one plan to help each other for common progress. The rate of academic success for the whole class has reached 98.6% which is higher than the required standards by the University. The students have been continuously learning from Lei Feng (a national hero on collectivism and noble ideals to serve the people selflessly) with their action for response to critical incidents. For example, when a fire was found in the suburbs far away from the campus, at nighttime this semester, they voluntarily rushed to participate in the fire fighting. They also regularly used their weekends to provide free financial consultation, serve the people in the streets, and help the vulnerable with their needs voluntarily. During the semester break at home, they voluntarily joined the local communities to fight the floods and rescue people.

The motto of the class is, "Your existence is the happiness of the people around you." According to the statistics and the compliment letters received from the community, the students have already voluntarily responded to critical events to help and serve the people and the community 152 persons/times. They have continuously participated in the performing arts and sports matches, and won awards for the University. As a class, collectively, they have also developed a sound relationship with other classes and tertiary institutes. They received multiple awards of Excellent Class from the University and the State, and commendation letters from the communities and individuals for numerous times for being unsung heroes. Being their Banzhuren, I am proud of the students. (Author, Working Diary, June 28, 1991)

In summary, the Chinese tertiary education policy and system respect people and life. It is for students' all-round development in the moral, intellectual, physical, and aesthetic aspects, accommodating student comprehensive needs. The educational practice is to cultivate better human beings who are not only for their basic needs but also for the realization of the harmonies and happiness of the human community. Chinese students have been highly influenced by the high cultural values of "being the first to become concerned with the world's troubles, and the last to rejoice in its happiness" originated from the classic by Fan Zhongyan (989–1052). Students have continuously been steered to participate in social practice for learning to integrate knowledge with action for a positive difference.

The national policy to value people and life as the first and paramount principle provides the macrostructural environment for student development. Nowhere has this been demonstrated more than the students' responses to the pandemic. For example, every person in China has been carefully tested and every patient has been carefully treated in the epidemic, regardless of their age, gender, ethnicities, nationalities, social, or economic status. In Wuhan, among the fully recovered, 3,000 patients are over 80 years old and 7 patients are over 100 years old. The average cost for treating a COVID-19 patient is 23,000 yuan. For an average patient in severe condition, the cost surpassed 150,000 yuan. In critical cases, each cost exceeded 1 million yuan. The highest cost is about 1.5 million yuan or US$211,372 for a patient over 70 years old cared for by more than ten medical workers for several weeks, with costs fully covered by the Government. All the patients, confirmed or suspected, received subsidies from the state finance for any medical bills not covered by their medical insurance or the medical assistance fund. About 4 million Chinese community workers worked in around 650,000 urban and rural communities to protect and help residents with daily needs (Xinhua, 2020).

Many Chinese people voluntarily donated money to the communities without leaving their names. There were people who worked extremely hard in building the hospitals and fighting the pandemic, but they refused receiving the payments or donated the payments immediately to hospitals. Some aged citizens determinedly asked communities to accept donations of their retirement savings. All the people are grateful and strong with spirits to care for each other, fighting to protect the vulnerable from the pandemic. Many students from foreign countries living in China during the epidemic outbreak expressed that they were feeling safe and even joined the Chinese students to become volunteers to help others. They said they were not outsiders (Sina xinwen zhongxin, 2020).

Finally, the well-developed information technologies such as WeChat, artificial intelligence, Big Data, and Cloud computing have been valued by many for keeping the students informed and connected. More than a quarter of a billion full-time students resumed their studies in mid-February through online platforms, which was the largest "online movement" in education history (Sengyee, 2020).

Discussion and Conclusions

COVID-19 pandemic is the most challenging event in China and the world in this century. Tertiary students in China faced it by presenting a vigorous response, which expressed their belonging, being, and becoming. It is viewed as a thought-provoking response to a big test for tertiary education policy and system, supported by the educational philosophies, and endorsed in the practice in China. Nurturing the student's strong sense of connection, mission, and vision with ideals, Chinese higher education policy has maintained consistency with the national policy in respecting people and life and accommodating human needs for all-round development of the students. Through a century-long striving to move from standing up to being prosperous, and then to become stronger with comprehensive development of the nation, particularly, since the Opening and Reform in 1978, Chinese higher education has become the national priority for development. The development of education is philosophized as a need for the development of the nation.

Globally, in the first two decades of the 21st century, human beings have continuously experienced attacks by SARS, H1N1, H5N1, H7N9, Cholera, MERS, Ebolavirus, and now COVID-19. Human beings in the world share the common fate of health and safety and have the same needs to be addressed for survival and the sustainability of the earth for the global community. Meanwhile, a report on September 2, 2019, was stirring the author's mind that each year there have been 800,000 people who have died of suicide. Suicide became the leading cause of death in young people aged 18–29. Every 40 seconds, one suicide happened in the world due to complex issues, requiring coordination and collaboration among multiple sectors of society, such as "education, labor, agriculture, business, justice, law, defense, politics, and the media" (WHO, 2019). People facing other conflicts, such as violence, exclusion, gaps, poverty, and climate change, often ask the same question: What is education for? Being an educator in higher education for decades, I realized that education may not have the power to fix the issues listed. But it is an educator's responsibility to call on educators and education policy-makers to pay more attention to the needs of the young people for their belonging, being, and becoming; for their survival and development; for a harmonious, safe, and sustainable environment, so that young students can equally share, care, and support each other; and all of us, together, the earth, the global home for all.

Acknowledgment

I would like to express my deep gratitude to Professor Darol Cavanagh of UNESCO-INRULED, Beijing Normal University, for his great support to this work with excellent advice on the drafts; to Professor Nanshan Zhong of Guangzhou Institute of Respiratory Health, China, for his excellent talk with insightful anti-pandemic information in China, presented to the China Studies Centre, the University of Sydney, invited by the Centre; to Professor Tian Xie of Wuhan University, Professor Qi Feng of Shanghai University, and Professor Dongmei Qu of Harbin Normal University, for their great support with insightful information on the university student management, and student response to the epidemic in China.

References

Cole, D., Newman, C. B., & Hypolite, L. I. (2020). Sense of belonging and mattering among two cohorts of first-year students participating in a comprehensive college transition program. *American Behavioral Scientist, 64*(3) 276–297. SAGE Publications. https://doi.org/10.1177/0002764219869417, journals.sagepub.com/home/abs

Jiaoyubu. (2020, June 29). Tong shijian saipao, yu yimo jiaoliang. Quanli chiyuan Hubei kangji xinguanfeiyan yiqing: Jiaoyuxitong jianjue daying yiqing fangkong zhujizhan xilie zhier [Race with time, fight with the epidemic, fully support Wuhan against the NCP: Chinese education system resolutely fight to win the epidemic prevention and control resistance war, Series II]. *Zhongguojiaoyu zaixian*. https://news.eol.cn/yaowen/202006/t20200629_1735712.shtml

Dong, K. (2020, April 2). *Zhongguo kangyi tujian laile! Yitu kandong zheliangeyue fashengle henme* [There comes the anti-COVID-19 picture! Understanding what happened in the two months in one picture]. [infographic]. Duzhe xinmeiti, Renminribao weixin, Woshi K Dong, Jiatingzazhi. https://www.wxnmh.com/thread-6958720.htm

Dong, K., Li, J., Tan, S., Zhou, Y. (Directors), Ye, N., Dong, K. (Writers), Cai, F., Bi, Jun., Chen, G., & Zheng, X. (Producers). (2020, April 8). Dute shijiao xiade guoshi dandang! [The national soldier's role from a unique perspective!]. [Film (Documentary)]. In G. Zheng, Y. Shi, F. Lei, & Q. Lin (Executive Producers), *Zhong Nanshan*. [Nanshan Zhong]. Guangdong Radio and Television Station; Zhonghongwang Company Limited, Guangdong Branch; Shenzhen Qianhaiweilan Network Culture Media Company Limited; Centre of External Communication, Guangdong Radio and Television Station (International Channel); Guangdong Radio and Television Station Dong Ke Studio. https://v.qq.com/x/cover/mzc00200b1552j2/y0947la5jxg.html

Doroud, N., Fosseyb, E., & Fortunec, T. (2018). Place for being, doing, becoming and belonging: A meta-synthesis exploring the role of place in mental health recovery. *Health and Place*, *52*, 110–120. https://doi.org/10.1016/j.healthplace.2018.05.008

Education Ministry of the People's Republic of China. (2020, June 29). Tong shijian saipao, yu yimo jiaoliang. Quanli chiyuan Hubei kangji xinguanfeiyan yiqing: Jiaoyuxitong jianjue daying yiqing fangkong zhujizhan xilie zhier [Race with time, fight with the epidemic, fully support Wuhan against the Novel Coronavirus Pneumonia: Chinese education system resolutely fight to win the epidemic prevention and control resistance war, Series II]. *Sino-Education Online. https://news.eol.cn/yaowen/202006/t20200629_1735712.shtml*

Fan, Z. (2020, February 23). Wuhan daxue xiangjia yiyang baohuzhe wo [Wuhan University has protected me like my family and home]. In L. Chen & X. Li (Eds.), *Fengcheng yiyue – wo he wo shenaide chengshi he xiaoyuan* [In one-month "lockdown" of the city - My beloved city and campus, and I]. Wuhandaxue xinwenwang. https://news.whu.edu.cn/info/1002/57410.htm

Feng, P. (2020, January 27). Kangji xinguanfeiyan yiqing, Hubei daxue xiang gaoxiao fachu changyi! [To combat the NCP epidemic, Hubei University issued an initiative to tertiary institutions!]. *Zhongguojiaoyu zaixian*. https://www.eol.cn/hubei/hubeinews/202001/t20200127_1707645.shtml

GMW.cn. (2020, February 10). China speed: Huoshenshan Hospital, built in 10 days. In ZY (Ed.), *Guangming online*. http://en.gmw.cn/2020-02/10/content_33541065.htm

Gong, W. (2020, February 26). Yige daxuesheng zhiyuanzhe Gong Wenjin de kangyi riji [An anti-epidemic diary by a college student volunteer]. In X. Peng (Ed.), *Qiandongnan ribao*. Zhongguo gansuwang. http://dxs.gscn.com.cn/system/2020/02/26/012327862.shtml

Guo, X. (2020, March 2). Kangji yiqing: yipian "lingling hou" daxuesheng zhiyuanzhede "zhanyi riji" [Fighting against the Epidemic: An "anti-epidemic" diary of a college student volunteer born "Post-2000"]. *Souhu*. https://www.sohu.com/a/377299890_120207034

Ke, T., & Gao, X. (2020, May 30). Zhongnanyiyuan zhanhuo liangxiang quanguo chuangxin zengxianjiang [Wuhan University Zhongnan Hospital won two National First Innovation Awards]. In L. Chen (Ed.), *The Second Clinical Collegeclinical college*. Wuhandaxue xinwenwang. https://news.whu.edu.cn/info/1002/60632.htm

Liang, Z., Zhou, Y. (Writers), He, Y., Li, X., Ouyang, Q., Liang, B., Hu, S. (Directors), Zhou, X., Shen, H., & Chen, B. (Producers). (2019, November 5). Liguozhiben [The fundamental to develop a nation] (Session 1) [TV series]. In Y. Sun, X. Li, M. Xu, X. Zhou, D. Cui, J. Zhang, L. Dong, H. Lu, & G. Quan (Executive Producers), *Jiaoyu qiangguo* [Education makes a powerful nation]. Zhongyang guangbo dianshi zongtai; Zhongguo jiaoyubu; *CCTV; Xinhuawang.* http://www.xinhuanet.com/video/2019-11/07/c_1210345242.htm

Maslow, A. H. (1943). A theory of human motivation. *Psychological Review, 50*(4), 370–396. http://dx.doi.org/10.1037/h0054346

Matthews, K. E., Andrews, V., & Adams, P. (2011). Social learning spaces and student engagement. *Higher Education Research & Development*, 105–120. https://doi.org/10.1080/07294360.2010.512629

Morgan, A. R., Rivera, F., Moreno, C., & Haglund, B. J. (2012). Does social capital travel? Influences on the life satisfaction of young people living in England and Spain. *BMC Public Health.* http://www.biomedcentral.com/1471-2458/12/138

Morningstar Analysts. (2020, November 5). China's rapid recovery on much firmer Footing. *Morningstar.* https://www.morningstar.com.au/credit/article/chinas-rapid-recovery-on-much-firmer-footing/206968

Raymond, C. (1992). Models as an effective research tool. In D. M. Cavanagh & G. W. Rodwell (Eds.), *Dialogues in educational research* (pp. 117–126). William Michael Press.

Renminwang. (2020, March 19). China's Wuhan marks no new coronavirus case, success of strict measures. *GlobalSecurity.org.* https://www.globalsecurity.org/security/library/news/2020/03/sec-200319-pdo07.htm

Robinson, S., Hill, M., Fisher, K. R., & Graham, A. (2020). Belonging and exclusion in the lives of young people with intellectual disability in small town communities. *Journal of Intellectual Disabilities, 24*(1) 50–68. https://doi.org/10.1177/1744629518765830, journals.sagepub.com/home/jid

Sengyee, L. (2020, April 8). How China's industrial internet is fighting COVID-19. *World Economic Forum.* https://www.weforum.org/agenda/2020/04/china-covid-19-digital-response/

Shi, J. (2020, February 14). *Kangyi yixian: Shoudu daxuesheng zaixingdong* [Anti-epidemic first-line: Capital university students in action]. Zhongguo jiaoyu xinwenwang. http://www.jyb.cn/rmtzcg/xwy/wzxw/202002/t20200214_295480.html

Sina xinwen zhongxin (Host). (2020, May 29). Disan ji: wozai Zhongguo [Session 3: I'm in China] [Video podcast episode]. In S. Wang (Ed.), *Zhongguo kangyi renwugushi* [People's anti-epidemic stories in China]. Zhonggong zhongyang duiwai lianluobu xinwen bangongshi; Guojia guangbo dianshi zongju guoji hezuosi; Jiangxi shengwei xuanchuanbu; Guangdong guangbo dianshitai xinwen zhongxin; Huayi fangyuan yingshi wenhua youxian gongsi. Sina. (cited from Renminwang). https://news.sina.com.cn/gov/2020-05-29/doc-iircuyvi5647627.shtml

Trieu, M. M. (2009). Identity construction among Chinese-Vietnamese Americans: Being, becoming, and belonging. In S. J. GoldG. Rubén, & R. G. Rumbaut (Eds.), *The New AmericansRrecent Immigration and American Society* (228 pages). A Series from LFB Scholarly Publishing LLC.

World Health Organization. (2019, September 2). Suicide. *World Health Organization.* https://www.who.int/news-room/fact-sheets/detail/suicide

World Health Organization. (2020a, January 5). Emergencies preparedness, response: Pneumonia of unknown cause – China, disease outbreak news. *World Health Organization.* https://www.who.int/csr/don/05-january-2020-pneumonia-of-unkown-cause-china/en/

World Health Organization. (2020b, February 11). Novel-coronavirus-2019/events-as-they-happen.

World Health Organization. https://www.who.int/emergencies/diseases/novel-coronavirus-2019/events-as-they-happen

Xie, Y. (2020, May 2). 2561 daxuesheng wei zhongxiaoxuesheng jiaqi "yunduanshuzhuo" [2561 Tertiary students set up "desk through clouds" for primary and secondary school students]. *Xinhuawang.* http://education.news.cn/2020-05/02/c_1125936215.htm

Xinhua. (2020, June 7). Full text: Fighting COVID-19: China in action. In Huaxia (Ed.), *Xinhuanet.* http://www.xinhuanet.com/english/2020-06/07/c_139120424.htm

Xinhua News Agency. (2020, September 8). Xi Focus: Chronicle of Xi's leadership in China's war against coronavirus. *PML Daily Content Partner.* https://www.pmldaily.com/investigations/special-reports/2020/09/xi-focus-chronicle-of-xis-leadership-in-chinas-war-against-coronavirus.html

You, T., & Blanchard, S. (2020, January 30). News: Wuhan's SECOND coronavirus hospital springs from the ground in time-lapse video as officials say it will be open in a week and global death toll hits 170. *Mail Online.* https://www.dailymail.co.uk/news/article-7942007/Time-lapse-footage-shows-Wuhan-building-second-coronavirus-hospital-1-600-beds.html

Zhongxinwang. (2020, June 7, 12:41). Jiankuzuojue, yongyuan mingji! 50 juhua huigu Zhongguo zhanyi licheng [Hard work, always remember! 50 sentences to review China's anti-epidemic war]. In Langlang (Ed.), *Zhongguo xinwenwang.* Xinlangkeji. https://tech.sina.com.cn/roll/2020-06-07/doc-iircuyvi7178291.shtml

Bio

Li Wang, Dr Teach, has been engaged in teaching and research in education, culture, literature, and language for the University of Sydney, University of Technology Sydney, and Charles Darwin University for the last decades. Dr. Li also worked for the Higher Education of the People's Bank of China, being an Associate Professor since 1994, and then a Visiting Professor for Shanghai University. Her recent academic book in education is *Culture Pedagogy: Teaching Chinese Culture in Australia.* E-mail: li.wang@sydney.edu.au

5 Coming in from the Cold

US-China Academic Relations after COVID-19

Joshua S. McKeown

Abstract

Academic relationships between Chinese and foreign higher education institutions have flourished for a generation, building upon intermittent outward-looking strategies since the late 19th century. International academic collaborations are an established practice for American institutions. Despite the urgency of the COVID-19 global pandemic, those with China are being challenged on national security grounds as the preferred method for state-directed acquisition of sophisticated science and technology, and other concerns. For US institutions founded on traditions of academic freedom, shared governance, and reciprocity, to be accused of negligence and naivete while China engages in such violations is a devastating affront both to the purpose of the university as known in the West and to the reputations and self-worth of many who work in them. More crucial than ever, US-China academic collaborations are facing heightened restrictions. Solutions to reforge and redefine this complex but enduring academic relationship in the post-COVID-19 era are discussed.

Key words

international education, international exchange, research collaboration, higher education, China, US-China relations, study abroad, education policy

Introduction

The novel coronavirus that caused the COVID-19 global pandemic was perhaps the one thing able to bypass border restrictions and walls, ignore tariffs and trade barriers, evade surveillance by state and big tech corporate actors, and shut down the mobility of people and supply chains worldwide. In an age sometimes described in terms of unfettered and borderless *hyperglobalization* (Murray, 2006), the virus reminded people worldwide of the fragility of what had seemed irreversible triumphs of globalization.

COVID-19 and global higher education have a similarly vivid story, particularly the near cessation of student and scholar mobility. Closer examination of recent trends tells a more nuanced story of when this slowdown in international educational exchange began, however (Fischer, 2019), particularly in the relationship between the two largest economies and most powerful states in the world: United States and People's Republic of China. The response to the pandemic tended to be a nationalist one, even though the crisis itself was global and international institutions arguably being the most efficient mechanisms to solve it (Richardson, 2020). Little public discussion occurred in the United States on how American institutions of higher education could work with Chinese or other foreign counterparts collaboratively. Whereas academics in China called for greater collaboration towards a more global scientific community able to tackle the pandemic and other challenges (Li, 2020), there was not a similarly urgent national discussion in the United States despite decades of advanced international partnerships.

Whether as one aspect of global great power rivalry (Colby & Mitchell, 2020), or as pawns in an emerging new Cold War (Layne, 2020), academic relationships between the United States and China had taken on a decidedly frostier tone before the pandemic. COVID-19 laid it bare. Why did this occur and what can be done to resolve it? This chapter seeks to provide insight into the enduring and complex academic relationship between China and the United States and provides considerations for reforging and redefining it towards new normalcy.

US-China Higher Education at a Crossroads

Global higher education is fundamentally about *education*. Done right, internationalization of higher education supports and transforms curricula through meaningful interactions of culture and language (Knight, 1994); it contributes to students' intellectual and academic development (McKeown, 2009; McKeown et al., 2021); it enables scholars and researchers to collaborate productively on the most effective solutions to global challenges (Xie & Freeman, 2021); and can extend higher education institutions beyond national borders towards their broader and more excellent forms (de Wit & Hunter, 2015).

Higher education institutions also reside within states. They are organizations incorporated inside borders of countries whose laws they are subject to, often founded by governments and resourced through political processes, and typically constructed to serve the interests of the state. Although they may have relative degrees of autonomy depending on the form of government where they operate, they are regulated by the state and typically exist in order to contribute to the prosperity of the nation's population and economy (Cantwell et al., 2018). While universities in the United States have arguably held a less clear acknowledgment of their role vis-à-vis the state (Pusser, 2018), and have been largely autonomous to pursue international interests free from significant government interference, those in China are very much under state control in general and Chinese Communist Party (CCP) direction in particular (Cai & Yan, 2017). While there are different university models in

China, with varying degrees of national control, it is nevertheless true that all Chinese institutions of higher education must follow state goals and objectives, including CCP political supervision (Lai, 2010) with incentives to develop graduates in strategic fields for key industries (Lau, 2020).

This "asymmetry in Sino-American exchange" (Hoover Institution, 2018), particularly the different governance structures and perceived academic objectives of US and Chinese higher education, underlies much of the recent criticism facing Chinese universities in their dealings with American counterparts. Seen this way, China is tactically exploiting gaps in an otherwise open system of collegial exchange with the United States. American institutions may not always be aware of what their faculty are doing overseas, for example, or the extent to which their researchers collaborate with Chinese state-run operations. Such lack of oversight is not typically what American institutions encounter from the Chinese government when working in China, however, what the Director of the FBI called "naivete on the part of the academic sector" (U.S. Senate, 2019).

Tough policies have been implemented because of this suspicion. The United States began revoking Chinese student and scholar visas over suspected ties to China's military, and some visiting Chinese scholars funded by their government were forced to leave the United States. On American campuses, administrators received sternly-written directives from the federal government, including a letter co-signed by the Secretaries of State and Education warning universities to "examine carefully" all China-related activities, to "push back against efforts to infiltrate and divide us," and that the "authoritarian influence" of the "CCP's totalitarian regime" should be guarded against (U.S. Departments of State and Education, 2020).

Strenuous policy guidance (U.S. Department of State, 2020) critical of Chinese Confucius Institutes, at one time totaling more than 500 on university campuses worldwide including in the United States before recent closures, were issued in 2020. Confucius Institutes are mutually agreed-to language and cultural centers staffed and funded by Chinese universities, hosted by partner universities. They have become lightning rods for criticism and scrutiny in the United States as "essentially political arms of the Chinese government" (U.S. Senate, 2019) operating on American university campuses. This reflects a chilling concern for US higher education regarding China: undue influence by the Chinese state on American campuses. It is particularly acute in sensitive technological and scientific research, free speech and academic freedom issues, and on-campus operations. Joint research collaborations between universities, a tradition of academic exchange and mobility programs, are now criticized as the "preferred method" (Hoover Institution, 2018) for Chinese state-directed acquisition of sought-after technologies from the United States. Seemingly harmless on-campus clubs and social groups under the Chinese Student and Scholar Association (CSSA) banner are seen as a "ready channel and entry point" (Hoover Institution, 2018) for intelligence gathering, as well as to stifle academic freedom by keeping in line Chinese campus peers through monitoring and reporting on those who stray from official CCP narratives on controversial topics like Tibet's autonomy, persecution of minorities in Xinjiang, democracy activists in Hong Kong, and the status of Taiwan.

The COVID-19 pandemic heightened official US rhetoric, blaming China for missteps managing the virus and bringing to the surface simmering disputes and grievances that impact the foundation of US-China academic relations. It also has raised concerns for US higher education and international education professionals that they and their universities are expected to be part of the official state apparatus designed to exclude, restrict, and monitor international partners rather than embrace, expand, and enrich what had until recently been considered a mutually beneficial exchange, perhaps confirming after all that even in the United States "(h)igher education is an inherently political activity" (Cantwell et al., 2018).

China's Unique Position

China's higher education sector has been on an accelerating modernization and internationalization process over the past two decades. It has grown through similar state-directed and state-funded agendas as other economic sectors, with the goal to improve academic offerings, expand research capacity and expertise, diversify and internationalize personnel (particularly in English language proficiency), and overall to become globally competitive.

The Chinese government has not hidden its efforts to include higher education in its engagement with and opening up to the world, indeed in many ways it has been explicit in its educational goals since its post-Cultural Revolution opening in 1978 ("Principal Documents," 2005). Further, the US government, still ensconced in the Cold War with the Soviet Union at the time of official recognition, understood that American technological and academic superiority made for an advantageous exchange relationship, including "the great reservoir of knowledge and ability in science and technology existing in American colleges and universities," and it was understood at the time that the thousands of students and scholars that China planned to send to the United States, almost all in science and technology disciplines, were something to include in its first formal diplomatic dialogues with China (Jimmy Carter Library, 1979). This effort occurred alongside China's overall economic growth and modernization strategy following guidance from global economic institutions including the World Bank (Ma, 2014).

Today the Chinese government encourages and funds international educational collaborations not just with the United States but worldwide, particularly to advance science and technology, and it has generally found willing university partners at every turn. The rush to recruit students from China, build academic and research linkages in China, and receive funds and institutes from China can be seen, therefore, as deliberate actions on the part of independent-minded, globally conscious US and other foreign universities. Whether because of ambition for global prestige and rankings, the necessity for additional financial and academic resources, or well-meaning naivete, the view from China might very well be that these US and other foreign universities were willing actors in a mutually beneficial, harmonious, win-win situation for both sides. By one measure, in the latest pre-pandemic data, over 372,000 students and over 47,000 visiting scholars came to the United States from China, dwarfing the number from any other country and comprising fully one-third of the total in the United States (IIE, 2020).

While clearly an important player in terms of scientific and technological development during a period of profound economic growth, as well as for massive delivery of educational opportunities during a period of immense societal transformation, higher education modernization and internationalization in China should be seen unequivocally as having been directed by the state. With that direction comes the assumption of centrality, power, and recognition that the resulting university system would serve the state, enforce its priorities, avoid unwelcome foreign influences, and preserve unique Chinese characteristics. This has included partnerships with American higher education which, again, was well understood by the US government at the time of recognition and diplomatic opening, particularly that "the Chinese would like to acquire the Western technology and equipment, master the ability to replicate and improve it, adapt it to their own needs, and remain independent of the West" (Jimmy Carter Library, 1979).

Particularly in the area of research collaborations, the Chinese government through its Ministry of Education has provided generous funding for experiences by visiting scholars abroad, most notably to the United States. As cited earlier, these relationships have been particularly controversial. While such funding priorities driven by state economic imperatives might imply a massive coordinated strategy worthy of suspicion, a closer look at how these Chinese scholars pursue their activities abroad, and how those state-funded experiences and skills are employed once they return to China, suggests that strong linkages are not always evident. After their time in the United States, Chinese scholars do not typically report working closely on their home institution's internationalization efforts or otherwise contributing directly to strengthening their global competitiveness once back in China (McKeown, 2021) and, in general, there has not been a wholesale copying or modeling of US and Western higher education structures in China despite the extent of academic collaboration and mobility (Liu & Scott Metcalfe, 2016).

This misunderstanding both undervalues the considerable soft power advantages held by the United States, as it continues to draw talented students and scholars from around the world, and likely overstates the emphasis on Chinese educational and cultural exchange with the United States as being part of a realist competition and ideological conflict as both strive for greater global influence (Lynch, 2013). Nonetheless, increasingly many consider a new Cold War between the two as either inevitable or already underway (Marginson, 2019) and whether higher education will be consumed by it.

Five Points to Reforge and Redefine US-China Academic Relations

The arrival of COVID-19 and the global tightening of borders, as well as the urgency to develop effective vaccines and ensure supply chains, has made US-China academic collaboration more difficult and more crucial than ever before. Due to the steady backsliding of what a short time ago was a lively, productive, and voluminous relationship, there are prudent and realistic ways to imagine global higher education in general and the US-China relationship in particular in order to restart in a more sustainable manner.

Point #1: The State Matters

At the first meeting I ever attended at the Ministry of Education in Beijing, what struck me was not the specifics of that day's meeting but rather the thoroughness of Chinese government involvement and preparation. The Ministry of Education (MOE) official had a list of all the agreements with all the universities that mine had previously signed in China, matched program by program and degree by degree, with our Chinese partners. That would never happen in Washington, DC. In retrospect, I was just a typical representative of a form of entrepreneurial and largely unregulated international education enterprise easily undertaken at that time. With respect to China at least, I would argue that those days are over.

American higher education professionals do not typically consider themselves to be directly part of a national security apparatus. As stated earlier in this chapter, a case can be made that just like universities worldwide US institutions have always been a part of their state structure. At the very least, vis-à-vis China, it is time to recognize that they are. The story of my first Beijing meeting certainly suggests that the Chinese government views university international relations as such.

For many US higher education professionals, especially those with a tradition of agnosticism regarding the relationship with the federal government, recognizing the role of the state more deliberately could bring about an important change in posture. We live in a democratic society with well-run institutions of government (recent concerns notwithstanding). As educators and professionals we will continue to be vigilant, proactive, and above all to advocate for our students and scholars, performing our work as we define it and intersect with the state as it requires us, no more and no less, giving to the state what is the state's: responsibility for matters of law enforcement, counter-espionage, surveillance of visiting scholars and students, and so forth, much of which has accelerated in recent years. As we delineate even more clearly than before the state's interest in and control over these activities, whether or not we agree with the policies responsible for them, it has the potential to relieve dedicated professionals from undue worry over accusations of negligence, naivete, or complicity as some recent criticisms hold.

If harnessed properly, this reforged role can allow us to relinquish what I would argue in retrospect were improperly developed and inaccurately held beliefs about our own agency as institutional actors on the global stage in the first place. We can be informed and in compliance regarding federal regulations and policies, not necessarily fervent and certainly not intimidated. We can be assured even if not entirely comfortable that in order for US-China academic relations to re-set properly it is for the best, and our counterparts in China will accept that as well. The joy and fulfillment lie in our academic collaborations and intercultural learning, regardless of any national security backdrop that ultimately is not our direct concern.

Point #2: Relationships Matter

An early career lesson I received from a seasoned mentor was that, essentially, a memorandum of understanding (MOU) with a foreign university is not worth the paper it is printed on, but real relationships endure. Given the speed with which many academic relationships are being severed between higher education institutions in China and the United States, one has to wonder how deep and meaningful those relationships ever were. Looking back on the recent robust period of US-China academic exchange, it seems fair to say that for many institutions MOUs were signed that were unable to be enforced due to national and jurisdictional incongruities, oftentimes filled with vague and superfluous language exalting the indubitable benefits of an international exchange without tangible outcomes or mutually agreed-to procedures.

It might be helpful to recognize better how our Chinese counterparts think. Chinese universities have their own goals, state-driven and party-controlled, as part of a well-established but dynamic national structure. What may be less understood outside of China is that as their country has developed at a rapid pace, they have ambitious new generations to educate and assuage. China's youth of today, born after the tumultuous Tiananmen Square period, is well aware of US culture and society and is generally favorable and open to experiencing it, sometimes motivated by China's recent history. However, China's youthful generations are not immune from, or always in disagreement with, CCP narratives and official positions on China's role in the world.

Those US institutions sincerely interested in working with Chinese counterparts should be mindful of this tenuous balance and consider carefully the expectations we have and the postures we embrace. Our standards, sometimes based on our own official or collegial narratives, may hold, for example, that our more open, liberal, democratic academic systems are superior and must therefore not be compromised in any context or in any way when working with Chinese partners. This may not be workable in a holistic sense, but achievements can be made on more transactional things. MOUs should be written and agreed to accordingly, explicit and detailed about what they seek to accomplish and only that. To seek overly broad engagements based on vaguely written MOUs built on universalistic approaches assumes an agreed-to goal for global higher education that is not universally shared.

Controversial as this may be to some well-meaning and sincere among us, by not adopting this posture, are we willing to risk cutting off academic collaboration and engagement with Chinese institutions? Clearly, this would not be in anyone's long-term interest, Chinese or American. Further, if we insist on enforcing our standards on Chinese (or indeed any foreign) institutions, is that not in some ways similar to the superior-minded, condescending mindset out of another century, believing that China must somehow change on terms we think best and otherwise be *opened*? At the very least, those US higher education professionals seeking to engage with Chinese counterparts might benefit from knowing that this is how they could be perceived. Student flows, research collaborations, artistic and academic endeavors can flourish, but must be planned, should be purposeful, and respectful of a partner who is an equal. This limited but clear academic relationship is preferable, even at the expense of more typical, unfettered collaborations based on academic freedoms that others, including our Chinese counterparts, may not recognize or be able to adopt fully at this time.

Point #3: US Soft Power Advantages Matter

I was fortunate to have had a giant in the field of international education as a professor during my undergraduate study abroad program. His name was less important than how he referred to himself: as "the doorman," literally opening doors for us to understand a country and a culture with otherwise inaccessible insights. For US academics recently jaded by domestic and world events, it should not be underappreciated how much our open and free system of higher education attracts and retains not only talented students and scholars but also encourages building and maintaining tight professional bonds internationally throughout careers and lives. That is an enormous soft power advantage that should be celebrated and reinforced. American cultural, political, and economic power still holds great advantages vis-à-vis China. America's creativity and vitality, embrace of cultural diversity and, generally speaking, support for immigration has kept it economically competitive and innovative at a level and scale other societies have not attained. All this said, it may take longer than anyone thought previously for the United States and China to come to mutually agreeable terms on many things.

If it is useful for us to recognize the importance of the state and how our Chinese academic counterparts see the world, it is also useful to understand how national security experts see us. US counter-espionage services consider China's visiting researchers and scholars to be non-traditional collectors of intelligence, and its considerable investment in *talents* initiatives, such as the recent Thousand Talents Program, to be deliberately designed to transfer knowledge and sensitive intellectual property to China, taking advantage of the relatively open and collegial academic research environment in the United States (OSAC, 2020).

This is understandable and depicts a worrisome challenge to US economic and geopolitical power. However, change seems to happen in China only incrementally and typically over a long period of time. If the United States is sincere about seeking a more open, democratic, and globally integrated

China, it might do well to remember that its greatest strength is its unequivocal embrace of freedom, confident in what it stands for and, therefore, attractive to others yearning for similar freedoms. We know that other nations have evolved from seeking higher education as only a tool of economic growth and power towards more cultural and enlightened purposes, and we know that the flow of Chinese students and scholars into the United States dwarfs the number in reverse (MOE, 2019). Despite the apparent near-term threats, it seems evident that China seeks as much to learn from and enjoy harmonious relations with the United States as it does to gain advantages. If the US plays to its advantages, in the long run, the opportunity remains to solidify its position not only with China but the rest of the world. Higher education can play an important part in that.

Point #4: Fixing US Higher Education Matters

For US higher education professionals, the COVID-19 pandemic not only brought home the insufficient status of national preparedness and coordination, but other existential domestic concerns including broad mistrust of scientific expertise and the urgency of addressing racial inequality in pursuit of social justice. For some powerful and influential political and media leaders, what began as blaming China for American economic and strategic decline seemed to morph myopically and uncritically into blame for the containment and management of the virus, manipulation of international organizations, and to some extremists for creation of the virus itself. Despite the unilateral US withdrawal of scientific and disease control experts from joint projects in China (Buckley et al., 2020), as well as American withdrawal from climate, trade, and other international accords and organizations, to blame China alone for the multitude of national crises seemed to some as possibly racist in its impunity to those laying the blame and its overarching completeness towards not just a government but an entire nation and people, including Americans of Chinese descent (Lee, 2020). At the very least, it seemed a too-convenient, hollow narrative designed to shift attention from what ailed the United States at home.

One of America's greatest needs is a better, more inclusive, and successful higher education system that graduates more of its students into productive careers and lives, in turn bringing economic prosperity to families and progress to communities. Quality and rankings of America's most selective institutions are unquestionable, yet so too are high costs and debt burdens, elitist perception, and overall lack of accessibility and inclusion representative of a diverse nation. The challenges of pandemic response can push us towards deeper questions: are we who lead and participate in global higher education contributing the way it is needed most, or are we isolated in silos? This is relevant for the US-China academic relationship because without a strong core there will be no sustainably successful outreach across borders. Remembering that China seeks to build and improve its universities for their own sake, not merely to compete with the United States; if American universities do likewise, and renew commitments to access, teaching, mentoring, advisement, and improving graduation rates, especially in the newly urgent remote and virtual learning space, and only then seek to renew and expand outward engagements, I believe we will be performing our international functions on firmer footing. Even experienced international educators often left out of these broader conversations should consider the urgency of this need and get involved right now.

Point #5: This Moment Matters Because Academic Decoupling Is Unimaginable

In early April 2020, as the realities of COVID-19 were ravaging New York, a brief story appeared in my local newspaper describing a video conference call between doctors and researchers at SUNY's Upstate Medical University in Syracuse and counterparts in Wuhan, China, where the first outbreak occurred. "Those on the call shared information about early identification and diagnosis, radiological exams, experimental drug use and other issues... (and) that the virus can be spread by people who do not have symptoms" (The Post Standard, 2020). That same SUNY hospital is home to a leading research institute whose director, a former US Army officer with global experience combating Zika, Ebola, and other devastating global diseases, was selected as the lead principal investigator worldwide for the development of one of the first COVID-19 vaccines (Mulder, 2020).

What would the world be like if international academic relationships such as those between the hospitals in Syracuse and Wuhan did not exist? If doctors and researchers had not built relationships and worked collegially so that, when a crisis hit, they were just a phone call away? What would the United States be like if its military officers, doctors, pharmaceutical innovators, research scholars, and academic professionals were not performing their work globally, constantly expanding networks and expertise? If the global spread of the virus taught us anything it is that national borders at best provide only an illusion of control; the world is a small and interconnected place. The new Cold War logic that too quickly entered the global dialogue is incompatible with responsible international academic relations post-pandemic. It is not an "either-or" world where one must choose the Chinese way or the American way, friendship with China or with the United States. Indeed researchers have concluded that academic decoupling with China would likely reduce and diminish US scientific output due to reduced collaboration with Chinese researchers (Lee & Haupt, 2020), which is not in America's long-term interests.

There are divergent views on how to proceed in the US-China academic context. Well-informed and experienced people in both countries, some of whom have spent their careers focused on this, find themselves at a crossroads along with their nations. That must be recognized and respected in this discussion. There are deep misunderstandings and misgivings in the United

States of Chinese organizational structures and systems, particularly how the state and the party influence Chinese universities, and there is great concern about how the Chinese government treats its minority populations in places like Xinjiang and Tibet, its censorship and opaque legal system, and more. There is deep suspicion in China of US policies and actions that are sometimes perceived as designed to perpetuate its global dominance, using its definitions of human rights and democratic ideals to solidify its own power. There are also deep social challenges in both countries. Despite this, the power of academic mobility and the mutual advantages resulting from this academic exchange have not diminished and, as the above story affirms, are more important than ever.

For academia, the US-Soviet Cold War was stifling in its restrictions on people-to-people interaction and intellectual collaboration. Thankfully that has not yet come to pass between the US and China, but tensions and restrictions have grown. While it is tempting to think in retrospect of some positive outcomes of the Cold War's intense global rivalry, such as the development of the internet and monumental achievements in space, the situation is different now. Global supply chains and financial markets are integrated, travel and communications have become faster and simpler, and information as well as a liberal education more attainable. If a Cold War metaphor is useful then let us consider it productively to rebuild ourselves not just to confront China, to focus on other moonshot goals for our country and all of humanity, and focus on "whole of society" progress, not just threats. With respect to the sober and divergent opinions on this consequential and strained matter, the question is not between being pro-China or anti-China, pro- or anti-American, it is understanding that China and the United States are both here, will be here, and how best to engage. Higher education can play a crucial role.

References

Buckley, C., Kirkpatrick, D. D., Qin, A., & Hernandez, J. C. (2020, December 30). 25 days that changed the world. *The New York Times.* https://www.nytimes.com/2020/12/30/world/asia/china-coronavirus.html

Cai, Y., & Yan, F. (2017). Universities and higher education. In W. J. Morgan, Q. Gu, & F. Li (Eds.), *Handbook of education in China* (pp. 169–193). Elgar.

Cantwell, B., Coates, H., & King, R. (2018). Introduction: The politics of higher education. In B. Cantwell, H. Coates, & R. King (Eds.), *Handbook on the politics of higher education* (pp. 1–7). Elgar.

Colby, E. A., & Mitchell, A. W. (2020). The age of great power competition. *Foreign Affairs, 99*(1), 118–130.

de Wit, H., & Hunter, F. (2015). The future of internationalization of higher education in Europe. *International Higher Education, 83*, 2–3. https://doi.org/10.6017/ihe.2015.83.9073

Fischer, K. (2019, April 5). The sunset of international education's golden era. *The Chronicle of Higher Education*, A12–A18.

Hoover Institution. (2018). *Chinese influences and American interests: Promoting constructive vigilance.* https://www.hoover.org/research/chinas-influence-american-interests-promoting-constructive-vigilance

IIE. (2020). *Open doors.* https://www.iie.org/Research-and-Insights/Open-Doors

Jimmy Carter Library. (1979). Memorandum. *Science and technology in China today.* Physical Sciences and Technology Division of the Office of Scientific Intelligence, Central Intelligence Agency, Brzezinski Material, NSA 5, Box 2.

Knight, J. (1994). *Internationalization: Elements and checkpoints* (research monograph, no. 7). Canadian Bureau for International Education.

Lai, M. (2010). Challenges to the work life of academics: The experience of a renowned university in the Chinese mainland. *Higher Education Quarterly, 64,* 89–111.

Lau, J. (2020, May 18). China offers students incentives to bolster 'strategic fields'. *Times Higher Education.* https://www.timeshighereducation.com/news/china-offers-students-incentives-tobolster-strategic-fields

Layne, C. (2020). Coming storms. *Foreign Affairs, 99*(6), 42–48.

Lee, J. J. (2020). Neo-racism and the criminalization of China. *Journal of International Students, 10*(4), i–vi. https://doi.org/10.32674/jis.v10i4.2929

Lee, J. J., & Haupt, J. P. (2020). Winners and losers in US-China scientific research collaborations. *Higher Education, 80,* 57–74. https://doi.org/10.1007/s10734-019-00464-7

Li, J. (2020, May 12). A more holistic approach to knowledge will help prevent future pandemics. *Times Higher Education.* https://www.timeshighereducation.com/opinion/more-holistic-approach-knowledge-will-help-prevent-future-pandemics

Liu, H., & Scott Metcalfe, A. (2016). Internationalizing Chinese higher education: A glonacal analysis of local layers and conditions. *Higher Education, 71,* 399–413.

Lynch, D. (2013). Securitizing culture in Chinese foreign policy debates: Implications for interpreting China's rise. *Asian Survey, 53,* 629–652.

Ma, J. (2014). Rethinking the World Bank agenda for Chinese higher education reform. *Frontiers of Education in China, 9,* 89–109.

Marginson, S. (2019, November 16). How should universities respond to the new Cold War? *University World News.* https://www.universityworldnews.com/post.php?story=20191112103413758

McKeown, J. S. (2009). *The first time effect: The impact of study abroad on college student intellectual development.* SUNY Press.

McKeown, J. S. (2021). Wasted talents? China's higher education reforms experienced through its visiting scholars abroad. *Journal of Contemporary China.* https://doi.org/10.1080/10670564.2021.1884961

McKeown, J. S., Celaya, M. L., & Ward, H. H. (2021). Academic development: The impact of education abroad on students as learners. In A. C. Ogden, B. Streitwieser, & C. Van Mol (Eds.), *Education abroad: Bridging scholarship and practice* (pp. 77–91). Routledge.

MOE Ministry of Education, the People's Republic of China. (2019, April 17). *Statistical report on international students in China for 2018.* http://en.moe.gov.cn/documents/reports/201904/t20190418_378692.html

Mulder, J. T. (2020, November 15). Upstate doctor takes on a new adventure with vaccine study. *The Post Standard.* https://www.syracuse.com/coronavirus/2020/11/latest-adventure-for-hotshot-at-upstate-medical-pfizers-covid-breakthrough.html

Murray, W. E. (2006). *Geographies of globalization*. Routledge.

OSAC Webinar. (2020, May 27). *Economic espionage*.

Sharpe, M. E. (2005). Principal documents issued by the Ministry of Education and relevant departments concerning study-abroad work. *Chinese Education and Society, 38*, 63–65.

Pusser, B. (2018). The state and the civil society in the scholarship of higher education. In B. Cantwell, H. Coates, & R. King (Eds.), *Handbook on the politics of higher education* (pp. 11–29). Elgar.

Richardson, L. (2020, April 9). Universities fill the void. *Foreign Affairs*. https://www.foreignaffairs.com/articles/world/2020-04-09/universities-fill-void

The Post Standard (2020, April 2). Syracuse doctors compare notes on the coronavirus with peers in China. *The Post Standard*. https://www.syracuse.com/coronavirus/2020/03/syracuse-doctors-compare-notes-on-coronavirus-with-peers-in-china.html

U.S. Department of State and U.S. Department of Education. (2020, October 9). *State-ED joint letter to university presidents and affiliates re PRC influence*. https://www2.ed.gov/about/offices/list/ope/state-edjointltrreprcinfluence1092020.pdf

U.S. Department of State, Bureau of Educational and Cultural Affairs, Private Sector Exchange. (2020, November 18). *Exchange visitor program – Confucius Institutes 2020–01*. https://j1visa.state.gov/wp-content/uploads/2020/11/2020-01-Confucius-Institutes.pdf

U.S. Senate, Staff Report, Permanent Subcommittee on Investigations, Committee on Homeland Security and Governmental Affairs. (2019). *China's impact on the U.S. education system*. https://www.hsgac.senate.gov/imo/media/doc/PSI%20Report%20China's%20Impact%20on%20the%20US%20Education%20System.pdf

Xie, Q., & Freeman, R. B. (2021). *The contribution of Chinese diaspora researchers to global science and China's catching up in scientific research*. NBER. https://www.nber.org/papers/w27169

Bio

Joshua S. McKeown, Ph.D., is an Associate Provost for International Education & Programs at SUNY Oswego and International Education Leadership Fellow at the University at Albany (SUNY). Under his leadership SUNY Oswego has earned national and international awards for international education from the American Association of State Colleges & Universities (AASCU), the Institute of International Education (IIE), Diversity Abroad, the Chinese Service Center for Scholarly Exchange (CSCSE), and achieved multiple top rankings in the annual Open Doors survey for education abroad enrollment and for student Fulbright awards. McKeown is a scholar-practitioner who authored *The First Time Effect: The Impact of Study Abroad on College Student Intellectual Development* (SUNY Press 2009), several book chapters including in *Education Abroad: Bridging Scholarship and Practice* (Routledge, 2020) and NAFSA's Guide to Education Abroad (NAFSA, 2014), numerous articles including in the *Journal of Contemporary China*, and has spoken and presented worldwide. He was a Fulbright-Nehru International Education Administrators recipient for India, a mentor with the IIE's Connecting with the World Myanmar program, and has served professional organizations such as the Forum on Education Abroad, CAPA, and Phi Beta Delta Honor Society for International Scholars. He holds a Ph.D. and bachelor's from Syracuse University, master's from Clarkson University, and teaches in the undergraduate Global & International Studies program at SUNY Oswego and the graduate program in International Education Management & Leadership (IEML) at UAlbany. E-mail: joshua.mckeown@oswego.edu

Part II

Looking into Existential Threats to Higher Education

6 COVID-19 Crisis and the Future of Higher Education

Perspectives from Kenya

Caroline S. Wekullo, John O. Shiundu, James B. Ouda, and Anthony Mutevane

Abstract

The chapter provides an understanding of the ways COVID-19 is affecting higher education and advances practical strategies for managing the challenges caused by the pandemic. To understand the effect of the COVID-19 pandemic on higher education, it is prudent to understand the context within which the institutions of higher learning operate. It also offers an overview of the education system in Kenya, followed by a situation analysis. It then explores how COVID-19 is affecting and shaping the future of higher education and based on literature, presents the strategies to manage the effects of the pandemic.

Keywords

future of higher education, COVID-19, Kenya, strategies for mitigating pandemics

Introduction

COVID-19 is the most devastating disease the world has ever experienced. Known to have originated in Wuhan, China in December 2019, the virus spread quickly around the world, and in less than a month, the number of COVID-19 confirmed cases were 3,634,172 worldwide, having claimed over 251,446 lives (World Health Organization [WHO], 2019). To control and curb the spread of COVID-19, WHO strongly recommended measures, such as social distancing, confinement, frequent washing of hands, and wearing face masks in public places. Since these measures seemed to work for China, countries across the world took up the same measures.

In education matters, the Government of Kenya (GoK) has developed a three-pronged approach to ensure the continuation of learning remotely, while adhering to the COVID-19 protocols of social distancing, quarantine, and self-isolation. The tertiary institutions (i.e., universities and other postsecondary institutions) have developed online content that can be accessed by students through various channels to ensure that uninterrupted learning continues for students in the country while they are at home. According to Nguyen (2015), online learning is a wide range of curricula that uses the internet to facilitate instruction and provide materials as well as interactions between teachers and students or even among a group of students. In the same line, Paschal and Mkulu (2020) conceptualized online education as a general mode of teaching and learning virtually with the assistance of digital platforms and technology tools. The success of online learning programs in tertiary institutions has largely depended on digital skills, availability of educational technologies, and good internet networks in the learning environment, for both students and teachers. There are several platforms as well as tools that teachers and learners use in online learning in Kenya. These include WhatsApp.com, Zoom, Youtube.com, Skype.com, and Google classroom. However, it must be appreciated that the online program in tertiary institutions is riddled with a lot of challenges (Ministry of Education, 2020; Nyerere, 2020; Tarus et al., 2015). This was expected because the development of online programs in tertiary institutions of learning does not happen overnight, they take time.

The internet has made teaching and learning conceivable during the pandemic, and many educators and scholars are interested in online learning to enrich accessibility of learning resources and improve students learning, mainly in tertiary institutions of learning (Horn & Staker, 2011; Page, 2010), The students in tertiary institutions as well as other institutions of higher education come from varied backgrounds. Some come from well-to-do families while others come from a middle-class background. Others also come from disadvantaged backgrounds including slums, remote locations as well as informal settlements. Some of the students also come from families who have lost livelihood as a result of the effects of the COVID-19 pandemic among other difficult circumstances. There are also students who are refugees while others suffer from various disabilities. Despite the prevailing circumstances, it is a right for every citizen to achieve the highest attainable standard of education, training, and research as enshrined in the Constitution of Kenya (Munene & Otieno, 2007; Republic of Kenya, 2010). This chapter will therefore look at the Coronavirus (COVID-19) crisis and its effect on the future of higher education in Kenya. The focus will be on the increased online teaching and learning, the institutionalization of online learning, the challenges experienced as well the management of staff and students' education needs during the COVID-19 pandemic in higher education in Kenya.

Higher Education in Kenya

In Kenya, there has been extraordinary growth in the number of higher education institutions. According to the Economic Survey, the number of universities increased by 69.6% from 7 public higher education institutions in 2011 to 23 in 2015 (Republic of Kenya, 2014, 2016). Currently, there are 71 universities: 35 public and 36 private institutions and several tertiary institutions

(CUE, 2017). The rapid expansion in the number of public institutions is partly because of the conversion of many middle-level technical colleges to university colleges status through granting of charters, the introduction of new programs, and opening of new satellite campuses (Republic of Kenya, 2015; Wekullo et al., 2018).

Since the 1990s, enrollment in both public and private universities in Kenya has been on the rise. Most of the growth in student enrollment in public higher education institutions was partly due to the emerging of "parallel stream" (Court, 1999) and partly due to liberalization for these institutions to diversify their funding streams. Most institutions took advantage of the opportunity to admit self-sponsored students also referred to as "fee-paying students" alongside the government-funded students. The fee-paying students made up a significant majority of the total enrolment in the largest and best-established public universities (Odhiambo, 2011).

According to the Kenya National Bureau of Statistics, enrollment in universities sharply declined by about 43,600 students in the academic year 2017/2018, making it the first drop since the massive increase in the 1990s (Republic of Kenya, 2016, 2018). The drop in enrollment was due to a reduction in the number of students who scored c+ and above the minimum grade required for university entry. Since public universities admitted all students who scored c+ and above, there has been a reduction in the pool of students to enroll in private universities and as parallel degree students (i.e., fee-paying students) in public universities. The decline in enrollment has worsened the institutions' cash flows (Igadwah, 2018).

Even with the decline in enrollment across universities in Kenya, teaching and learning is characterized by a large class size, which limits opportunities for students to engage in critical reflection and dialogue. Institutions of higher learning are also characterized by inadequate and poorly maintained physical infrastructure. Odhiambo (2011) observed that in public universities, windows, and doors were falling apart, residential halls were stinking, there was little to no subscriptions to journals. Also, there were no tutorials and that large lecture halls lacked efficient microphones.

Quality has become a significant challenge in most institutions of higher education. It all started when middle-level colleges were "upgrading" to university status, and several small campuses of established universities were set up in interior towns, often with precarious infrastructure. While public universities have the greatest concentration of highly qualified academic staff and research activity, they suffer from overcrowding, insufficient numbers of lecturers, and degraded facilities. Private universities have lower student-to-staff ratios, but also have severe challenges with staff with lower qualifications working in multiple institutions. Interestingly, the one significant group whose dissatisfaction cannot always be heard is the students themselves, yet as explored by McCowan (2016), the lack of a clear critical voice from students.

Currently, the Commission for University Education (CUE) has taken up actions to enhance the quality of higher education. The Inter-University Council for East Africa also has played an important role in quality assurance and has run a capacity-building program to develop institution-level practice. However, while these initiatives have brought some important changes, they are yet to ensure that quality across the system is enhanced, especially now during the COVID-19 pandemic and the health protocols that come with it.

Human Development Index

The Human Development Index (HDI) is a composite score used to rank countries based on their average achievement in three basic dimensions; life expectancy, education, and per capita income. A country has a higher HDI when it has a higher life expectancy, higher education level, and a higher gross national income per capita (United Nations Development Programme [UNDP], 2019a). Africa is one of the fastest-growing continents in its human development, but it also has the lowest average levels of human development compared to other regions in the world (UNDP, 2016). Kenya's HDI has steadily progressed in increasing people's choices in health, living standards, and education through its "big four agenda" of ensuring food security and nutrition, universal health care, affordable housing, and manufacturing (Republic of Kenya, 2018). Even though the pace of growth is slower, Kenya's HDI stood at 0.590 in the year 2019, a margin improvement of 0.042 from the year 2014. Kenya was ranked 142 out of 189 countries—a rank that placed the country into the category of medium HDI (UNDP, 2019b). Similarly, Kenya's life expectancy increased by 4.7% from 61.6% in the year 2014 to 66.3% in the year 2019. The expected years of schooling also increased by 0.1 from 11.0 years in 2014 to 11.1 years in 2019 (UNDP, 2019b).

Kenya's HDI was expected to further grow by 2020. Alas, this may remain a dream due to the global economic depression that is likely to devastate the economies of many nations and their higher learning institutions. Nevertheless, there is a need to create an awareness where the three basic achievements can be felt by a majority of the citizens who are still marginalized. Thus, affecting the HDI negatively.

On 15 March 2020, Schools and higher education institutions in Kenya abruptly closed in response to COVID-19, affecting over 17 million learners nationwide (Parsitau & Jepkemei, 2020). Even as some sectors, such as the economy and health reopened, and cessations in some counties were removed, schools and higher education institutions were still closed. The abrupt closure and the measures taken to curb the spread of the COVID-19 pandemic have had serious effects on the operations of higher learning institutions. While some effects of COVID-19 have been felt immediately, the consequences of some effects on the operation of higher education institutions will be felt for years to come (Mohamedbhai, 2020). At the onset of COVID-19, the winds of change started blowing through higher education, shaping and influencing various activities including the transition to online learning, enrollment, mobility of scholars, funding, focus on higher education, access, and equity. COVID-19 has affected higher education institutions in several ways.

Theoretical Framework and Philosophical Stance

The study is anchored on the Classical Liberal Theory of Equal Opportunities whose proponents are Sherman and Wood as cited by Njeru and Orodho (2003). The theory advances the perspective of the need for equal opportunities in education for all students. The philosophy of the classical Liberal Theory of Equal Opportunities is that every student is born with some ability, which is congenital and cannot be substantively changed. Therefore, education structures and systems need to be structured in a way that eliminates challenges of whatever form including but not limited to social, political, gender, and economic problems that may hinder ingenious learners from taking full gain of innate talents, which may fast-track their social promotion. The Classical Liberal Theory implies that social mobility would be motivated by the equal opportunity of educational structures for all students. According to this theory, education structures and systems need to be planned with the aim of eliminating obstacles or challenges of any form which may inhibit students from achieving their full potential including their talents.

The outbreak of the COVID-19 pandemic led to unexpected prolonged closures of learning institutions. As a result, online classes were the popular option to ensure continued learning in institutions of higher education. The shift to online classes ensured that institutions continued engaging their students during the lockdown and social distancing (Marinoni et al., 2020). Going online, however, has not been easy due to challenges such as limited connectivity, limited access to the internet, and power interruptions, not to mention smartphones, laptops and data (Gillett-Swan, 2017). Since several of these institutions have no adequate capacity and infrastructure to reach all students online, the move to online learning in some institutions will stop no sooner than they begin (Wang, 2020). In other instances, only a fraction of the learners will access the online classes. This means that some students will be marginalized due to a variety of reasons including but not limited to their socio-economic background. For successful online learning, proper infrastructures must be put in place at the beginning.

Method

We used a desktop analysis approach with careful consideration of the quality of the information sources. To create an effective and rigorous status update on the way COVID-19 is affecting and shaping the future of universities in Kenya, reliable sources needed to be used. A total of 52 sources were used. The emphasis was on information emerging from universities and government sources. Supplement information was derived from News articles, University World News, Higher Education News, and other forms of communications (i.e. e-mails to staff and students) (see Table 6.1). Content analysis was used in analyzing the information from the sources. Various themes were derived on some of the ways COVID-19 is affecting and shaping the future of higher education institutions in Kenya. The findings are presented below.

Table 6.1 Sources of information used for findings

Sources	Number	Percentage (%)
News articles	10	19.23
University World News	8	15.39
Higher education news	6	11.54
Government information	10	19.23
University communication	11	21.15
Other courses(i.e., social media)	7	13.46
Total	52	100

Findings: How COVID-19 Is Affecting and Shaping the Future of Higher Education in Kenya

A Shift to Online Teaching and Learning

The closure of higher education institutions as a measure to control and curb the spread of COVID-19 disrupted studies of over 9.8 million students in Africa, including those in Kenya (United Nations [UN], 2020). The fear of contacting COVID-19 triggered institutions to opt for online teaching as an alternative to face-to-face learning. The sudden shift to online activities was also caused by the need for institutions to continue engaging their students during the lockdown and social distancing (Li, 2020; Marinoni et al., 2020; Napier et al., 2011). Going online, however, has not been simple for a nation that has challenges with limited connectivity, limited access to the internet, and power interruptions. Since several of these institutions had no adequate capacity and infrastructure to suddenly reach all students online, the move to online learning in some institutions stopped no sooner than it started.

For successful online learning, proper infrastructures must be put in place at the beginning. According to Schroeder (2001) providing infrastructure to support online learning is equivalent to building a new physical campus similar to the pre-existing ones. Similarly, Students taking online classes have similar or more needs compared to their counterparts on the physical campus. Equally, faculty teaching online classes have similar requirements as their counterparts in face-to-face classes (Schroeder, 2001). Surprisingly, most institutions had little capacity and inadequate infrastructure for online learning.

The wisdom and necessity to increasingly invest in information and communication technology (ICT) infrastructure to support online and distance learning can no longer be denied. Before COVID-19, most institutions of higher learning in Kenya had a small capacity that served few students. Currently, most institutions are investing in greater and heavy bandwidth to ensure steady connectivity, serve many students, and access the needed content. In the same efforts, several higher education institutions are increasingly seeking to partner with internet providers, such as Safaricom and

Kenya Education Network (KENET) to negotiate access to specific education websites at a reduced cost (KENET, 2020). Also, individual institutions are providing data bundles for their staff and students.

Given that most institutions had minimally invested in ICT infrastructure for online and distance learning, most faculty members were unprepared for this sudden shift to online teaching (Andrews & Moulton, 2009; Marinoni, 2020). Very few faculty members, staff, and students understood working virtually (Kashorda & Waema, 2014; Tarus et al., 2015). As Andrews and Moulton (2009) observed, online teaching requires a different teaching approach from the usual face-to-face teaching. Most institutions quickly held one-day capacity training workshops to equip faculty with new software and skills to enable them to move to online teaching. While some faculty members were good to go with only one training, some needed continual support in constructing online content for various courses. Yet most institutions had very few technical support staff to assist faculty members.

The unpreparedness of faculty and institutions in online delivery may further affect the quality of education offered at higher education institutions (Brooks et al., 2020). According to Mohamedbhai (2020) quality online learning can only be achieved when professional instructional designers are engaged in preparing teaching material, lecturers are adequately trained to deliver the courses and program, and students are equally exposed to strategies and approaches of learning online. Unfortunately, institutions had not adhered to most of these online quality requirements. As a result, a majority of the faculty members have resulted in either posting lecture notes or recording videos and sending them to students. Others are afraid of sharing their notes. On the one hand, some faculty members feared losing their status as experts. On the other hand, institution leadership had not established and communicated a clear policy on knowledge sharing.

While online teaching is taking shape, it was abruptly implemented without consulting all students and other stakeholders. In reality, students taking courses online have higher learning expectations compared to the traditional face-to-face setting (Andrews & Moulton, 2009; Schroeder, 2001). It was, therefore, prudent that students receive technical training and support similar to that of their faculty to be able to navigate the online platform, conduct research, download class materials, submit assignments, communicate with their professors and peers, and get support services (Schroeder, 2001). Unfortunately, the majority of the students except for those taking courses through distance learning had not received the training. In some institutions like the Masinde Muliro University of Science and Technology, virtual training for students on how to navigate the online platform was organized. Indeed, not all students received communication for training leave alone, taking part in the actual training.

The increasing championship for online teaching, as the alternative mode of learning, has been met with resistance from students. Students from various universities have voiced serious concerns about the system, excluding their marginalized colleagues with little or no access to internet services and those with no money to buy laptops. Some students expressed their dissatisfaction with being forced to take online classes. For instance, some university students were actively engaged in a trending discussion on Twitter on 30th March 2020. A student by the Pseudonym Prince tweeted

> You want me to take online classes. I live in Turkana (in far-off remote northern Kenya). Does this university even care that I obviously can't access [the] internet. It is University of Main[pseudonym] ..., not University for people of Main.

Another student by the Pseudonym May tweeted "Training is an inevitable part of any business but depending solely on an e-learning platform can make learning less personal, less engaging, and in the process, less effective. We urge comrades to boycott such shenanigans by the university."

This was just but a sign that not all students embraced online learning. Further, students of one public university took the university management to court because they felt it was not right for them to take examinations online. This has made some institutions to suspend online learning and postpone examinations for the semester (Austrian et al., 2020).

The shift to online depended on discipline. While online learning was implemented with ease in social sciences and humanities, it was a challenge in technical and practical courses (Marinoni et al., 2020). Technical courses are the most crucial for Kenya's development. Thus, they cannot be offered online, but required blending online and face-to-face.

Changes in Student Enrollment

COVID-19 has hurt student enrollment for the new academic year 2020/2021. The admission and recruitment process is also bound to change. Like elsewhere, higher education institutions in Kenya select students for admission from those who have completed the Kenya Certificate for Secondary Education (KCSE), the National Examinations. Now that the KCSE national examination has been postponed, it will eventually affect the 2021 intake of first-year students. Higher education institutions will have to come up with a new approach to selecting their new cohort of students. This may include re-evaluating the current admission practices and being flexible with admission dates.

Internationalization of University Education

The COVID-19 has also changed the perspective and prospects of students from Africa, Kenya included, about studying abroad. Wuhan, the city in China, where the virus was first reported, is home to over 25 universities that attract international students across the world. Approximately, there are about 4,600 students from over 12 African countries in Hubei province, where

Wuhan is located (Sawahel, 2020). Overall, there are about 81,562 African students in higher education institutions in China, representing 16.57% of the continent's international students (Sawahel, 2020). With the outbreak of COVID-19, the findings of a survey showed that COVID-19 has affected the plans of some students to study abroad. Out of about 2,000 students from Africa, Asia, and Australia surveyed, three in ten students had changed their plans of studying in China due to the Virus (Marguerite, 2020).

The lockdowns and travel constraints implemented by various national governments as a way to curb the spread of COVID-19 have left many nations and institutions of higher learning to wonder who would be their future students. With the closure of learning institutions across the world, most international students including those from Kenya were caught in and held up by countries and cities, lockdowns, and travel bans. Even with support from their home country, most of these students preferred going home and being quarantined there than in a foreign country.

Apart from living in fear of conducting COVID-19, some international students from Africa were stigmatized, discriminated against, and suffered stress related to their visa status. There was limited to no direction on safety and protection against the hostile environment international students were exposed to in foreign countries. What international students experienced during the COVID-19 pandemic is evidence that universities are far away from the customer experience such caliber of organizations needs to develop to be successful. This could be a replica of what happens during learning, where there is less focus on different needs, abilities, and teaching and learning support for international students. Moreover, the uncertainty of such pandemics relapsing has caused most international students, including those from Kenya to prefer studying from home and in universities close to their homes (Jaschik, 2020; Svanholm, 2020). It is no doubt that the future of higher education in Kenya and elsewhere will depend on institutions' ability to recruit international students after the crisis.

Changes in Funding for Higher Education Institutions

The economic impact of coronavirus on higher education institutions in Kenya, like elsewhere, is quite significant. Tamrat and Teferra's (2020) analysis of the effect of coronavirus on over 2,000 higher education institutions in Africa showed that funding for colleges and universities could be affected severely because of the competing demands from sectors such as healthcare, agriculture, and business. Higher education institutions are likely to suffer from the decline in government budget allocation, yet these institutions should be considered a priority in helping the country overcome such challenges and many other economic and development issues.

Apart from causing a decrease in state budget allocation for higher education, the COVID-19-induced recession is likely to have severe short- and long-term effects, including an increase in tuition fees institutions charge.

Like other recessions, the COVID-19-induced recession is likely to cause a state of financial uncertainty in institutions that will make them shift from long-term to short-term planning. In such cases, students together with their parents are likely to dig deeper into their pockets to finance higher education. This has its implications; higher education will no longer be the public good. It will lock out most students - mainly from low-income families- with the inability to pay tuition at all.

Given the expected harsh financial climate, public universities are likely to merge. Private universities, which entirely depend on tuition and fees for their operations, are already hard hit. Currently, most private and some public universities are struggling to pay employees' salaries and allowances. In the aftermath of the COVID-19 pandemic, some private universities are likely to close some of their branches or completely close, as they do not receive any support from the government.

The focus on higher education institutions has also reduced. As Marinoni et al. (2020) observed, COVID-19 has seriously affected higher education institutions' partners in that they could no longer offer financial support to these institutions. Also, COVID-19 has weakened institutional partnerships as institutions have to concentrate resources on local issues (Marinoni et al., 2020). Moreover, higher education institutions have experienced huge drop in support from development partners, mainly for research and collaborations, which institutions have heavily depended on in the past (Tamrat & Teferra, 2020). On the contrary, COVID-19 has provided an opportunity for creating new partnerships and strengthening the existing partnerships, shown when researchers from various institutions coordinated their efforts to respond to COVID-19 (Marinoni et al., 2020).

Access and Equity in Higher Education

Like other nations, Kenya had no choice but to close its higher education institutions as part of lockdown measures to control and curb the spread of the virus. These institutions had no option but to shift to online learning. The process has exacerbated the existing inequity in learning institutions. The shift from face-to-face to distance learning strategies and ensuring that these strategies provide access and equity have been a challenge (Mohamedbhai, 2020). It is estimated that about 96% of students in Africa have been left out because of a lack of access to technological resources, devices, and support needed for effective online learning. Only 4% of the students in Africa have forged on with learning through sophisticated soft and hardware, high performing devices with well-trained faculty (Berry & Hughes, 2020; Crawfurd, 2020). Similarly, in Kenya, very few students, mainly those living in urban areas have access to online learning. Whereas, the majority of students from rural areas, and the vulnerable groups or communities in urban slums, and refugee camps can barely afford to access internet services.

Coronavirus is laying out new layers of economic disparities that may end up setting our society back even further. Coronavirus has reduced the economic capacities of most families and those who cannot pay are likely to drop out. Also, those with insufficient funds to enroll in higher education may opt for technical colleges even if they qualify for University. Right now, students from low- and middle-income families are deciding if they will start college or defer.

COVID-19 has also exposed deep gender inequality and inequity that exist in higher education institutions. As the economic effect of the pandemic continues, women are likely to bear the greater brunt. Women are likely to become unemployed as some institutions have resulted in stopping all contracts and casual workers as a way of coping with COVID-19. A majority of women are affected because they fall into this category of workers. With the upending of daily life and the shift to virtual learning that is a challenge to everyone, women take on additional work as households and caregivers. Moreover, women are likely to be used to cushion families' income. The situation exposes women to risks of sexual exploitation and gender-based violence (Parsitau & Jepkemei, 2020), which is likely to put women students at high risk of dropping out when universities reopen compared to males. The statistics already show an increase in pregnancy among adolescents in Kenya.

Although the future is uncertain, the COVID-19 crisis has proved that education institutions will never be the same as it has always been. It is, therefore, important to consider equitable access to resources in covering up for the lost time during institution closures. Meeting the needs of all students, especially girls and those from low-income families, students living with disabilities should be a priority for the nation and all institutional leaders.

Management of Staff and Students' Needs during COVID-19

Higher education institutions were at the forefront in responding to COVID-19. The level of response to the pandemic, however, depends largely on institutions' leadership, whose decisions may affect the future. As institutional leaders are likely to deploy resources and time to what they consider as a major priority.

The abrupt closure of learning institutions left many faculty members, staff, and students struggling to keep a sense of normalcy besides experiencing their uncertainties, fears, and anxieties. At such time it was prudent that higher education institutions come up with a mechanism to assist staff, faculty, and students to deal with the psychological and social effects of COVID-19 during the pandemic. At such time everyone be it staff, faculty, and students seek compassion, caring, and communication that acknowledges the brunt of the pandemic they face (Wu et al., 2020). It is imperative that higher education institutions reach their community and assure each of flexible and reasonable accommodation, to show that the institution cares for their wellbeing. Institutional leaders could also create a virtual community that allows staff and faculty to check in with each other, resonate with each other's experience and make room for a new normal.

Surprisingly, there was no evidence on how higher education institutions in Kenya addressed the effects of abrupt closure of learning institutions and social distancing on students. Yet, students' mental health has been reported to have a high effect on students' outcomes, such as well-being, readiness to learning, and completion (Chessman & Taylor, 2019; Wu et al., 2020).

Discussion of Strategies for Responding and Managing the Effects of COVID-19 Pandemics in Higher Education

Following the coronavirus (COVID-19) pandemic outbreak, the World Health Organization led the world in an effort to respond to the virus. The WHO warned the virus could spread and all nations needed to do everything they could to prepare for the pandemic (UNESCO, 2020). Since there was no panacea to the pandemic, the WHO recommended that nations carry out several activities currently, namely testing, contact tracing, quarantining, social distancing, wearing of masks, and staying home. These efforts enhanced response capacity to the pandemic.

To ensure adequate response to emerging challenges, Higher education institutions must focus on quality, relevance, and quickness. This can be achieved through a more coordinated and collaborative system inclusive of not only institution leaders, administrators, faculty, and students, but funders, government policymakers, and international agencies (United Nations, 2020). For instance, one of the major effects of COVID-19 in higher education institutions includes a reduction in funding and cash flow. Institutions have lost cash that was emanating from auxiliary services, hostels, and cafeterias, besides the high cost of mounting online learning. To respond to the challenge of a reduction in cash flow, Friedman et al. (2020) suggested that institutions need to restructure their operations to fit their already thin budget. Moreover, institution leaders need to consultatively develop a rolling forecast of their revenues and expenses and closely monitor it (Friedman et al., 2020). Though forecasts are never perfect, they can help detect any shortfalls that need to be addressed.

The move to online teaching and learning as a new normal in an attempt to maintain social distance came with challenges related to student engagement, socialization, and the need to modify the curriculum to fit the current situation. Powerful learning occurs only when students are engaged, energetic, and focused (World Economic Forum, 2020). This aspect, however, is completely missing in online learning. As institutions adopt online learning as the new normal, they must modify the curriculum, contact time, and teaching strategies to ensure students stay engaged during remote learning.

Moreover, as much as institutions are working to ensure online learning is effective, they need to be aware of other factors such as anxiety, fear, and isolation that come with COVID-19. Faculty, therefore, need to think about building a community of learning where students can reach out to others to share their experiences.

Besides, enhancing infrastructures for online learning, holding technical training workshops for faculty, staff, and students, higher education institutions should plan to have an inclusive approach at the time of crisis. This will ensure that marginalized students including those living with disabilities are not left out. Besides, institutions should develop a comprehensive plan and a rigorous follow-up structure to ensure that faculty and students properly use digital platforms (Tamrat & Teferra, 2020). Moreover, as McWilliams Nsofor stated, it is imperative for each institution to have an epidemic preparedness and rapid response team to guide and advise the university on how to detect, prevent, and respond to infectious virus outbreaks (Sawahel, 2020).

Since it would be hard for institutions to project their enrollment as most students are likely to study in universities close to home or will defer studies because of inability to pay fees in this harsh economic time, institutions already in financial stress or are operating in deficit may consider merging some campuses or shutting down some units. The decision to do so may be reinforced by the uncertainty in state funding and the short-term unanticipated expenses. For instance, private and public universities alike are closing down some of their campuses.

Coronavirus has caused some form of a recession that is projected to last for at least five years (Bethwell, 2020; Meredith, 2020). The coronavirus induced recession on higher education in developing countries in Sub-Saharan Africa and South Asia is projected to have a significant effect on the flow of scholars between countries. Until the recovery period, countries together with their higher education need to rise as regional and local hubs in providing education during the recovery period. In that effort, national governments in developing countries need to create new markets for higher education. Before the pandemic, few countries and cities had gained the title of premier institutions, known for the quality degree. Of course, tuition and fees in these institutions are a bit high, but most individuals have been able to bear and are willing to sacrifice. COVID-19 crisis has presented countries with an opportunity to diversify markets for international students. As those would contribute to the nation's economic development and ensure affordability and quality in the education offered.

As a future strategy, higher education institutions need to increase partnerships and collaborations as an alternative way of operating. As Thornton (2020) stated, institutions need to re-evaluate their operations and structures to maximize shared services, increase centralization, and reduce duplication of duties.

Higher education institutions can only thrive when the staff, students, and faculty are mentally and emotionally healthy (Wu et al., 2020). Looking ahead, COVID-19 has taught institutions to keep mental health a priority by maintaining consistent and clear communication, supporting faculty and staff as they respond to the needs of students, planning, and budgeting for mental health, and ensuring equity in addressing issues related to mental health.

Moving forward, the COVID-19 pandemic offers an opportunity for higher education institutions to better prepare to deal with a similar crisis in the future. Though most institutions are still coping with the crisis of the situation, it is a learning moment for institutions to equip themselves with crisis management skills. This will increase institutions' resilience and agility when dealing with unforeseen circumstances in the future.

Conclusion

This chapter discusses some of the ways COVID-19 has influenced and shaped the future of higher education institutions. The literature showed that the COVID-19 crisis has disrupted activities and the operations of higher learning institutions in several ways. Due to the closure of learning institutions, institutions of higher learning abruptly shifted to online learning to continue engaging their students. While immediate online learning was considered as the best alternative, it was received with mixed feelings from stakeholders. Yet, it may be here to stay as a new normal. The literature showed that the COVID-19 crisis is likely to cause a decline in funding levels and resources for higher education institutions, a decline in student enrollment, a reduction in mobility of students and scholars across countries, and an increase in access and equity disparities that already exist in higher education institutions. Whereas some effects of the COVID-19 crisis are already being felt, others will be felt in the future.

To some extent, coronavirus brought some positive aspects to higher education. For instance, COVID-19 has forced institutions to accept and adopt the technology. Online learning may be considered as a cheaper and more advanced option of learning in the long run. Also, students and faculty may be reluctant to turn back to traditional face-to-face learning after experiencing an alternative mode of learning at a cheaper cost. The experiences during the COVID-19 are a catalyst for institutions to improve their digital interactions with students and other stakeholders.

The chapter also illuminates strategies for responding and managing the effects of the COVID-19 crisis in higher education institutions. As noted from the literature, these strategies are intertwined and require a coordinated and collaborative system that is inclusive of not only institution leaders, administrators, faculty, and students, but funders, government, policymakers, and international agencies. Moreover, while the strategies and the management approaches suggested may not be an all-encompassing canon to resolving pandemics in higher education institutions, they certainly are a step towards getting institutions of higher learning prepared to handle pandemics of such magnitude in the future.

References

Andrews, C., & Moulton, S. (2009). Effects of an e-learning support help desk on the implementation of e-learning technologies by university faculty. In *E-Learn: World Conference on E-Learning in Corporate, Government, Healthcare, and Higher Education* (pp. 3429–3434). Association for the Advancement of Computing in Education (AACE).

Austrian, K., Pinchoff, J., Tidwell, J. B, White, C., Abuya, T., & Kangwana, B. (2020). COVID-19 related knowledge, attitudes, practices and needs of households in informal settlements in Nairobi, Kenya. [Submitted]. *Bull World Health Organ.* E-pub: 6 April 2020. http://dx.doi.org/10.2471/BLT.20.260281

Berry, G. R., & Hughes, H. (2020). Integrating work–life balance with 24/7 information and communication technologies: The experience of adult: students with online learning. *American Journal of Distance Education*, 1–15. https://doi.org/10.1080/08923647.2020.1701301

Bethwell, E. (2020, March 26). Coronavirus: Global student flows to suffer 'massive hit' for years. *The World University Rankings*. https://www.timeshighereducation.com/news/coronavirus-global-student-flows-suffer-massive-hit-years.

Brooks, C. D., Grajek, S., & Lang, L. (2020, April 9). Institutional readiness to adopt fully remote learning. Creative Commons BY-NC-ND 4.0 *International License*. https://er.educause.edu/blogs/2020/4/institutional-readiness-to-adopt-fully-remote-learning.

Chessman, H., & Morgan, T. (2019, August 12). College student mental health and well-being: A survey of presidents. Higher *Education Today (blog), American Council on Education*. https://www.higheredtoday.org/2019/08/12/college-student-mental-health-well-survey-college-presidents/

Commission for University Education. (2017). Accredited Universities in Kenya – March 2017. http://www.cue.or.ke/images/phocadownload/Accreditted_Universities_March_2017.pdf

Court, D. (1999). *Financing higher education in Africa: Makerere: The quiet revolution*. The World Bank.

Crawfurd, J. (2020). *History of the Indian archipelago*. Routledge.

Friedman, S., Hurley, T., Fishman, T., & Fritz, P. (2020). COVID-19 impact on higher education. *Deloitte*. https://www2.deloitte.com/us/en/pages/public-sector/articles/covid-19-impact-on-higher-education.html#1

Gillett-Swan, J. (2017). The challenges of online learning: Supporting and engaging the isolated learner. *Journal of Learning Design*, *10*(1), 20–30. http://dx.doi.org/10.5204/jld.v9i3.293

Horn, M., & Staker, H. (2011). The rise of K-12 blended learning. *Innosight Institute*. http//www.innosightinstitute.org/innosight/wp-content/uploads/2011/01/The-Rise-of-K-12-Blende d-Learning

Igadwah, L. (2018, April 26). 43,614 enrolment fall hits varsities cashflow. *Business Daily*. https://www.businessdailyafrica.com/economy/43-614-enrolment-fall-hits-varsities-cashflow/3946234-4523934-e5n8v1z/index.html

Jaschik, S. (2020, April 9). Will students show up? *Inside higher ed.* https://www.insidehighered.com/admissions/article/2020/04/09/survey-shows-potential-impact-coronavirus-enrollment

Kashorda, M., & Waema, T. (2014). *E-Readiness survey of Kenyan Universities (2013) report*. Kenya Education Network.

Kenya Education network [KENET]. (2020). *Kenya education network: E-learning discounted bundle.* https://registration.kenet.or.ke/

Li, C. (2020, April 29). The COVID-19 pandemic has changed education forever. This is how. *World Economic Forum.* https://www.weforum.org/agenda/2020/04/coronavirus-education-global-covid19-online-digital-learning/

Marguerite, D. (2020, March 28). How will higher education have changed after COVID-19. *University World News.* https://www.universityworldnews.com/post.php?story=20200324065639773

Marinoni, G., Van't Land, H., & Jensen, T. (2020). *The impact of COVID-19 on higher education around the world.* International Association of Universities (IAU) Global Survey Report. UNESCO House, France.

McCowan, T. (2016). Universities and the post-2015 development agenda: An analytical framework. *Higher Education, 72*(4), 505–525.

Meredith, S. (2020, May 14). WHO warns it could take up to 5 years before the coronavirus pandemic is under control. *Health and Science.* https://www.cnbc.com/2020/05/14/coronavirus-who-warns-it-could-take-up-to-5-years-to-control-pandemic.html

Ministry of Education (MoE). (2020). *Kenya basic education sector COVID-19 emergency response plan.* Ministry of Education.

Mohamedbhai, G. (2020, April 9). COVID-19: What consequences for higher education? *University World News.* Africa Edition. https://universityworldnews.com/post.php?story=20200407064850279

Munene, I. I., & Otieno, W. (2007). Changing the course: Equity effects and institutional risk amid policy shift in higher education financing in Kenya. *Higher Education, 55*(2008), 461–479. http://dx.doi.org/10.1007/s10734-007-9067-3

Napier, N. P., Dekhane, S., & Smith, S. (2011). Transitioning to blended learning: Understanding student and faculty perceptions. *Journal of Asynchronous Learning Networks, 15*(1), 20–32.

Nguyen, T. (2015). The effectiveness of online Learning: Beyond no significant difference and future horizons. *Journal of Online Learning and Teaching, 11*(2), 34–49.

Njeru, E., & Orodho, J. (2003). Education financing in Kenya: Secondary school bursary. *Policy Analysis and Research.* http://erepository.uonbi.ac.ke/bitstream/handle/11295/12060/IPAR_Education%20Financing%20in%20Kenya%20-%20Prof.%20E.%20Njeru.pdf?sequence=1

Nyerere, J. (2020, May 12). Moving online huge challenge for Kenya's Higher Education. *Social Science Space.* https://www.socialsciencespace.com/2020/05/moving-onlone-huge-challenge-for-Kenya's-higher-education/

Odhiambo, G. O. (2011). Higher education quality in Kenya: A critical reflection on key challenges. *Quality in Higher Education, 17*, 299–315.

Page, L. (2010). Blended teaching and Learning. *School Administrators, 67*(4), 16–21.

Parsitau, D. S., & Jepkemei, E. (2020). How schools closures during COVID-19 further marginalized vulnerable children in Kenya. *Education Plus Development.* https://www.brookings.edu/blog/education-plus-development/2020/05/06/how-school-closures-during-covid-19-further-marginalize-vulnerable-children-in-kenya/

Paschal, M., & Mkulu, D. G. (2020). Online Classes during COVID-19 Pandemic in Higher Learning Institutions in Africa. *Global Research in Higher Education, 3*(3), 1. http://dx.doi.org/10.22158/grhe.v3n3p1

Republic of Kenya. (2010). *Constitution of Kenya 2010.* Government Printer.

Republic of Kenya. (2015). *Economic survey 2015; Kenya National Bureau of Statistics. Keeping you informed.* ISBN: 9966-767-47-9. https://www.knbs.or.ke/economic-survey-2015-2/

Republic of Kenya. (2016). *Economic survey 2016; Kenya National Bureau of Statistics. Keeping you informed.* Kenya National Bureau of Statistics (KNBS) - April, 2016. ISBN 9966-767-52-5. http://www.knbs.or.ke/index.php?option=com_content&view=article&id=369:economic-survey-2016&catid=82:news&Itemid=593

Republic of Kenya. (2018). *Economic survey 2018. Nairobi: Kenya National Bureau of statistics: Keeping you informed.* https://www.knbs.or.ke/?wpdmpro=economic-survey-2018

Republic of Kenya. (2018). *Parliamentary Service Commission Parliamentary Budget Office: Eye on the "Big Four".* http://www.parliament.go.ke/sites/default/files/2018-09/Budget%20Watch%202018.pdf

Sawahel, W. (2020, January 28). Coronavirus outbreak-what should universities be doing? *University World News.* https://www.universityworldnews.com/post.php?story=20200128093852832

Schroeder, R. (2001). Institutional support infrastructure for online classes. *Metropolitan Universities, 12*(1), 35–40.

Svanholm, A. G. (2020, April 24). The impact of COVID-19 on study abroad: Latest survey results. *Higher Education Marketing.* https://institutions.educations.com/insights/student-survey-covid-19-and-study-abroad

Tamrat, W., & Teferra, D. (2020, April 9). COVID-19 poses a serious threat to higher education. *University World News.* https://www.universityworldnews.com/post.php?story=20200409103755715

Tarus, J. K., Gichoya, D., & Muumbo, A. M. (2015). Challenges of implementing E-Learning in Kenya: A case of Kenyan Public Universities. *International Review of Research in Open and Distance Learning, 16*(1). http://dx.doi.org/10.19173/irrodi.v16i1.1816

Thornton, G. (2020, July 2). *COVID's impact on higher education strategy: Key consideration for the road ahead.* https://www.grantthornton.com/library/articles/nfp/2020/COVIDs-impact-on-higher-education-strategy.aspx

United Nations. (2020, May 2). COVID-19 and higher education: Learning to unlearn to create education for the future. *Academic Impact.* https://academicimpact.un.org/content/covid-19-and-higher-education-learning-unlearn-create-education-future

United Nations Development Programme. (2016). *Africa Human development report 2016: Accelerating gender equality and women empowerment in Africa.* http://hdr.undp.org/sites/default/files/afhdr_2016_lowres_en.pdf

United Nations Development Programme. (2019a). *Human development report 2019: Beyond income, beyond averages, beyond today: Inequalities in human development in the 21st century.* http://hdr.undp.org/sites/default/files/hdr2019.pdf

United Nations Development Programme. (2019b). *Human development index trends, 1990–2018.* http://hdr.undp.org/en/content/table-2-human-development-index-trends-1990%E2%80%932018

Wang, A. (2020, March 30). The Coronavirus outbreak and the challenges of online-only classes. *The Coronavirus Crisis.* https://www.npr.org/2020/03/13/814974088/the-coronavirus-outbreak-and-the-challenges-of-online-only-classes

Wekullo, C. S., Nafukho, F. M., & Muyia, M. H. A. (2018). *Conflict management in Kenya's public universities.* In N. T. Watson, M.J. Etchells, & L. Xie (Eds.), *Cultural impact on conflict management in higher education.* A volume in the series: International Higher Education (pp. 17–36).Information Age Publishing.

World Economic Forum. (2020, May 6). *What lessons from the coronavirus pandemic will shape the future of education?* https://www.weforum.org/agenda/2020/05/A-lockdown-future-education/

World Health Organization [WHO], (2019, December). *WHO statement on cases of COVID-19.* https://www.who.int/news-room/detail/07-03-2020-who-statement-on-cases-of-covid-19-surpassing-100-000

Wu, A. W., Buckle, P., Haut, E. R., Bellandi, T., Koizumi, S., Mair, A. … Newman-Toker, D. (2020). *Supporting the emotional well-being of health care workers during the covid-19 pandemic: Strategies for leaders to support campus well-being.* https://www.acenet.edu/Documents/Mental-Health-Higher-Education-Covid-19.pdf

Bios

Caroline S. Wekullo, PhD is a Research Scientist affiliated with the Directorate of Research at Masinde Muliro University of Science and Technology, Kenya. Dr. Wekullo received her Doctoral Degree in Higher Education Administration, Leadership and Policy from Texas A& M University, College Station, Texas, U.S.A. Her research centers on policy and financial issues influencing the operation of higher education institutions. Her research interest also focuses on student access, retention, engagement, and completion/achievement, as well as the measures of faculty performance, global aspects of talent development, and conflict management in higher education institutions. Dr. Wekullo is an editorial board member, copy editor, series editor, and reviewer of several top-tier journals in her field. She has published 14 peer reviewed journal articles, 1 book, 7 book chapters, and made over 15 presentations nationally and internationally. Caroline has written several grant applications and has won university-wide, National and international awards. E-mail: ccs18wekullo@gmail.com

John O. Shiundu, PhD is a Professor of Education, Masinde Muliro University of Science and Technology, (MMUST), Kenya. John specializes in curriculum instruction. He teaches curriculum, introduction to teaching and school operations, research methodology, and educational management. Advising students on school attachment and supervising graduate students. Helping students to develop academic portfolios. Writing and Reviewing textbooks and articles for journals. Designing and Developing Curriculum. Areas of Research Interest include Social Policy, Education and Development, with special reference to Elementary Education, Non-formal Education, and Vocational Education. He is currently the Director of the Institute of Indigenous Knowledge and Cultural Studies, MMUST. E-mail: jshiundu@mmust.ac.ke

James B. Ouda, PhD is a lecturer in the Department of Psychology, Masinde Muliro University of Science & Technology (MMUST), Kenya. An expert in Monitoring and Evaluation (M&E), he obtains his Post-Doctoral Research Fellowship (PDRF) from University of Venda (UNIVEN), South Africa. He has over ten years' experience in university education and is involved in placement and advising students on school practice as well as project and research supervision of undergraduate and postgraduate students, respectively. James has been involved in developing and reviewing curriculum as well as training of teachers. He has written book chapters as well as journal articles. Areas of research interest include education and development as well as M&E at all levels of education including Early Childhood Education, Teacher Education and University education. Currently he is the Chair of the PostGraduate Committee (PGC), School of Education, MMUST. E-mail: jouda@mmust.ac.ke

Anthony Mutevane, MBA is a director at African Canadian Continuing Education Society, Kakamega, Kenya. He obtained an MBA in Strategic Management from Jomo Kenyatta University of Agriculture and Technology. His research interests focus on business management and practice especially on strategic business management. E-mail: anthonymutevane@gmail.com

7 Coronavirus Disruptions to the Private Higher Education Sector in Malaysia

Benny Lim

Abstract

The COVID-19 pandemic has taken the world by storm. On March 18, Malaysia was put into a countrywide lockdown, where all non-essential businesses have to close, including shutting down the campuses of institutions of higher learning. Many institutions have no choice but to go forward quickly with online modes of teaching and learning. Based on an autoethnographic research, it is concluded that private institutions faced financial challenges brought about by students' decisions to defer and/or delay their studies. The institutions also encounter challenges in the disruptions of their teaching and learning activities, including the internship program. Moving forward, private institutions need to embrace online modes of teaching and learning. Furthermore, faculty members and students should also develop resilience through enhancing their social and cultural capital.

Keywords

COVID-19 Pandemic; Online Teaching and Learning; Private Higher Education in Malaysia; Resilience Building; Digital Thinking

Introduction

The coronavirus (or COVID-19) outbreak has taken the world by storm. What started out as an epidemic was soon upgraded to a pandemic status on March 11, 2020, by the World Health Organization. The pandemic has triggered many countries to lock down their borders, and impose strict internal restrictions for all activities, businesses, and otherwise. By late March, the chief of the International Monetary Fund asserted that the global economy has entered a recession due to the pandemic, which would eventually lead to a foreseeable surge in business closures and unemployment rates. Malaysia is not spared from the impacts of the pandemic. On March 16, the Malaysian prime minister declared a sudden two-week countrywide lockdown (effective two days after) known as the Movement Control Order (MCO). Under the

MCO, all non-essential businesses have to close, including shutting down the campuses of institutions of higher learning.

Many institutions, especially private higher education institutions (PHEIs), have no choice but to go forward quickly with online modes of teaching and learning. The initial two-week closure of campuses would eventually last for seven weeks for staff members and much longer for the students. A portion of the students was allowed to return to their campuses for face-to-face classes in July and October, while the remaining students would have to continue learning online till the end of the year. This chapter seeks to detail the challenges faced by PHEIs in Malaysia during the MCO based on an autoethnographic research, given my personal involvement then as a member of the senior leadership team in a Malaysian private university college. Drawing from Bourdieu's theory of social and cultural capital, the chapter also attempts to envisage the crucial issues surrounding the "new normal" of Malaysia's private higher education sector post-COVID-19, specifically on how faculty members and students could develop resilience.

The Rise and Fall of Malaysia's Private Higher Education

While Malaysia is a multicultural country, the society has always been divided along racial and religious lines, with Malays and Islam practices dominating almost every aspect of politics, civil service, and people's day-to-day lives (Wise, 2009). The national policies favor Malays alongside the indigenous population collectively known as Bumiputera, and higher education is no exception (Koh, 2017; Mellström, 2010). Preference of enrollment to subsidized public higher education institutions is accorded to Bumiputera, and this led to a large proportion of minority races such as the Chinese and Indians having to either seek costly higher education overseas or give up hope of ever earning a degree. This situation led to the establishment of private colleges in the 1980s, mainly by businessmen who are themselves from minority races (McBurnie & Ziguras, 2007). These colleges often collaborate with Australian and British universities to offer transnational offshore higher education academic programs.

Most PHEIs in Malaysia are for-profit entities without any form of government subvention. Simply put, the bulk of PHEIs' revenue comes from the fees paid by the students. In 1997, the government launched an initiative to provide loans to partially cover tuition fees of accredited higher education programs according to students' household income levels. This initiative has definitely accelerated neoliberal practices in private higher education, and the number of PHEIs grew exponentially thereafter. Furthermore, to enroll more students, it is common for PHEIs to usually have three or four intakes a year, as compared to only one intake per year by public higher education institutions. Despite so, the private higher education sector is strictly governed by the Ministry of Higher Education, and the academic programs by the institutions are subjected to accreditations and rigorous checks by the Malaysian Qualifications Agency (MQA).

Since the late 1990s and early 2000s, colleges with proven track records have been upgraded to university college status that comes with degree awarding powers. In the last 15 years, many university colleges fulfilled the requirements for further upgrade to full university status (Da Wan & Morshidi, 2018). The private higher education sector is also tasked to attract a pool of international students into the country, and brand Malaysia as a global hub for higher education. As of 2018, there are 447 PHEIs in Malaysia, which include 53 universities, 10 branch campuses of foreign universities, 37 university colleges, and 347 private colleges. These institutions enrolled over 666 thousand students, of which 131 thousand are international students (Ministry of Education, 2020). It is surmised to say that the private higher education market in Malaysia is both saturated and highly competitive.

Main Challenges Faced by PHEIs during the Lockdown

Financial Implications

The economic downturn brought about by the pandemic has greatly impacted the financial standing of many PHEIs, which are dependent on tuition fees to sustain and survive. Unemployment rates in Malaysia skyrocketed at 5.3% in May 2020, the highest ever since 1990 (Shanker, 2020). Amongst those who lost their jobs or had their salaries cut include parents of students pursuing higher education. Local students from lower-income families often take on part-time jobs to support their higher education. However, with the MCO in place, these students are likely to have lost a part, if not all, of their income. Due to the difficulty in paying for the hefty tuition fees, many affected students in PHEIs have no choice but to defer their studies to later semesters, and some students only intend to return to their institutions in 2021. Existing foreign students who left Malaysia during the pandemic or new international students who intend to study in Malaysia were not given the go-ahead to enter the country, resulting in some of these students unable to start a new semester with their respective PHEIs in April/May. It is expected that the total enrollment of PHEIs would drop by 37% by the end of 2020 (Chung, 2020).

The months of April and May are the peak enrollment period for most private institutions, where students complete their secondary education and are seeking to register into either pre-university or diploma programs in PHEIs. Similarly, a proportion of new students chose to delay their studies due to financial stress, particularly when government loans are not available to students in their first semester of study. Financial reasons aside, there was also a group of students who delayed/deferred their studies in April/May due to the uncertainties in teaching and learning, especially when institutions had yet to receive the go-ahead to recommence face-to-face teaching then. To a certain extent, this implies students' (and parents') skepticism towards the shift to online learning.

Given the enrollment and deferment situation, coupled with the absence of a stimulus package by the government for the private higher education sector, many PHEIs fell into severe financial devastation and cash flow problems. Even prior to the pandemic, the enrollment situation in PHEIs was already highly uneven, with many institutions falling short of their targets to break even or make a profit. According to a recent report, a 15% reduction in income would render 50% of the PHEIs financially insolvent (Hunter, 2020).

To reduce the number of deferments due to financial difficulties, many PHEIs rolled out flexible installment and payment schemes so that students could still continue with their studies. In late May, the ministry of higher education released a circular, announcing that all classes are to remain online till the end of the year (Landau, 2020). Nevertheless, a later circular was sent out in July notifying PHEIs that diploma and degree students who need to undertake practical classes could return to campus (Liew, 2020). Foreign students were also given the go-ahead to enter Malaysia subjected to a series of conditions.

Disruptions to Teaching and Learning

While MQA did not restrict the use of technology in teaching prior to the pandemic, many PHEIs have failed to fully embrace the possibilities of technology in education. While most institutions subscribe to some form of online learning management systems (LMS), the commonly used functions are often limited to the mere creation of new announcements and the sharing of learning materials with students. It should also be noted that investments in education technologies could be especially costly for PHEIs, some of which are facing continued financial difficulties due to the immense competition from within the sector. It comes as no surprise that many PHEIs stuck on to the conventional face-to-face teaching methodologies, such as lectures, tutorials, and practical sessions. Sad to say, many PHEIs were not prepared to handle online modes of teaching and learning when the MCO was implemented.

During the onset of the MCO, PHEIs were discouraged from conducting real-time online teaching as there were concerns over students' access to internet connections. Therefore, some faculty members pre-recorded lectures and made them available on the LMS, while others uploaded learning materials and engaged in informal discussions with students over messaging applications such as WhatsApp. The lack of clear directives from both the ministry and MQA on the execution of practical classes for culinary arts, hotel management, and design programs, etc. has left many PHEIs hanging. Many students in PHEIs also reflected that the asynchronous mode of teaching and learning was disengaging. Eventually, real-time synchronous online teaching was given the go-ahead by the ministry, provided that individual institutions offered support to students who faced difficulties with connectivity.

The fortnightly announcement of the MCO extension also affected the operations of the final examinations for many PHEIs, especially when April is the month for final examinations of undergraduate programs. Almost all PHEIs ended up offering alternative modes of assessments. Depending on the nature of the courses, alternative assessments included real-time examination (examination scripts are made available on LMS) with online invigilation carried out via Google Meet or Zoom, or written assignments to be submitted by a given deadline. Students are not the only ones who are marginalized in the digital divide. Faculty members, too, face connectivity issues, such as having subscribed to lower speed and threshold internet plans at home, and/or staying in locations that have a weaker internet connection. With the campuses closed, some faculty members are also confronted with the lack of a private domestic space to teach online and some ended up not showing their faces on the screen while delivering a lecture. Apart from the issues of internet access, faculty members had to quickly adapt to online teaching within days, and in most cases, with minimal training initially. Academics who are less tech-savvy experienced a wider cultural lag and found the switch a lot more challenging.

Disruptions to Internships

In Malaysia, most PHEIs focus mainly on employment-ready programs (Cheong et al., 2018). This resulted in the lack of humanities and liberal arts undergraduate programs in private institutions. Even certain social science areas, such as sociology and geography, are at most offered as electives. The focus on employment explains why an internship is such an integral component of most homegrown diploma and degree programs in PHEIs.

On completion of their secondary education, students could apply to pre-university programs (foundation or "A" levels', etc.) or diploma programs. With a diploma qualification, some students would opt to join the workforce. Many diploma graduates would proceed to enroll in a three-year 120-credit bachelor program with exemptions up to 60 credits, depending on the equivalency of courses. Since both diploma and bachelor programs lead to employment, it is therefore common for both programs to each include an internship component in students' final (or second last) semester of study. Simply put, students who graduate from bachelor programs via the diploma pathway are likely to have completed two separate internships.

Through a three- to a four-month internship, students could apply the theories they learn from lectures into actual work situations and at the same time, reflect on their personal capabilities in their chosen field of study (Jawabri, 2017). Knowledge aside, soft skills, such as teamwork, communication, time management, adaptability, to name a few, are equally important for interns to succeed (Patacsil & Tablatin, 2017). Moreover, internships provide opportunities for students to network and enhance their resumes with the much-needed initial work experience. Several PHEIs go as far as to conduct preparatory courses and psychometric tests on their students so that they could excel in their internships. Students aside, the providers of the internship opportunities stand to benefit from the process as well. For one, being digital natives, interns might offer innovative, out-of-the-box ideas, especially in engaging the youth segment. Full-time junior employees of companies could also develop professionally through managing interns. Last but not least, companies could make use of their internship programs to spot potential permanent talents from the pool of interns.

Given the border restrictions alongside the economic recession, internship programs globally face the reality of being disrupted. Companies with reduced operations or financial difficulties might cut back on the number of internship places, or even cancel the provision of internships altogether. Despite the implementation of the MCO, students are not allowed to replace internships completely with other credit-bearing modules. Furthermore, students are often sent out for internships only in the later stage of their studies, for they have completed enough courses to develop the necessary knowledge and skillsets to effectively carry out their work. Unlike universities in Singapore, which allowed students to defer their internships to later semesters, PHEIs in Malaysia have limited flexibility for such postponements.

PHEIs have to identify possible alternatives to internships within the guidelines of MQA when both physical and remote modes of internships become impossible. Institutions must continue to ensure that whatever internship opportunities are left in this trying time should still adhere to students' learning outcomes and that the learning experience for the students would not be undermined. Depending on the nature of the work involved, some internships could be carried out remotely. For instance, the exponential growth of online events during the pandemic, such as business meetings, festivals, and webinars, has boosted the demand for event technologists. These digital events are likely to welcome the support of interns specializing in communication and events management. One recommendation by MQA is for PHEIs to replace internships with industry-based projects. Institutions are encouraged to work with their respective industry partners to develop suitable projects for students. Some companies have developed special projects relevant to the pandemic for interns, while others have provided opportunities for students to initiate and run their own projects by identifying gaps in the current marketplace.

Malaysia's Private Higher Education Sector in the Post-COVID-19 Era

The COVID-19 pandemic is returning for the second or third waves in many countries, including Malaysia. Even if a vaccine is available in the mid or longer-term, the private higher education sector will continue to face arduous challenges. The public will generally be more conscious and cautious in participating in large group learning, and/or crossing borders for the pursuit of higher education. This section discusses the growing importance of technology in education, and how faculty members and students could develop resilience in the post-COVID-19 era.

Embracing Technology in Education

In his Teachers' Day speech on May 16, Malaysia's prime minister clearly mentioned that online learning would be the future, and urged teachers to continue enhancing their online teaching capabilities. The circulars issued by the ministry of higher education reiterated the prime minister's speech and emphasized that online teaching and learning will be the new norm for higher education institutions.

For most city dwellers in Malaysia, it is almost impossible to imagine going by a day without any form of technological support. Technologies serve as extensions to the limitations of our human body (Goody, 2011; Sigwart, 2016). Yet, despite our heavy reliance on technology, the idea of pursuing higher education through online means is still frowned upon by many. E-education is often perceived as less favorable, citing concerns about the quality of teaching and learning (Fain, 2019). Regardless of the skepticisms, more universities, including top-ranked UK universities such Oxford and Cambridge, have created e-learning platforms to offer both short courses and full academic programs. Many established universities are also putting aside resources to encourage the development of e-learning. Globally, millions of students are enrolled in some form of online degree programs, making e-education a multi-billion dollar enterprise (Valverde-Berrocoso et al., 2020). Undoubtedly, the future of higher education is virtual.

The term "e-education" could be interpreted in at least two ways. First, academic programs offered by e-universities are considered a form of e-education. In Malaysia, there are only four such institutions, and none are major players in the private higher education sector. Two institutions are relatively well-known lifelong learning universities, while the other two focused more on professional business programs, such as online MBAs or DBAs. These institutions are fully capable of transferring knowledge to students. However, little has been discussed on how they develop students' emotions, values, ethics, and networks. Eventually, there would be an entire philosophy on how whole person education could be achieved through digital means.

Another type of e-education refers to the online programs offered by campus-based universities. These online programs are above and beyond the current suite of campus-based programs and could collectively be offered by one teaching unit of an institution, or managed by respective schools and departments. Such a mode of e-education is sometimes described as distance learning, although 'distance learning' does not always involve the use of digital technologies. In Malaysia, there seems to be a growing trend of online distance learning programs offered by campus-based PHEIs, especially professional business programs designed for busy working executives. PHEIs should continue in this direction and eventually, expand into a wider range of disciplines. Instead of viewing each other as competitors, PHEIs are more likely to benefit from collaborations, especially in their e-education offerings. At this stage, it might seem unthinkable that students could complete credits for different courses online from a pool of PHEIs to earn a bachelor's degree. With MQA's approval and adequate planning, this could well happen in the near future.

The COVID-19 pandemic has no doubt disrupted face-to-face classes. Yet, the sudden shift to online teaching is not all doom and gloom. Digital technologies, such as Zoom and Google Meet, are catching up to the demands of education. In the weeks and months since the implementation of the MCO, many PHEIs have arranged additional training for their faculty members to better equip them with the capabilities to adopt a range of digital learning tools. The shift has also led to increased conversations and sharing between academics and institutions on effective and creative online teaching methodologies. Months into the MCO, PHEIs are definitely better prepared for e-education and should continue to develop new competitiveness in the online sphere so as to capture a wider pool of local and international students.

Nevertheless, mastering a range of technologies for education does not necessarily translate into expertise in online teaching and learning, especially when delivery technologies evolve all the time. Furthermore, using technologies to merely mirror how faculty members would normally teach in a face-to-face environment is certainly not reflexive of an advancement. Training workshops should also revisit the methodologies in carrying out the flipped classrooms and problem-based learning (PBL) through digital platforms. PBL, for instance, can be adopted in online mission-based assignments where students are expected to be self-directed learners, equipped with the necessary skills to seek useful information online. Gamification techniques, such as the award of achievement badges, can also be incorporated into the learning process. As for internships, should there be a significant reduction in the number of placements due to the pandemic, PHEIs could redesign the program into pockets of remote practicums, whereby learning takes place through observing, rather than doing.

Developing Resilience in Faculty Members and Students

If anything, the pandemic serves as a good reminder that adversities could happen anytime and from all directions. Resilience thinking, as opposed to automatic thinking, is about identifying opportunities in times of adversities through forming new perspectives via human-centric critical and reflexive approaches (Schiraldi, 2017). Scholars have suggested the relevance of Bourdieu's theory of social and/or cultural capital in developing resilience (Gnieciak & Wódz, 2020; Grenfell, 2014; Promberger et al., 2019; Wilson, 2012). Social capital refers to a person's mutual obligations and networks whereas cultural capital relates to one's culturally relevant skills, knowledge, and achievements (Bourdieu, 1986). Both social and cultural capital could be "cashed out" under certain conditions (Chiang, 2009).

The private higher education sector is supported by 23,000 faculty members, of which, only 21.1% are doctoral holders, while another 52.3% are qualified at the Master's degree level (Ministry of Education, 2020). As compared to academics from public universities, faculty members in PHEIs are somewhat subordinated. For one, public universities' academics could easily move to PHEIs, but the reverse is not as straightforward. Moreover, MQA usually appoints public universities' academics to conduct audits and reviews on PHEIs. Once again, the reverse is rare.

Given the external economic environment and the financial challenges faced by many PHEIs, the fear of being laid off lingers amongst their faculty members. Academics should seriously contemplate the outlook of the sector, and develop action plans to better prepare themselves to contribute to the post-pandemic higher education landscape. A way forward for academics in PHEIs is to upskill and/or upgrade their qualifications. While a higher qualification does not bring about guaranteed success, it enhances one's competitiveness and mobility.

All PHEIs in Malaysia subscribe to outcome-based education (OBE). Institutional and program audits conducted by MQA have mainly focused on whether the institutions fulfill their stated outcomes. This has resulted in PHEIs devoting substantial resources in instilling the OBE mentality into faculty members. Moving forward, part of the resources could be diverted to developing digital thinking amongst faculty members, so that they could critically reflect societal shifts brought about by the digital age, as well as identify and implement new teaching and learning methodologies and digital tools (Kumar et al., 2020). Academics have to become what Spanish sociologist Manuel Castells (2012) describes as "self-programmable labor", who is ready to take on new tasks and challenges in this network society.

Faculty members should explore the potential of various social media platforms, especially LinkedIn. The platform offers vast opportunities for personal branding, networking, as well as sharing of new trends in the higher education sector. It would be increasingly possible for an academic to teach remotely for a few institutions in different geographical locations (including overseas). Demand for curriculum developers for programs conducted through online distance learning is also expected to grow. Even before the pandemic, PHEIs, unlike public institutions, were not able to commit much funding for their faculty members to participate in international academic conferences. The pandemic has accelerated the acceptance of online conferences or conferences with virtual components. Academics in PHEIs should make use of this opportunity to gather insights and develop new networks through participating in these conferences.

The pandemic has also brought about a hike in unemployment rates, coupled with categorical changes in the employment market. Students who are entering the job market soon are naturally concerned about their employment prospects. Faculty members in PHEIs should walk alongside students in identifying trends and gaps in the post-COVID-19 road to recovery within their respective professional fields. Moreover, students are generally unfamiliar with the potential of online learning. Hence, PHEIs should initiate workshops to also instill digital thinking capabilities in students, so that they can make the best out of their online learning experience. This includes facilitating online learning in ways where they could become self-directed learners and producers of digital learning content.

The main arguments so far seem to further propel private higher education towards neoliberal practices. PHEIs should bear in mind that the overemphasis on employment is a double-edged sword, resulting in the subordination of humanities and liberal arts in the curriculum of many private institutions. General education courses in PHEIs focus mainly on improving students' language competencies, communication skills, and teamwork. Students might find it hard to actualize their resilience, and any negative emotions could easily shake up their stand. This is especially true for many millennials studying in Malaysia's PHEIs, who have a better quality of life than that of their parent's generation. PHEIs should introduce courses that delve into philosophical investigations of a wide spectrum of dilemmas and failures in past and contemporary societies.

Furthermore, there should be regular windows for students to share their personal fears and worries with their lecturers and peers (including alumni). These exchanges could take place in a form of face-to-face conversations, or via digital video conferencing tools. In a nutshell, our leaders of tomorrow ought to be equipped with the right capabilities to deal with the ever-evolving globalized informational society.

Conclusion

Institutions of higher learning, universities or otherwise, have reacted and responded to a myriad of changes in the last hundreds of years. The belief is that they will continue to evolve with new adversities and challenges in the years to come. In Malaysia, PHEIs have contributed substantially to providing education opportunities to many Malaysians, especially the ethnic minority. They have also positioned Malaysia as an international higher education hub. Yet, the sector is also more affected by the pandemic than its public counterpart. PHEIs must recognize that disruption is not necessarily a bad thing, especially since societies and human behaviors in the digital age have constantly been impacted by disruptive technologies. In fact, disruptions necessitate a rethinking of how the higher education sector should evolve in the near future. Online modes of learning are here to stay—faculty members and students alike have to internalize digital thinking and to develop resilience through enhancing their social and cultural capital.

References

Bourdieu, P. (1986). The forms of capital. In J. Richardson (Ed.), *Handbook of theory and research for the sociology of education* (pp. 241–258). Greenwood.

Castells, M. (2012). *Networks of outrage and hope: Social movements in the Internet age.* Polity Press.

Cheong, K.-C., Hill, C., Leong, Y.-C., & Zhang, C. (2018). Employment as a journey or a destination? Interpreting graduates' and employers' perceptions – A Malaysia case study. *Studies in Higher Education*, 43(4), 702–718. https://doi.or g/10.1080/03075079.2016.1196351

Chiang, M. (2009). *The cultural capital of Asian American studies: Autonomy and representation in the university*. NYU Press.

Chung, C. (2020). *Private institutions seeking govt help*. https://www.thestar.com.my/news/nation/2020/06/08/private-institutions-seeking-govt-help

Da Wan, C., & Morshidi, S. (2018). The evolution of corporatisation of public universities in Malaysia. In J. C. Shin (Ed.), *Higher education governance in East Asia: Transformations under neoliberalism* (pp. 89–105). Springer. https://doi.org/10.1007/978-981-13-2469-7_6

Fain, P. (2019). *Takedown of online education*. https://www.insidehighered.com/digital-learning/article/2019/01/16/online-learning-fails-deliver-finds-report-aimed-discouraging

Goody, A. (2011). *Technology, literature and culture* (Vol. 3). Polity Press.

Gnieciak, M., & Wódz, K. (2020). Cultural aspects of resilience from the perspective of everyday practices of households affected by economic crisis. In M. Promberger, M. Boost, J. Dagg, & J. Gray (Eds.), *Poverty, crisis and resilience* (pp. 105–123). Edward Elgar Publishing. https://doi.org/10.4337/9781788973205.00017

Grenfell, M. J. (2014). *Pierre Bourdieu*. Bloomsbury Publishing.

Hunter, M. (2020). *The collapse of Malaysian private universities*. https://www.asiasentinel.com/p/the-collapse-of-malaysian-private

Jawabri, A. (2017). Exploration of internship experience and satisfaction leading to better career prospects among business students in UAE. *American Journal of Educational Research*, 5(10), 1065–1079. https://doi.org/10.12691/education-5-10-8

Koh, S. Y. (2017). *Race, education, and citizenship: Mobile Malaysians, British colonial legacies, and a culture of migration*. Palgrave Macmillan. https://doi.org/10.1057/978-1-137-50344-2

Kumar K., Zindani, D., & Davim, J. P. (2020). *Design thinking to digital thinking*. Springer. https://doi.org/10.1007/978-3-030-31359-3_5

Landau, E. (2020). *University lectures to go online until Dec 31, except for 5 groups*. https://www.nst.com.my/news/nation/2020/05/595758/university-lectures-go-online-until-dec-31-except-5-groups

Liew, E. (2020). *University & college students to return to physical classes in phases starting July 2020*. https://worldofbuzz.com/university-college-students-to-return-to-physical-classes-in-phases-starting-july-2020/

McBurnie, G., & Ziguras, C. (2007). *Transnational education: Issues and trends in offshore higher education*. Routledge.

Mellström, U. (2010). New gender relations in the transforming IT-industry of Malaysia. In S. Booth, S. Goodman, & G. Kirkup (Eds.), *Gender issues in learning and working with information technology: Social constructs and cultural contexts* (pp. 25–47). IGI Global. https://doi.org/10.4018/978-1-61520-813-5.ch002

Ministry of Education. (2020). *Way forward for private higher education institutions: Education as an industry (2020–2025)*. https://issuu.com/sharafuddin/docs/inside_ctb_kpm_full_

Patacsil, F. F., & Tablatin, C. L. S. (2017). Exploring the importance of soft and hard skills as perceived by IT internship students and industry: A gap analysis. *Journal of Technology and Science Education*, *7*(3), 347–368. http://dx.doi.org/10.3926/jotse.271

Promberger, M., Meier, L., Sowa, F., & Boost, M. (2019). Chances of 'resilience' as a concept for sociological poverty research. In B. Rampp, M. Endreß, & M. Naumann (Eds.), *Resilience in social, cultural and political spheres* (pp. 249–278). Springer. https://doi.org/10.1007/978-3-658-15329-8_13

Schiraldi, G. R. (2017). *The resilience workbook: Essential skills to recover from stress, trauma, and adversity.* New Harbinger Publications.

Shanker, A. C. (2020). *Malaysia unemployment rate escalates to 5.3% in May.* https://www.theedgemarkets.com/article/malaysia-unemployment-rate-escalates-53-may

Sigwart, H. J. (2016). *The wandering thought of Hannah Arendt.* Palgrave Macmillan.

Valverde-Berrocoso, J., Garrido-Arroyo, M. D. C., Burgos-Videla, C., & Morales-Cevallos, M. B. (2020). Trends in educational research about e-Learning: A systematic literature review (2009–2018). *Sustainability*, *12*(12), 5153. https://doi.org/10.3390/su12125153

Wilson, G. (2012). *Community resilience and environmental transitions.* Routledge.

Wise, A. (2009). Everyday multiculturalism: Transversal crossings and working class cosmopolitans. In A. Wise & S. Velayutham (Eds.), *Everyday multiculturalism* (pp. 21–45). Palgrave Macmillan. https://doi.org/10.1057/9780230244474_2

Bio

Benny Lim is currently a Professional Consultant with the Department of Cultural and Religious Studies, the Chinese University of Hong Kong. He is also an Adjunct Professor of the Master's program in Communication and Media Studies with Università Telematica Pegaso (Italy). He was formerly an Associate Professor and Dean of the Faculty of Liberal Arts, Berjaya University College (Malaysia). E-mail: bennylim@cuhk.edu.hk

8 Innovating in the Face of the COVID-19 Pandemic

Case Studies from Nigerian Universities

Samuel Adeyanju, Oluwatoyin Ajilore, Oluwafemi Ogunlalu, Alex Onatunji, and Emmanuel Mogaji

Abstract

This chapter critically examines the impacts of the coronavirus pandemic on tertiary education in Nigeria and highlights outstanding indigenous innovations within tertiary institutions prompted by the pandemic. The Coronavirus pandemic and the associated lockdown measures have led to the suspension of in-person instruction and learning in many higher education campuses globally. In Nigeria, school closure has negatively impacted the already fragile educational system, causing further hardships for students—who previously grappled with frequent school closures due to incessant strike actions and unrest. Unlike more developed climes—where schools have quickly transitioned to online teaching, poor infrastructural facilities (ICT and Internet) make online teaching and learning an arduous task for the hundreds of higher institutions present in Nigeria. We offer managerial implications relevant for University administrators and managers towards the development of a workable post-COVID-19 education strategy and response plan.

Keywords

E-learning; COVID-19; Innovation; Nigeria; School closure; Universities

Introduction

In the 20th century, three different pandemic outbreaks of influenza ravaged the world in 1918, 1957, and 1968 (Kilbourne, 2006). One of the worst was the 1918 influenza pandemic which claimed an estimated 50–100 million lives worldwide between 1918 and 1919 (de Almeida, 2013). On 11 March 2020, the World Health Organization (WHO) declared COVID-19 caused by the coronavirus as a global pandemic. The earliest cases were discovered in Wuhan, China, and reported to the WHO Country Office in China on 31 December 2019 (World Health Organisation—WHO, 2020a).

This new coronavirus seems to be very contagious and has swiftly spread globally. Reports show that the virus has spread to 191 countries and regions with more than 81 million confirmed cases and over 1.7 million deaths recorded as of 29 December 2020 (Johns Hopkins University, 2020). Furthermore, the pandemic has taken a toll on economies, public health, education, and the daily lives of people worldwide.

The severity of the COVID-19 pandemic has prompted local and global efforts to contain the spread of the virus. Governments worldwide have responded by instituting various public health, social and economic measures (Ihekweazu & Agogo, 2020; Porcher, 2020, Roser et al., 2020). These containment measures could be broadly grouped into social, public health, and economic measures. The social measures include border closures, suspension of international and domestic travels, business and school closures, cancellation of public events and gatherings, and stay-at-home restrictions. The public health measures include molecular testing, intensive surveillance, and case-finding. The economic measures include income support and debt relief (Porcher, 2020).

In Nigeria, the first case was confirmed on 27 February 2020 (Ihekweazu & Agogo, 2020). It has increased to over 86,576 reported cases and about 1,278 deaths as of 30 December 2020 (Nigeria Centre for Disease Control, 2020). To curb the spread, the Government introduced a travel restriction on both local (inter-state) and international travel (CNBC Africa, 2020). Before the initial lockdown announcement, all schools in Nigeria were closed by the Government on 19 March 2020 (Abdulsalam, 2020), leading to the suspension of in-person instruction and learning at all levels of education.

According to the United Nations Educational, Scientific and Cultural Organisation (UNESCO), over 60% of the world's student population were unable to attend school due to school closures (Figure 8.1), representing 1.5 billion children and youth in 195 countries, from pre-primary to higher education as of mid-April 2020 (UNESCO, 2020a, 2020b). In Nigeria, almost 40 million learners have been affected by the nationwide school closures and over 4% (1,513,371 students) are in Higher Education Institutions (HEIs) (UNESCO, 2020b). This number is spread across all the higher education institutions in Nigeria. The closure has negatively impacted the already fragile educational system, causing further hardships for students—who previously grappled with frequent learning disruptions and school closures due to incessant strike actions and unrest (Wahab, 2018). Unlike in more developed climes—where schools have quickly transitioned to online teaching within weeks (Burke, 2020; Kedraka & Kaltsidis, 2020), the poor infrastructural facilities (ICT and Internet) make online teaching and learning an arduous task for the hundreds of HEIs in Nigeria (Adeoye et al., 2020).

In this chapter, we draw on survey questionnaire data, literature and news publications, our personal experience, and research in Nigeria to critically examine the impacts of the coronavirus pandemic on tertiary education in that country and highlight outstanding indigenous innovations within tertiary institutions prompted by the pandemic. We offer suggestions on the practical

School closures during the COVID-19 pandemic, Jul 31, 2020

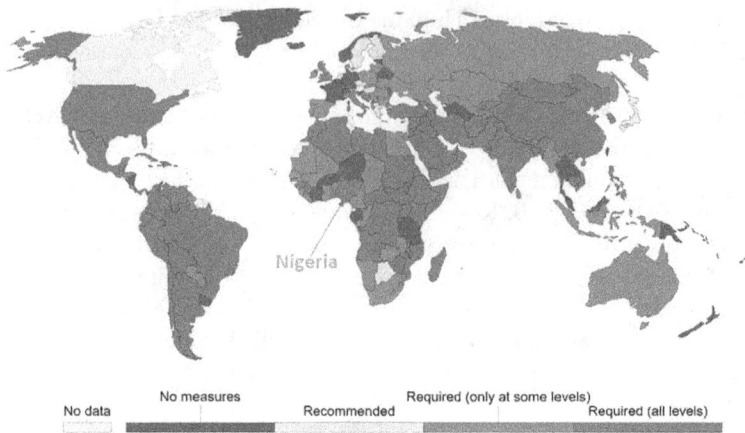

Figure 8.1 Map of global school closures during the Covid-19 pandemic as of 31 July 2020 (Roser et al., 2020). This map is licensed under a very permissive "Creative Commons" (CC) license: The CC-BY license is free to use. See here for the permission to use note https://ourworldindata.org/how-to-use-our-world-in-data#how-is-our-work-copyrighted

implications for the various stakeholders (the Federal Ministry of Education, Higher Education Institutions, Local and International Education NGOs, etc.) in the Nation's tertiary education sector towards the development of a workable post-Covid-19 education strategy and response plan. The chapter begins with a literature review on the status of Higher Education in Nigeria and the impact of the Coronavirus Pandemic on Higher Education in that country. Followed by the methodology, result, and discussion sections, this chapter closes with important conclusions and identifies the main implications and recommendations for policy and practice.

Literature Review

The Status of Higher Education in Nigeria

Nigeria is the most populated nation in Africa, with over 200 million people (Akinpelu, 2020a). There are huge numbers of youths who aspire for higher education in the country. Every year, many prospective students write the Unified Tertiary and Matriculation Examinations (UTME) which is a requirement for securing admission into Nigeria University (Adeyanju et al., 2020). However, the demand for a university place is higher than the supply of universities due to the limited number and capacity of universities in Nigeria. In 2020, two-thirds (over 1.1 million) of the 2 million students who applied for tertiary education were not admitted due to limited spaces available in all tertiary institutions in Nigeria (Akinpelu, 2020a).

Therefore, these market dynamics make university spots in Nigeria very competitive, especially in public universities mainly due to the lower tuition fees, reputation, and ranking of public universities (Adeyanju et al., 2020). The total population of students enrolled in Nigerian universities is over 2 million, which presents a considerable challenge for prospective students (Premium Times, 2020). There are 174 Universities in Nigeria, consisting of public universities that are supported by the Federal Government (43 universities), State Government (53 Universities), and privately owned (79) (Farinloye et al., 2020). The numbers of private universities in Nigeria are also increasing (from the first three established in 1999 and now 79 in 2019) (Farinloye et al., 2020). They address some of the challenges facing the Nigerian education system and for example, ensuring that their students finish their degree at the stipulated time (Olaleye et al., 2020).

Despite these opportunities, there are inherent challenges for higher education in Nigeria which questions its status in Africa and even worldwide. Nigeria has a much bigger education system in Africa, but unfortunately, there are concerns about its overall quality, unlike higher education in South Africa and Egypt (Ndofirepi et al., 2020). Nigeria has four universities in the overall Times Higher Education World University Rankings. The highest-ranking university in Nigeria is Covenant University (a private university), ranked at number 401–500 (Times Higher Education, 2020).

The Nigerian universities are underfunded which is reflected in the quality of facilities for student learning, research output, and the job prospect of the students. Nigeria allocated 6.7% of its 2020 budget to education, compared to its 2019 budget which had 7.05%, (Amoo, 2019). This reduction highlights funding problems for Nigeria's education sector especially as it is lower than the 15–20% government's budget recommendations by UNESCO (UNESCO, 2015).

There have been many disruptions to academic calendars because of industrial action by the staff protesting for funding for their Universities. Since 1999 when Nigeria moved to democratic rule, the Academic Staff Union of Universities (ASUU) has been on strike for over 15 times for a cumulative period of three years (Wahab, 2018). For instance, ASUU members are currently on a nationwide strike (Adedigba, 2020). This funding issue is however not much of a problem for the private university as their struggle is more on maintaining their reputation, facilities and accreditation process, posing some limitations on the courses they offer (most private universities offers classroom-based, easy to teach courses and less of medicine or engineering which requires more facilities) (Olaleye et al., 2020).

With these disruptions to the academic calendar, the stiff competition for University placement, and the poor perception about the Nigerian education system, many Nigerian students seek quality higher education abroad. According to UNESCO Global Flow of Tertiary-Level Students (UNESCO, 2020c), the United Kingdom, United States of America, Malaysia, Canada, and Ghana were the top destinations for Nigerian students. In 2018, 12, 642 students went to the UK while 6,506 studied in Ghana. This educational tourism costs Nigeria a considerable amount of money as data from the Institute of International Education shows that Nigerian students spend $514 million to study in the United States (Kazeem, 2019).

Impact of Coronavirus Pandemic on Higher Education in Nigeria

The impact of the COVID-19 on higher education in Nigeria cannot be overemphasized, as total suspension of on-campus academic activities has led to the disruption of various activities such as lectures, exams, research, thesis defenses, and graduation ceremonies (Obiakor & Adeniran, 2020; Ogunode, 2020). Since the coronavirus outbreak was reported in Nigeria and an accompanying lockdown in most of the Nation's biggest states, there has been a progressive crippling of key economic activities across all sectors (Mogaji, 2020). The educational sector—a very vital aspect of nation-building is not left out of this quagmire. Students across the board—from elementary schools to tertiary institutions have been on lockdown since 19 March with no structured alternatives to cushion the effects of the pandemic on their education (Abdulsalam, 2020; Ogundipe et al., 2020). After frequent statements released during the daily briefings of the Presidential Task Force on COVID-19 to debunk series of fake news on school resumption spreading across social media (Edeh, 2020), the Federal Government gave a list of conditions for reopening schools after calls for reopening from various stakeholder groups (Abdulsalam, 2020).

While acknowledging that the pandemic is affecting higher education on a global scale, universities in emerging countries like Nigeria have additional challenges to deal with. Generally, access to stable electricity, high quality, and affordable Internet facilities are some of the major infrastructural deficits that Nigerians have suffered for decades. The significance of these facilities (especially electricity and Internet) to educational services has gained prominence due to the lockdown and school closures occasioned by the COVID-19 pandemic (Nwaogwugwu, 2020). To provide some context, nearly 60% of Nigeria's population (186 Million) had access to electricity in 2015 (according to the World Bank), which is 86% of its urban population and 41% of its rural population (Sustainable Energy for All—SE4ALL, 2020). However, 57% of the national population experience a blackout every day (Nwaogwugwu, 2020). Internet penetration in Nigeria stood at 42% (85.49 million of the total population) in January 2020. The average speed of mobile Internet connections in Nigeria is 15.32 Mbps compared to the United Kingdom and Australia with 35.57 Mbps and 67.66 Mbps respectively (Kemp, 2020). On average, across Internet providers, one gigabyte of data costs N1,000 Naira ($USD 2.62) which is equivalent to spending nearly 3% of the national minimum wage (N30,000 Naira - $USD 78.70) on monthly Internet access (Ekenimoh, 2019). Electricity and Internet facilities are essential for learning, teaching, and research. Students use the Internet for research, widen the scope of reading, tackle assignments, and prepare for examinations using a combination of self and peer learning (Apuke & Iyendo, 2018; Nwaogwugwu, 2020). In addition, without a regular power supply, technological gadgets and Internet facilities are useless, since users will run out of power/battery within hours (Apuke & Iyendo, 2018).

Similarly, many Nigerian HEIs are not prepared to adopt e-learning strategies except for some privately-owned institutions (Adeoye et al., 2020). Meanwhile, the unavailability of personal computers and poor Internet connectivity poses a challenge to online teaching and learning in Nigeria. Consequently, it is challenging to teach students in a style that is consistent with modern-day technology or carry out cutting-edge scientific research (Nwaogwugwu, 2020). Further, many lecturers (especially those in the uppermost cadre) do not have adequate literacy in computer use, which poses a fundamental challenge to running academic instructions remotely. All these summed up frustrate efforts to meaningful transition to online education (Idowu et al., 2017).

The coronavirus pandemic ravaging the world continues to place a threat to the dreams of higher education students. One of the most significant effects in Nigeria is the complete disruption of the universities' academic calendars. Unlike in developed countries with fixed academic calendars, Nigerian universities have an unstable calendar reflected in universities' varying resumption times across the country (Ejiogu & Sule, 2012). This is due to failure to maintain the same calendar over the years occasioned by industrial strikes, inadequate planning, and security concerns in certain parts of the Nation (Wahab, 2018). The advent of coronavirus has worsened the complexities involved and university administrators have to grapple with major calendar changes in the post-Covid world.

Students must undertake a three to six months internship in many Nigerian universities as part of their degree requirements. For many of these students, the pandemic started just before the resumption period for their internships. While some with internship offers were still rounding up semester exams, others were in the process of submitting applications for placement. The pandemic has largely halted this process as university administrators have little clarity on the new academic calendar. On the other hand, private establishments are also reporting job freezes and retrenchment (Adesoji, 2020). In a 2020 report by the National Bureau of Statistics, four out of every ten Nigerians have lost their jobs due to the pandemic (Akinpelu, 2020b). This is a significant threat to students looking for companies to fulfill their internship requirements and a bigger blow to fresh graduates looking for jobs. University staff are not exempted from job losses, a private university—American University of Nigeria (AUN), located in the city of Yola laid off 400 staff members as part of its restructuring for sustainability (Alao, 2020). There have been many burdens and mental toll that the pandemic has placed on the University community—leaving much anxiety about degree completion, job security, and return to normalcy (Sahu, 2020).

Method

This research extensively consulted and analyzed various news reports, university documents, and recent research publications to compile the various innovative products rolled out by Nigerian universities in the wake of the COVID-19 pandemic. To complement the findings from journal articles, university websites, and online news outlets, we carried out a survey among the university community (student and staff) to know their awareness of the innovative efforts of the universities in the country.

In July 2020, students and staff from any university in Nigeria were recruited through various online media and known contacts to participate in an online survey. The online media used for recruiting respondents include WhatsApp, Twitter, Facebook. The categories of university staff recruited included lecturers, technicians, lab attendants, non-academic staff. Google Forms survey platform was used for collecting the data for this research. At the end of the survey, 105 respondents comprising 82 students and 23 university staff members participated in the survey.

For this study, we adapted the definition of "innovation" from Brennan et al. (2014),

> Innovation is a new or significantly improved product, process, organizational method or an organization itself developed by or having a significant impact on the activities of a higher education institution, other higher education stakeholders and the larger society.

Results

Items Produced by Nigerian Universities in Response to COVID-19 Pandemic

Based on the analysis of various news reports, university documents, and recent research publications, the various innovative products rolled out by universities are categorized in Table 8.1.

We identified four major innovations:

1. Locally made liquid soap and hand sanitizer (Durotoye et al., 2020; Standards Organisation of Nigeria – SON, 2020)
2. Dual-purpose hand sanitizer machine (Dada, 2020)
3. COVID-19 Self-Test App (Onaleye, 2020)
4. Ventilator (Bayero University Kano, 2020; Observer Times, 2020; SON, 2020)

Innovative Products from the Universities According to the Survey Respondents

Figure 8.2 shows out of 105 participants, 32% of innovations are hand sanitizer products, 22% of innovations are hand washing machine, 13% were

Table 8.1 An overview of items produced by Nigerian universities in response to the Covid-19 pandemic

S/N	Item	Description (features and uniqueness)	Manufactured by
1.	Production of liquid soap and hand sanitizer	• The production made use of local products and produced at a cheaper cost.	University of Ilorin (Durotoye et al., 2020) University of Benin - UNIBEN (SON, 2020)
2.	Production of a dual-purpose hand sanitizer machine	• Hand sanitizer machine that functions in two ways - either as manual (enables users to use pedal systems) or automated machine. Thus, users do not need to interact with the device. • It can be used in places with erratic/lack of electricity supply. • The user places the hand close to the dispenser while the device dispenses soap, water which runs for 20 seconds following WHO recommendation and sanitizer in succession at regulated times.	The Federal University of Technology, Akure (Dada, 2020)
3.	Covid-19 self-test app	• The mobile self-test app will help Nigerians self-diagnose and find out if they are infected with the virus. Thus, reducing the number of visitors to the testing centers due to false symptoms. • The mobile app has been tested and certified by the Lagos State University College of Medicine (LASUCOM), Ikeja. • Available for Android download on Play Store from 7 April 2020.	Lagos State University (Onaleye, 2020)
4.	Locally fabricated ventilator	• The prototype was developed using locally made materials. • Low cost of production: cost of fabrication was less than N500,000 Naira. • The ventilator can be used for two patients at a time and it can be easily taken to interior villages. The machine can work at least 24 hours without power supply due to the battery stored energy. • The machine is adjustable and it works for both the children and the adults.	The Federal University of Agriculture, Makurdi (Observer Times, 2020). UNIBEN (SON, 2020) Bayero University, Kano (Bayero University Kano, 2020)

Innovation products

■ Hand Sanitizer   ■ Hand Washing Machine   ■ Facemask
▨ Drug/Vaccine   ■ Locally-made Ventilators   ■ Virtual Learning and Exams

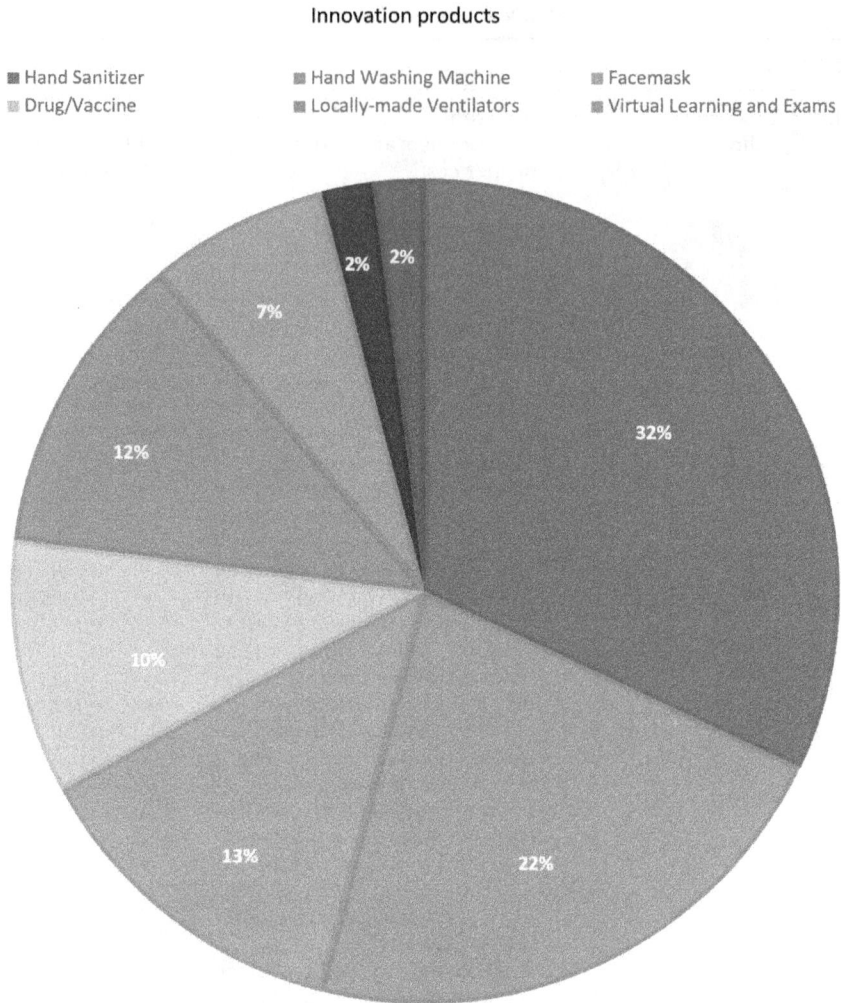

Figure 8.2 The lists of innovation products being carried out by the universities according to the survey respondents ($N = 105$).

face masks, 12% were locally made ventilators, 10% were potential herbal drugs or vaccines, virtual learning and exam platforms were 7% while robots for scans and COVID-19 testing apps were 2% each.

The Level of Awareness of the Respondents of Innovative Efforts in Response to COVID-19 Pandemic

Figure 8.3 shows that of the total 105 respondents (students and university staff), 37% of respondents chose "yes", 48% chose "no", and 15% of respondents are unsure in terms of their knowledge/awareness of innovative

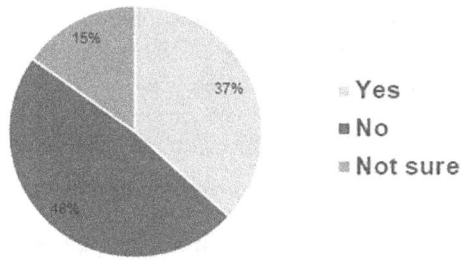

Figure 8.3 The respondents' level of awareness of the innovative efforts (vaccine developmentoranyothermaterial/equipment)oftheiruniversitiesinresponseto the Covid-19 pandemic. (N = 105).

efforts of the universities. Meanwhile, for student respondents (N = 82), 29.3% of student respondents chose "yes", 56.1% chose "no", and 14.6% of student respondents are unsure in terms of their knowledge/awareness of innovative efforts of the universities. For university staff (N = 23), 65.2% of respondents chose "yes", 21.7% chose "no", and 13% of respondents are unsure in terms of their knowledge/awareness of innovative efforts of the universities.

Discussion

According to Brennan et al. (2014), higher education institutions have three principal functions which are providing education (knowledge transmission), undertaking research (knowledge creation), and a "third" mission of service to society (knowledge transfer). In Nigeria, providing education (mainly teaching) has been limited due to the pandemic. However, despite enormous infrastructural and funding challenges facing HEIs, many Nigerian universities have undertaken innovative actions in the wake of the pandemic. Universities are producing essential materials and equipment needed to fight against COVID-19 and exploring new avenues to engage students in remote learning and offering online resources.

Some universities have made commendable efforts to provide alternative learning opportunities for their students. Foremost among public universities is the Lagos State University (LASU), which leveraged upon its existing online learning platform (ENVIVO) to provide quizzes and pre-recorded lecture videos to all students in April 2020 (Abubakar, 2020). Besides, Edo University in Iyamho town deployed the University's CANVAS Learning Management System and the Academic Information Systems (AIS) platform for its second-semester academic session in April 2020 (Ibileke, 2020). Meanwhile, for private universities such as Covenant University, the university's existing online repository of educational resources was upgraded to include real-time learning platforms such as Zoom and class-attendance management opportunities such as the admin features by WhatsApp and Telegram group services to provide real-time online learning. Other privately-owned universities such as Crawford University, Joseph Ayo Babalola University, and Babcock Universities also use similar innovations (Abubakar, 2020).

As the world races to find a cure to the COVID-19 pandemic, global leaders have united to ensure people can access new vaccines (WHO, 2020b). In Nigeria, traditionalists and university researchers have also submitted some potential cures for the virus to the Government (Adejoro, 2020; AfricaNews, 2020; Figure 8.2). For instance, the National Universities Commission has revealed that 32 Nigerian universities are at different research stages to develop COVID-19 vaccines and other treatments (Igomu, 2020). Also, the production of critical medical supplies has been rolled out to promote quality health in society (Table 8.1). Universities are also creating awareness about the disease in their communities and enforcing safety and physical distancing protocols on their premises (Durotoye et al., 2020).

The knowledge of the innovations is different between the two groups (i.e., students and university staff. The university staff (65.2%) has a higher knowledge of innovations than the students (29.3%). This could be because staff members are superior to students and receive more correspondence from the university than students.

Conclusion

The coronavirus pandemic has exposed the dysfunctional state of the Nigerian education sector especially its Higher Education Institutions (HEIs). Over 1 million HEI students in Nigeria remain unengaged in academic learning for over five months and are still counting due to school closure occasioned by the pandemic. Most HEIs are not prepared for the rapid transition towards blended learning due to inadequate infrastructural facilities and virtual learning environments which is indicative of the agelong infrastructure deficit endemic in the nation. However, the efforts of several universities in Nigeria to produce some innovative products needed during the pandemic suggest a commendable local capacity within the country's HEIs. If supported by relevant government agencies with adequate funding, these institutions could produce cutting-edge technologies in various fields, reducing the country's overdependence on foreign goods.

Recognizing that many people were not aware of the innovations by the universities, the universities must take pride in their innovation and their contribution to society. These innovations and other research activities should be communicated to all stakeholders in form of press releases, social media posts, and possible demonstrations. This awareness can raise the reputation of the university, attract more funding and international collaborations.

Recommendations

This study presents practical implications and recommendations for University management, teaching staff, and students. These recommendations are in the areas of innovation, entrepreneurship, research, and development.

- University Managers should make an effort to address their infrastructural deficit, particularly in virtual learning. This deficit can be tackled by formulating policies that support hybrid learning (virtual & physical), the Government's political will to make necessary changes, and the involvement of donor agencies (international NGOs, private foundations, etc.). We further propose that universities should seek out a public-private partnership with EdTech companies and multinational organizations to provide needed digital infrastructure and education for teaching staff and students. In addition, the university management needs to improve its correspondence with members of its university community especially students by communicating current and ongoing research embarked upon by university faculty. This can inspire creativity as well as a sense of pride in their institution in the students.
- The Teaching Staff are also expected to develop their research expertise, build their network, and improve their teaching skills to effectively support students to be more innovative and creative. We recommend that the teaching staff prioritize continuous improvement in their pedagogy, especially in the areas of virtual teaching and learning.
- The students should take responsibility for their learning. The infrastructural deficit should not be an excuse but a motivation to be more innovative and creative − to solve problems and improve the wellbeing of society. Students should improve their ICT skills by taking advantage of various free Massive Open Online Course platforms including Alison, Cousera, FutureLearn (Ifijeh & Yusuf, 2020).
- Local and International Education NGOs can offer technical support and funding to the Ministries of education and schools in adopting various online meeting and presentation platforms as well as other virtual technologies (Ifijeh & Yusuf, 2020).

References

Abdulsalam, K. (2020, June 16). COVID-19: FG lists 6 conditions for reopening of schools. *DailyTrust*. https://dailytrust.com/covid-19-fg-lists-6-conditions-for-re-opening-of-schools

Abubakar, I. (2020, June 2). Without online learning platforms a few Nigerians Universities are using WhatsApp. *TechCabal*. https://techcabal.com/2020/06/02/without-online-learning-platforms-a-few-nigerian-universities-are-using-whatsapp/

Adedigba, A. (2020, March 23). ASUU begins 'indefinite' strike. *Premium Times*. https://www.premiumtimesng.com/news/top-news/383371-just-in-asuu-begins-indefinite-strike.html

Adejoro, L. (2020, May 27). Three of numerous claims of COVID-19 herbal cure validated —PTF. *Punch Newspaper*. https://healthwise.punchng.com/breaking-three-alleged-covid-19-herbal-cure-validated-ptf/

Adeoye, I. A., Adanikin, A. F., & Adanikin, A. (2020). COVID-19 and E-Learning: Nigeria tertiary education system experience. *International Journal of Research and Innovation in Applied Science (IJRIAS)*, 5(5), 28–31.

Adesoji, B. S. (2020, June 8). Covid-19: Survey confirms job losses, hardship for Nigerians. *Nairametrics*. https://nairametrics.com/2020/06/08/covid-19-survey-confirms-job-losses-hardship-for-nigerians/

Adeyanju, S., Mogaji, E., Olusola, J., & Olaniyi, M. (2020). Factors influencing students' choice of a Federal University: A case study of a Nigerian Federal University. In E. Mogaji, F. Maringe, & R. E. Hinson (Eds.), *Higher education marketing in Africa - Explorations on student choice* (pp. 135–163). Springer.

AfricaNews. (2020, May 29). Coronavirus - Nigeria: Efforts to find local remedy for COVID-19 underway – Mamora. https://www.africanews.com/2020/05/29/coronavirus-nigeria-efforts-to-find-local-remedy-for-covid-19-underway-mamora//

Akinpelu, Y. (2020a, June 20). 2019 UTME: Two in three students who applied for admission into Nigerian institutions not admitted. *Premium Times*. https://www.premiumtimesng.com/news/headlines/398679-2019-utme-two-in-three-students-who-applied-for-admission-into-nigerian-institutions-not-admitted.html

Akinpelu, Y. (2020b, June 7). Coronavirus: About 4 in 10 Nigerians lost their jobs in April – NBS. *Premium Times*. https://www.premiumtimesng.com/news/headlines/396472-coronavirus-about-4-in-10-nigerians-lost-their-jobs-in-april-nbs.html.

Alao, O. (2020, May 5). America University of Nigeria sacks 400 staff. *The Nation*. https://thenationonlineng.net/america-university-of-nigeria-sacks-400-staff/

Amoo, A. (2019, October 11). Nigeria allocates 6.7% of 2020 budget to education ministry. *EduCeleb*. https://educeleb.com/nigerian-2020-budget-education-ministry/

Apuke, O. D., & Iyendo, T. O. (2018). University students' usage of the internet resources for research and learning: Forms of access and perceptions of utility. *Heliyon*, *4*(12), e01052. https://doi.org/10.1016/j.heliyon.2018.e01052

Bayero University Kano. (2020, May 3). Covid-19: BUK produces locally manufactured ventilator. https://www.buk.edu.ng/?q=node/300

Brennan, J., Broek, S., Durazzi, N., Kamphuis, B., Ranga, M. & Ryan, S. (2014). Study on innovation in higher education: Final report. European Commission Directorate for Education and Training Study on Innovation in Higher Education, Publications Office of the European Union, Luxembourg. ISBN 9789279350818. http://eprints.lse.ac.uk/55819/

Burke, L. (2020, March 9). Colleges move online Amid Virus fears. *Inside Higher Ed*. https://www.insidehighered.com/news/2020/03/09/colleges-move-classes-online-coronavirus-infects-more

CNBC Africa. (2020, March 29). *COVID-19: Lagos, FCT & Ogun State to go into lockdown*. https://www.cnbcafrica.com/coronavirus/2020/03/29/covid-19-lagos-fct-ogun-state-to-go-into-lockdown/

Dada, P. (2020, May 26). FUTA manufactures dual purpose sanitiser machine. *Punch Newspaper*. https://punchng.com/futa-manufactures-dual-purpose-sanitiser/

de Almeida, M. A. P. (2013). Epidemics in the news: Health and hygiene in the press in periods of crisis. *Public Understanding of Science*, *22*(7), 886–902. https://doi.org/10.1177/0963662512473212

Durotoye, I., Odunola, R., Adeyemi, O., Akanmu, A., Bolarinwa, O., Adeboye, M., Abdullahi, A., Bolajoko, Z., Durosinmi, W., Adebisi, G., & Aduloju, V. (2020). Pertinent roles of African higher institutions in the COVID-19 pandemic response: The University of Ilorin, Ilorin, Nigeria; An African Model. *The*

International Journal of Health Planning and Management, 35(5), 1257–1259. https://doi.org/10.1002/hpm.2984

Edeh, H. (2020, June 9). Again, PTF says no resumption date for schools reopening. *Business Day.* https://businessday.ng/coronavirus/article/againptf-says-no-resumption-date-for-schools-reopening/

Ejiogu, A., & Sule, S. (2012). Sixty-five years of university education in Nigeria: Some key cross cutting issues. *Higher Education, Lifelong Learning and Social Inclusion, 4,* 257–264.

Ekenimoh, I. (2019, April 11). Overpriced: Why Nigerians pay so much for data. *Stears Business.* https://www.stearsng.com/article/overpriced-why-nigerians-pay-so-much-for-data

Farinloye, T., Adeola, O., & Mogaji, E. (2020). Typology of Nigeria Universities: A strategic marketing and branding implication. In E. Mogaji, F. Maringe, & R. E. Hinson (Eds.), *Understanding the higher education market in Africa* (pp. 168–198). Routledge.

Ibileke, J. (2020, April 25). Lockdown: Edo varsity commences 2nd semester. *P.M. News.* https://www.pmnewsnigeria.com/2020/04/25/lockdown-edo-varsity-commences-2nd-semester-via-canvas-learning/

Idowu, A., Esere, M., & Iruloh, B. R. (2017). Computer accessibility, usage and lecturers' perception of innovative ICT based assessment in a Nigerian University. In F. Maringe & E. Ojo (Eds.), *Sustainable transformation in African higher education* (pp. 215–226). SensePublishers.

Ifijeh, G., & Yusuf, F. (2020). Covid–19 pandemic and the future of Nigeria's university system: The quest for libraries' relevance. *The Journal of Academic Librarianship, 46*(6), 102226. https://doi.org/10.1016/j.acalib.2020.102226

Igomu, T. (2020, August 5). 32 Nigerian universities researching COVID-19 vaccines, treatment –NUC. *Punch Newspaper.* https://healthwise.punchng.com/32-nigerian-universities-researching-covid-19-vaccines-treatment-nuc/

Ihekweazu, C., & Agogo, E. (2020). Africa's response to COVID-19. *BMC Medicine, 18,* 151. https://doi.org/10.1186/s12916-020-01622-w

Johns Hopkins University. (2020, December 29). *COVID-19 case tracker.* https://coronavirus.jhu.edu/map.html

Kedraka, K., & Kaltsidis, C. (2020). Effects of the Covid-19 pandemic on University Pedagogy: Students' experiences and considerations. *European Journal of Education Studies, 7*(8), 17–30. http://dx.doi.org/10.46827/ejes.v7i8.3176

Kemp, S. (2020, February 18). Digital 2020: Nigeria. *Data Reportal.* https://datareportal.com/reports/digital-2020-nigeria?rq=digital%202020%3A%20nigeria

Kilbourne, E. D. (2006). Influenza pandemics of the 20th century. *Emerging Infectious Diseases, 12*(1), 9–14. https://doi.org/10.3201/eid1201.051254

Kazeem, Y. (2019, November 25). Nigerians are spending half a billion dollars to school in the United States. *Quartz Africa.* https://qz.com/africa/1755266/nigerians-spend-half-a-billion-dollars-to-school-in-the-us/

Mogaji, E. (2020). Impact of COVID-19 on transportation in Lagos, Nigeria. *Transportation Research Interdisciplinary Perspectives, 6,* 100154. https://doi.org/10.1016/j.trip.2020.100154

Ndofirepi, E., Farinloye, T., & Mogaji, E. (2020). Marketing mix in a heterogenous higher education market: A case of Africa. In E. Mogaji, F. Maringe, & R. E. Hinson (Eds.), *Understanding the higher education market in Africa.* (pp. 241–262). Routledge.

Nigeria Centre for Disease Control. (2020). *Covid-19 Nigeria.* https://covid19.ncdc. gov.ng/

Nwaogwugwu, C. (2020, June 23). Until schools reopen, adaptation is the name of the game. *Stears Business.* https://www.stearsng.com/article/ until-schools-reopen-adaptation-is-the-name-of-the-game

Obiakor, T., & Adeniran, A. (2020, April 7). *Covid-19: Impending situation threatens to deepen Nigeria's education crisis.* Center for the Study of the Economies of Africa, Abuja, Nigeria. https://www.africaportal.org/publications/ covid-19-impending-situation-threatens-deepen-nigerias-education-crisis/

Observer Times. (2020, May 21). *Breaking: University of Agriculture Makurdi presented a ventilator to action committee on COVID-19.* https://observerstimes.com/ breaking-university-of-agriculture-makurdi-presented-a-ventilator-to-action-committee-on-covid-19/

Ogundipe, S., Obinna, C., Wahab, A., & Uchechukwu, I. (2020, June 15). COVID-19: Doctors, parents, teachers caution FG against opening of schools. *Vanguard Newspapers.* https://www.vanguardngr.com/2020/06/ covid-19-doctors-parents-teachers-caution-fg-against-opening-of-schools/

Ogunode, N. J. (2020). Impact of COVID-19 pandemic school close down on the research programme of higher institutions. *International Journal of Advances in Data and Information Systems, 1*(1), 40–49. https://doi.org/10.25008/ijadis. vli1.189

Olaleye, S., Ukpabi, D., & Mogaji, E. (2020). Public vs private universities in Nigeria: Market dynamics perspective. In E. Mogaji, F. Maringe, & R. E. Hinson (Eds.), *Understanding the higher education market in Africa.* (pp. 19–36). Routledge.

Onaleye, T. (2020). Lagos State University develops COVID-19 self-test app for Nigerians. *TechNext.* https://technext.ng/2020/04/02/lagos-state-university-develops-covid-19-self-test-app-for-nigerians/

Porcher, S. (2020, May 12). *'Contagion': The determinants of governments' public health responses to COVID-19 all around the world.* https://halshs.archives-ouvertes.fr/ halshs-02567286

Premium Times. (2020, January 25). Nigeria university enrolment 'near crisis' with only 2 million students — NUC. https://www.premiumtimesng.com/ news/headlines/374344-nigeria-university-enrolment-near-crisis-with-only-2-million-students-nuc.html

Roser, M., Ritchie, H., Ortiz-Ospina, E., & Hasell, J. (2020). Coronavirus pandemic (COVID-19). https://ourworldindata.org/coronavirus

Sahu, P. (2020). Closure of universities due to coronavirus disease 2019 (COVID-19): Impact on education and mental health of students and academic staff. *Cureus, 12*(4), e7541. https://doi.org/10.7759/cureus.7541

Standards Organisation of Nigeria (SON). (2020, May 6). *SON conducts inspection of UNIBEN ventilator, hand sanitizer in response to Covid-19 pandemic.* https://son.gov. ng/son-conducts-inspection-of-uniben-ventilator-hand-sanitizer-in-response-to-covid-19-pandemic

Sustainable Energy for All (SE4ALL). (2020). *Country data - Nigeria.* https://www. se4all-africa.org/seforall-in-africa/country-data/nigeria/

Times Higher Education. (2020). *Study in Nigeria.* https://www.timeshighereducation. com/student/where-to-study/study-in-nigeria

UNESCO. (2015). Education for All 2000–2015: Achievements and challenges; EFA global monitoring report, 2015. Paris, France. https://en.unesco.org/gem-report/report/2015/education-all-2000-2015-achievements-and-challenges

UNESCO. (2020a, April 29). *1.3 billion learners are still affected by school or university closures, as educational institutions start reopening around the world, says UNESCO.* https://en.unesco.org/news/13-billion-learners-are-still-affected-school-university-closures-educational-institutions

UNESCO. (2020b). *Education: From disruption to recovery. Interactive map and updated figures.* https://en.unesco.org/covid19/educationresponse

UNESCO. (2020c). *Global flow of tertiary-level students.* http://uis.unesco.org/en/uis-student-flow

Wahab, B. (2018, May 11). All the times ASUU has gone on strike since 1999. *Pulse NG.* https://www.pulse.ng/communities/student/all-the-times-asuu-has-gone-on-strike-since-1999/5jtb8cs

World Health Organisation (WHO). (2020a, March 11). *WHO director-general's opening remarks at the media briefing on COVID-19.* https://www.who.int/dg/speeches/detail/who-director-general-s-opening-remarks-at-the-media-briefing-on-covid-19---11-march-2020

World Health Organisation (WHO). (2020b, April 24). *Global leaders unite to ensure everyone everywhere can access new vaccines, tests and treatments for COVID-19.* https://www.who.int/news-room/detail/24-04-2020-global-leaders-unite-to-ensure-everyone-everywhere-can-access-new-vaccines-tests-and-treatments-for-covid-19

Bios

Samuel Adeyanju is a Research Assistant and incoming Ph.D. student at the University of British Columbia, Canada where he completed a master's degree in Forestry in 2020. His research focuses on SDG 4 (Quality education), SDGs 13 and 15 (Climate Action and Life on Land) in sub-Saharan Africa. His profile can be found on https://samueladeyanju.carrd.co/. E-mail: samadeyanju@alumni.ubc.ca

Oluwatoyin Ajilore is an Assistant Lecturer in the Department of Geology, University of Ibadan, Nigeria. Her research interests lie in the areas of economic/mining geology, environmental geology, and geoscience education. E-mail: olutoyinajilore@gmail.com

Oluwafemi Ogunlalu is a Chemistry Ph.D. Candidate at Purdue University. His research interests broadly cut across polymers for energy and food applications. Additionally, he writes commentaries that address infrastructural gaps in the educational systems of developing economies. E-mail: oogunlal@purdue.edu

Alex Onatunji is the Program Officer at Save Sahara Network, Nigeria. His research and work interest are in promoting forest education in the continent of Africa and he recently co-authored the book: "Building a Successful

Forestry Career in Africa: Inspirational Stories and Opportunities". Alex is also currently an MSc. student in Erasmus Mundus Master Programme in Mediterranean Forestry and Natural Resources Management (MEDfOR) at the University of Padova, Italy. His profile can be found on https://www. linkedin.com/in/alex-onatunji/ E-mail: alexonatunji@gmail.com

Emmanuel Mogaji, Ph.D., is a lecturer in Advertising and Marketing Communications at the University of Greenwich, London, UK. His research interests are in artificial intelligence, digital marketing, and service brand management. Emmanuel has previously worked as a marketing communication executive, responsible for creative designs and managing marketing campaigns, liaising, and building relationships with a range of stakeholders. He has published peer-reviewed journal articles and book chapters and presented his works in many national and international conferences. His publications have appeared in the *International Journal of Information Management, Journal of Product and Brand Management, Australasian Marketing Journal,* and *International Journal of Bank Marketing.* E-mail: e.o.mogaji@greenwich.ac.uk

Part III
Understanding Institutional Policies, Resources, and Technology Priorities

9 Student Attitudes and Experiences with COVID-19

A Case of One Research University in California

David Edens and Emily Kiresich

Abstract

This chapter examines student attitudes and issues regarding the rapid pivot to virtual instruction in March 2020. Results indicated that students reported well-prepared and comfortable in the online environment, but the transition and overall life experience of this time left them feeling frustrated, anxious, and worried. They expressed specific concern about the current and future readiness for next courses and careers, amplified by having concerns for their health, the health of others, and their finances. Their responses indicated that open and transparent communication with instructors and about expectations and being included in decision-making about future changes to courses would have provided them with comfort. Training in technology and open communication for educators and students is essential to improving student success and satisfaction during this time of unprecedented change.

Keywords

Change Management; Online Teaching; Student Impact; Survey Research; Student Success

Introduction

COVID-19 has had a tremendous impact on the United States and the world. As of this writing, there have been approximately 122 million cases worldwide, with over 30 million cases and 550,000 deaths in the United States (*Coronavirus Update (Live): Worldometer*, 2021). In response, many states established procedures to limit the risk of transmission through policies such as social distancing, closing non-essential businesses, and moving all education, including higher education, to an online or virtual format.

Higher education responded to the coronavirus crisis by limiting face-to-face instruction and closing campuses (Gluckman, 2020). College campuses are risky as students, faculty, and staff are in classrooms, labs, and offices and often in close quarters. Additionally, campus housing is usually densely populated. Beyond these proximity issues, many of the curricular and co-curricular activities on campus require people to be in close contact. Wood (2020) noted that "a properly run college is a series of super-spreader events." Limits, for many universities, went beyond just changing instructional modalities. Many universities closed all campus services, including housing, food service, and research labs.

This study was designed to assess students' experiences in response to the rapid change in teaching at a large public university in Southern California. Using a sliding scale, students were asked to reflect and assess their attitudes towards the change and how the semester's remainder progressed. The results provide insight into what has affected the students through this time of rapid change and adaptation. Students were affected by the change in instruction and many other life and socioeconomic changes that occurred because of the pandemic.

In March 2020, the university ceased all face-to-face instruction and moved all teaching, including labs and activities, to a virtual environment. Beyond instruction, housing and limited food service on campus remained open. As the pandemic progressed, many of these services also became further limited or closed entirely. At the end of the semester, only essential personnel were allowed on campus. Necessary administrative offices and animal units were staffed by university personnel on a rotating basis. The campus was essentially closed to faculty, staff, and students for the final two months of instruction. The university was conducting all Summer session instruction online and was planning to offer most, if not all, classes online in Fall 2020 (Burke, 2020).

Literature Review

Student Success

Student success has been a fruitful topic of research. Historically, researchers have focused on traditional success measures, such as grade point average, retention, persistence, and degree completion (Astin, 1993; Pascarella & Terenzini, 2005).

Recently, student satisfaction is a topic of interest. When students are satisfied with their learning and the learning environment, they tend to invest more in their education and persist (Beltyukova & Fox, 2002; Billups, 2008; Elliot & Shin, 2002; Juillerat & Schreiner, 2004). Students who are motivated and self-directed tend to succeed in college (DeWitz et al., 2009; Dweck, 2006, 2007; Kuh et al., 2006).

Student interaction with faculty, both inside and outside of the classroom, is a strong predictor of student success (Cole, 2010; Fuentes et al., 2014; Umbach & Wawrzynski, 2005). When students trust, talk to and develop mentorship relationships with faculty, they tend to perform better and persevere.

Online Learning

Online learning takes many forms. Models range from web-assisted courses to fully online, asynchronous course delivery (Ainsworth, 2013). Web-assisted courses use learning management software to deliver materials to students while the course meets face-to-face. Fully online courses meet virtually in a synchronous or asynchronous mode with no face-to-face instruction. Synchronous courses meet at a scheduled time, while asynchronous course delivery allows students to progress at their own pace. Hybrid courses blend both face-to-face and online delivery.

Online Learning and Student Success

Historically, much of the research on student success has focused on traditional students attending traditional four-year universities and colleges. However, online learning and non-traditional college environments have become popular delivery models for modern students with many outside demands and pressures. Drummond (2008) defined the factors that lead to student success in online learning as having excellent instructors, meaningful learning objectives, effective teaching practices, hands-on learning opportunities, real-world applications, rigorous assessments, and communication tools that assist with the learning process.

A challenge in the online environment is engagement. Students in online courses tend to be less engaged and withdraw more often than their peers in face-to-face courses (Glazier, 2016). Models that utilize practices such as personal e-mails, video introductions, and methods, build rapport and a sense of community and also support student engagement while online (Glazier, 2016; Winger, 2016). As with traditional instruction, students benefit from and are more satisfied with their learning experiences when they have meaningful faculty interaction (Lewis, 2010). Additional factors such as student readiness, student preparation, and student support from the university also improve success and retention in online courses (Harrell, 2008). University support, in terms of tutorials and help centers, improve the online student's self-efficacy with both learning and technology (Miltiadou & Savenye, 2003).

Faculty development programs that support eLearning are valuable (Orozco et al., 2012). Students will be more engaged when the course outcomes, assessments, and materials are well-designed and meaningful. Providing training opportunities supports the faculty as they design classes or transition to eLearning.

Change Management

Specific divisions of scholarly activity are dedicated to change management. Hayes (2018) discusses the process of identifying several models used to examine change in an organization. These models often have similar phases used to identify and manage change, including recognizing the need for change, and planning, implementing, leading, and managing, and assessing outcomes. Beyond these duties, management must communicate with all stakeholders. Gill (2002) argues that leading change is the management's priority. Change is often framed in the negative and can develop fear and uncertainty in an organization (Antonacopoulou & Gabriel, 2001). This negative response is especially true in times of rapid change, where uncertainty levels are often very high. Therefore, leaders must react, communicate, and guide their constituents through the process (Gill, 2002).

Much of the existing research on change in higher education focuses on adaptations that arise from policy changes, funding shortfalls, accreditation pressures, and many other factors (Gumport & Sporn, 1999). Student success has also been studied in relation to change. Kezar (2003) adds that students can benefit from a higher education change that supports collaboration between student affairs and academic affairs. Much of the change in higher education occurs over time, such as an academic year. The pace of change is dictated by the shared governance models that exist in most American universities. However, there has been little research that reviews the effects of rapid change within an organization, such as the response to the COVID-19 pandemic.

Research Method

This research was conducted at a large, public university in Southern California. Participants were recruited from a single department at that university. The department has 628 students currently enrolled in three different degree options. After obtaining IRB approval (protocol #20–82), all students in the department were sent a Qualtrics[XM] (SAP, 2013) link. The students were sent three e-mails between May 5, 2020, and May 18, 2020, encouraging participation. Participants were disqualified if they were not currently enrolled in courses in the department for the Spring 2020 semester or did not provide consent. Participants were asked questions about their comfort level with virtual learning before the COVID-19 transition, their feelings about their own ability to adapt to the virtual environment, and several questions about their reactions to and involvement in the transition to online learning in their department courses. Additional questions allowed reflection about mental and physical health, major concerns during this transition (related and unrelated to the transition to online learning), and their perceived implications of this transition for their academic and professional futures.

SPSS 25 (International Business Machines Corporation, 2017) was used for all analyses. Sliding scales from 0 to 10 were used to quantify reactions to each question. For analysis and aggregation responses were transformed into very low (0–2), low (3–4), moderate (5–6), high (7–8), and very high (9–10). Counts within each category were converted into percentages and presented as within-category percentages of the total possible answers.

Participants

Most of the respondents (57%) were 18–24 years of age, followed by 25–30 years of age (27%), reflecting a slightly older population when compared to the department and university overall. The majority female (76%) closely resembles the department and is higher than the university overall. Race/Ethnicity reflects the department and the university at majority Hispanic/Latino, followed by Asian/Pacific Islander and White. Nearly 50% of respondents have completed 90 units. Most have taken online courses, with 3–4 courses (33%) being most common. Important to note, this department requires many laboratory and activity courses; of the respondents, nearly one-third (32.5%) reported being enrolled in a laboratory course in the Spring of 2020.

Results

Survey Responses

Between May 5 and May 27, 2020, 95 surveys were started. There were 83 usable surveys for analysis after disqualifications. For 95% Confidence Interval, 10% margin of error in our department population of 628 students, a sample size of 84 was ideal.

Readiness for Virtual Transition

To begin, we asked students about their perception of comfort in the virtual environment; 53.7% responded with high or very high (7–10) comfort before this rapid mandatory transition. The system of which this University is a part moved to a virtual learning approach in March 2020. Upon learning of this transition, our respondents' answers reflect uncertainty about being ready to tackle the challenge of online instruction (19% moderate, 17% high, 15% very high) and about the support they needed to be successful (16% moderate, 17% high, 15% very high), see Figure 9.1. There was a larger percentage of respondents who reported higher levels of agreement for these categories, but not a strong majority.

Initial Emotional Response

Many respondents scored high for stress, anxiety, and worry while 15% or fewer reported high or very high feelings for excited, angry, motivated, bored,

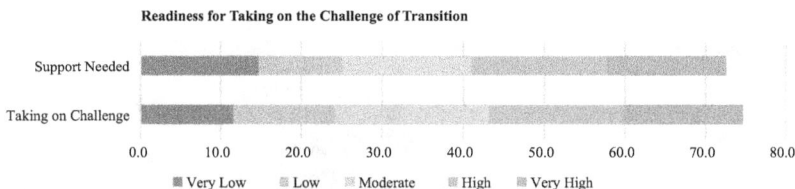

Figure 9.1 Comfort in taking on the challenge of transition to virtual instruction.
Note: Percentage of respondents within five categories of agreement: (0–2 [very low], 3–4 [low], 5–6 [moderate], 7–8 [high], 9–10 [very high]).

shock, relief, shame, curiosity, or calm. Strong feelings of anxiety (30% high or very high), worry (25% high or very high), stress (39% high or very high), and frustration and loneliness (>25% high or very high, each). These reflect several challenging emotional and mental conditions to be operating under while trying to successfully complete course requirements for nearly half of a semester.

Personal Impact of COVID-19 and Related Policies

In the next set of responses, we investigate the personal impact of COVID-19 and factors that may be of concern during this time. Students responded with high levels of concern, >25% reporting very high for 3 of the 4 categories, and at least 40% of respondents reporting high or very high concern for all categories listed: financial situation, own health or the health of others, and work-life balance (see Figure 9.2).

Elements of Course Transition

This portion of the survey allowed students to reflect on their response to college, department, and course-specific changes and their interaction with instructors during that transition. Some positive feedback about courses included strong positive responses for feeling they had information needed (35.8% high or very high), had the opportunity to ask questions (39% high or very high), and had their questions answered (38.9% high and very high). Of note for future consideration, strong negative response for "I felt I was part of the decision-making process" (30.5% very low). On a whole, students responses reflected clear understanding and support for the change to a virtual setting, considering the pandemic environment (see Figure 9.3), overwhelmingly very high (51–64%) agreement that the change was needed for safety, that virtual was the correct choice for instruction, that the need was urgent to make a change, and in understanding the need for a transition to virtual.

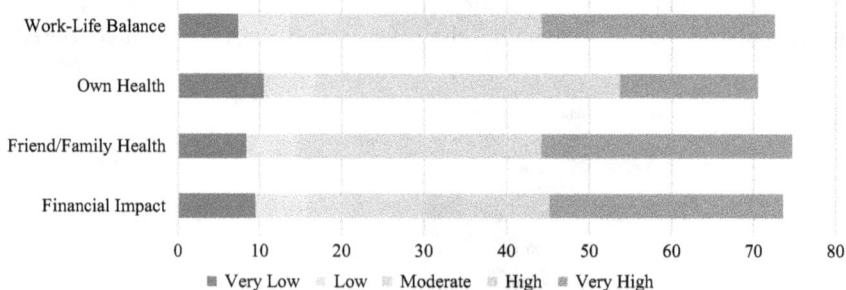

Figure 9.2 Personal impact of Covid-19 changes.
Note: Percentage of respondents within five categories of agreement: (0–2 [very low], 3–4 [low], 5–6 [moderate], 7–8 [high], 9–10 [very high]).

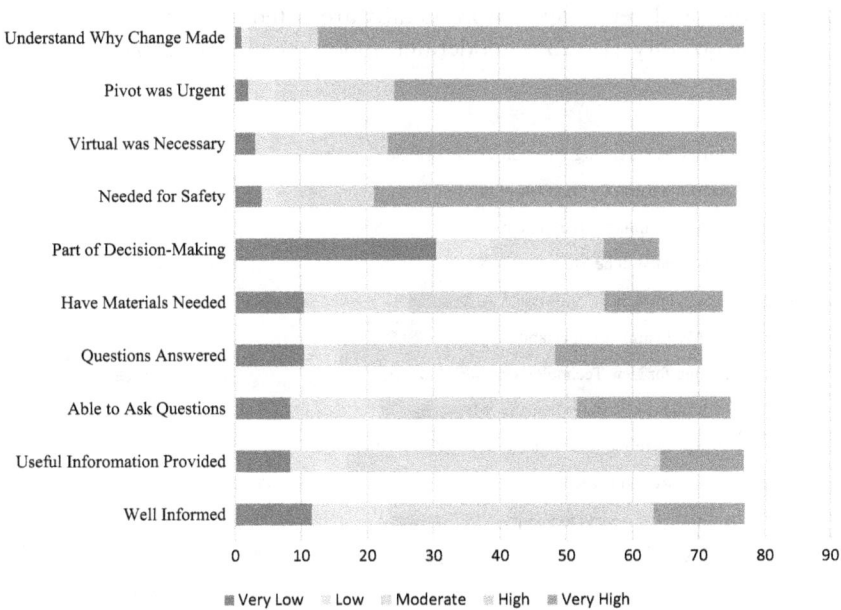

Figure 9.3 Respondent impression of the transition within department-specific courses.

Note: Percentage of respondents within five categories of agreement: (0–2 [very low], 3–4 [low], 5–6 [moderate], 7–8 [high], 9–10 [very high]).

Impact on the Learning Environment for This and Next Semester

Students were asked to reflect on their level of concern over elements of their physical and social environments as they relate to this transition to virtual instruction. Items, found in Figure 9.4, that were frequently scored of high concern were access to teachers and to peers (respectively 36.9% and 37.9% high and very high) and access to University services (38.9% high and very high). More course/class-specific concerns were: the ability to influence future changes related to COVID-19 (30.5% high and very high), will have adequate training (35.8% high and very high), classes meeting their learning expectations (44.2% high and very high), this environment creating more work than a traditional course (42.1% high and very high), the learning environment to being effective for the content (40% high and very high), and that this transition will cause them to be under-prepared for the next class or level of education (40% high and very high).

Will This Semester Have a Long-term Impact?

Students most strongly responded to the transition having a negative impact on their prospects of getting a job or internship (33.7% high and very high), and that this will have a negative impact on their success in classes/major (32.6% high and very high). More details are listed in Figure 9.5, which reflect uncertainty (13–25% moderate) about the future impacts of this transition.

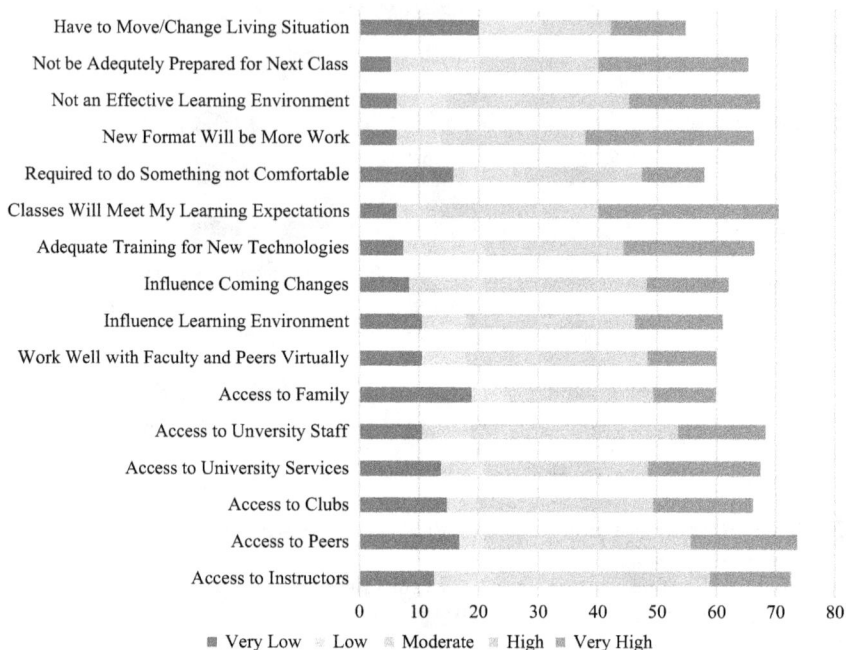

Figure 9.4 Student concerns moving through and beyond the Spring semester of instruction.
Note: Percentage of respondents within five categories of agreement: (0–2 [very low], 3–4 [low], 5–6 [moderate], 7–8 [high], 9–10 [very high]).

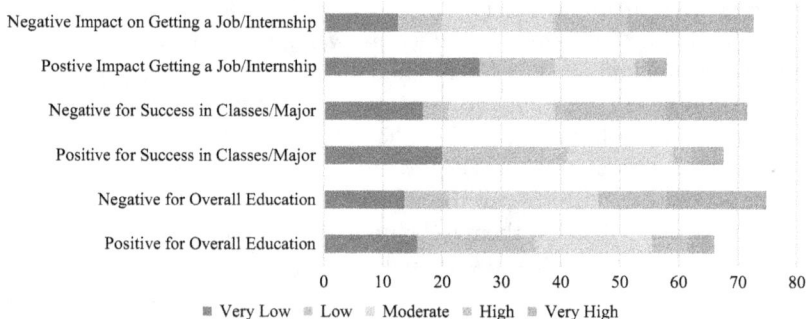

Figure 9.5 Student perceived impact of virtual instruction on future.
Note: Percentage of respondents within five categories of agreement: (0–2 [very low], 3–4 [low], 5–6 [moderate], 7–8 [high], 9–10 [very high]).

*Personal Beliefs about the Environment of Their Classrooms
after This Transition*

Strong agreement was shown in the following: my instructor cared about my ability to work on tasks for the class (37.4% high and very high), my instructor expressed concern about my well-being outside of schoolwork (44.2% high and very high), and my instructor tried to keep a personal connection after virtual transition (23.1% high and very high). Disagreement is noted for the rigor of the course being decreased after transition (37.9% low and very low) and the expectations of [their] performance being decreased after transition (29.5% low and very low). Another area of attention is: my instructor seemed confident in the material after transition (27.4% low and very low), and course rigor was increased (20% high and very high). Results are represented in Figure 9.6.

Final Emotional Response

These responses are compared to their answers for an initial response after having been working for weeks and nearing or at the semester's end. Promising responses include possibility of improving mental and emotional health, decreases in frustration, worry, and stress. Noteworthy, there were increases in average boredom, feeling overwhelmed, annoyed, and angry, also small increases in motivation and feeling ashamed. Emotional responses that continued to be strong for these respondents included anxiety (30.5% high and very high), stress (39% high and very high), disappointment (27.4% high

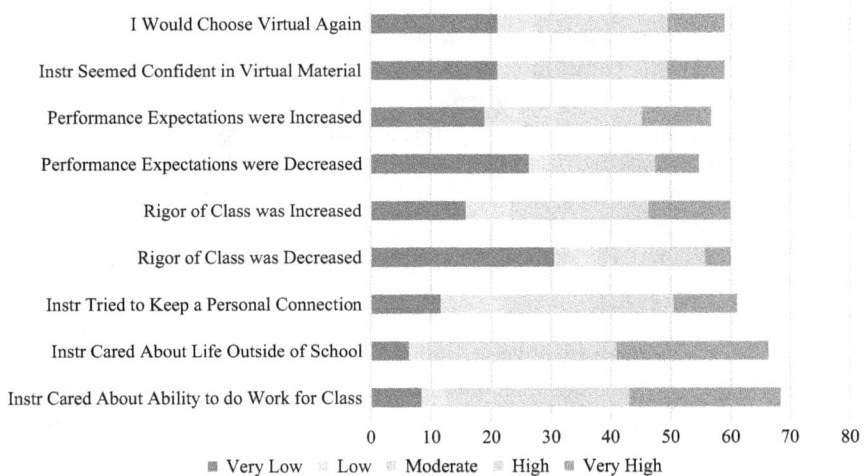

Figure 9.6 Classroom response and environment after virtual pivot.
Note: Percentage of respondents within five categories of agreement: (0–2 [very low], 3–4 [low], 5–6 [moderate], 7–8 [high], 9–10 [very high]).

and very high), frustration (23.6% high and very high), annoyance (26.3% high and very high), and lonely (25.2% high and very high).

Discussion and Conclusions

Students Readiness for Transition to Virtual Instruction

Despite student or educator preparedness for the online transition, the move to virtual instruction was mandated in mid-March, citing Centers for Disease Contol and Prevention (CDC) guidelines for safety during the COVID-19 pandemic. Fortunately, more than 30% of students in our survey were confident about their readiness for taking on the challenge of online transition (Figure 9.1). This may be attributable to the high number of students, more than 50%, who stated comfort in the virtual learning environment prior to this required and rapid transition. An additional element to consider is the demographic makeup of this department, 37% reporting 25 years of age or older. Though older (non-traditional) students report lower use of technology, they often prefer virtual, asynchronous learning environments (Johnson, 2019). Non-traditional and older students are likely to be focused, learning-driven, and have commitments outside of the university that make more flexible options appealing (Rabourn et al., 2018). Though many students reported feeling prepared for this change, nearly 25% of students did not feel prepared or that they had the support they needed for this transition.

Student Response

Though students were asked about their feelings and emotions as a response to the COVID-19 transition, it may have been difficult to separate the normal stress of the progressing semester, which was approaching mid-term examinations, and the additional stress of rapid change. Not surprisingly, students' initial responses to the virtual transition were that of stress, anxiety, and worry. Andrews and Wilding (2004) found that between pre-term and mid-term, anxiety and depression scores increased among university students. In addition to anxiety, worry, and stress, students reported frustration and loneliness.

Elements of timing have been cited as too rapid when it was unexpected, or when participants were unable to collaborate on decision-making (Smollan et al., 2010) and that students may benefit from change when allowed to collaborate (Kezar, 2003). Students were in support of this change, and it happened in a wave of other institutions making a similar pivot, unlikely a surprise to the students. As Figure 9.3 demonstrates, the students understood the reasons for changing to a virtual teaching model. However, the students expressed the desire to be part of the process, according to Figure 9.4. This concept of a student partnership in governance and curriculum design is a new and emerging field of study (Matthews et al., 2019). There is a feeling that partnering with students in decision-making is beneficial and improves overall success and engagement (Brooman et al., 2015).

The student experience and likelihood of success are indicated not only by the academic approach but are also influenced by other factors in their whole lives. In analyzing adverse life events, financial difficulties, personal injury or illness, the physical suffering of a close other, and relationship difficulties (separation), have been recognized as significant barriers for student success (Andrews & Wilding, 2004). Additionally, relationship difficulties, close other's illness, and financial difficulties were all significantly related to anxiety. In terms of online course success, unexpected emergencies and responsibilities apart from class (job, family, and health) can also negatively affect students' success (Yukselturk & Bulut, 2007). The student population for this survey indicated that the personal impact of the pandemic and its resultant mandated distancing policies, weighed heavily as they worked towards completing their academic semesters for Spring of 2020 (Figure 9.2).

After having a few weeks to acclimate to the new normal, students continued to have feelings that mirrored initial reactions, echoing established factors related to an expected response to rapid change. Of note, when allowed to provide an open response, students mentioned new challenges with childcare and the need for clear communication via e-mail and in assignment guidelines and expectations. This reiterates the view that allowing student collaboration and effective communication are imperative.

Classroom Environment

Student reflection of the classroom environment after transition revealed challenges including a perceived increase in course materials' rigor and a lack of perceived instructor-confidence in materials post-transition (Figure 9.6). Instructors had three days to work on the transition from original formats to entirely virtual, which could contribute to overall uncertainty felt by faculty and students. These perceptions may not reflect actual confidence but a response to the transparency of policy changes or instructor experience in the virtual environment. This transition required all faculty to go online, regardless of prior experience in any virtual formats. As cited by (Orozco et al., 2012), faculty support in eLearning is imperative for faculty success and translates to student success and satisfaction.

Concern for Future and Long-term Impact

Immediately, the students are concerned about their learning and success in the program. There is little research on the impact of rapid changes in education delivery. Higher education's response to the COVID-19 crisis will provide an opportunity to review the effects of rapid change on learning. The students' concerns over learning and outcomes reinforce the movement in higher education over the last several years towards a more learner-focused method of delivery, supported by strong student learning outcomes (Barr & Tagg, 1995). The students in this survey expressed concern about adequate preparation and success. By developing courses around strong learning outcomes verified by an assessment program, faculty should improve student readiness for the remainder of their student and professional careers.

Additionally, the students expressed concern over access to both faculty and university support services. Student-faculty interaction, especially outside of the classroom, is an essential factor in student success (Umbach & Wawrzynski, 2005). Beyond the classroom, faculty and administrators must work to develop alternate means for students and faculty to interact and work together, such as research and open online sessions (Gresh & Mrozowski, 2000).

Implications

The COVID-19 pandemic and ultimate pivot to virtual learning affected many campuses across the United States. This research mirrors other recent research on how students were affected by the rapid response (Blankstein et al., 2020). Students understood the need to change and expressed concern about the quality of education, academic preparation, and career preparation. Students had concerns about emotional and physical health, and importantly, they expressed a loss of belonging and connection to others, including faculty. Managing assignments and completing the semester changed to a crisis-management situation, and policies that reflect as much could support student success. Flexibility in classroom policies, especially after an upheaval, may provide students the room to maneuver the challenges they are experiencing within and outside the classroom

Addressing the student experience during and after this pivot needs to include support for technical skills and capacity in a new environment as well as be sensitive to emerging physical and mental health concerns. It is essential to understand that the students who participated in this survey were under stress because of the changes occurring at the university and the sweeping changes that were happening due to the COVID-19 pandemic. Allowing students to have some voice could permit them to feel as if they gained some control back of at least one element of their lives during the pandemic. Acknowledging the students and having them interact with the faculty about how their courses would proceed during the shelter-in-place could provide some consolation. Going forward, especially as universities potentially plan for a new standard, student participation in decision-making may help engage the students and give them a voice in the process.

Student collaboration for course decision-making may be unfamiliar to instructors, on top of many having limited or no experience in virtual teaching. The most important characteristics of the online teacher are effective communication, timely and precise interactions through various formats including e-mail, chat, live class questions, and assessment and feedback (Roddy et al., 2017). Reiterated by finding that student success and satisfaction, especially online, are often highest when there is effective communication and meaningful faculty interaction (Lewis, 2010). For instructors accustomed to face-to-face interaction, learning effective e-communication will take practice. Even in the absence of rapid change, faculty development in online instruction can foster deep learning in students (Restauri, 2006). Continued opportunities for faculty and staff skills development and support in creating interactive and effective online learning environments are essential for student and faculty success and satisfaction.

References

Ainsworth, J. (2013). *Sociology of education: An A-to-Z guide*. SAGE Publications, Inc. http://proxy.library.cpp.edu/login?url=http://search.ebscohost.com/login. aspx?direct=true&AuthType=ip, uid&db=e000xna&AN=592550&site=ehost-live&scope=site

Andrews, B., & Wilding, J. M. (2004, January 14). The relation of depression and anxiety to life-stress and achievement in students. *British Journal of Psychology, 95*, 509–521.

Antonacopoulou, E. P., & Gabriel, Y. (2001). Emotion, learning and organizational change. *Journal of Organizational Change Management, 14*(5), 435–451.

Astin, A. W. (1993). *What matters in college?: Four critical years revisited* (1st ed.). Jossey-Bass.

Barr, R. B., & Tagg, J. (1995). From teaching to learning - A new paradigm for undergraduate education. *Change, 27*(6), 12–25.

Beltyukova, S. A., & Fox, C. M. (2002). Student satisfaction as a measure of student development: Towards a universal metric. *Journal of College Student Development, 43*, 161–172.

Billups, F. D. (2008, October 23). *Measuring college student satisfaction: A multi-year study of factors leading to persistence*. Northeastern Education Research Association Annual Conference, Rocky Hill, CT.

Blankstein, M., Frederick, J. K., & Wolff-Eisenberg, C. (2020). *Student experiences during the pandemic pivot*. https://doi.org/10.18665/sr.313461

Brooman, S., Darwent, S., & Pimor, A. (2015). The student voice in higher education curriculum design: Is there value in listening? *Innovations in Education and Teaching International, 52*(6), 663–674.

Burke, L. (2020). *Cal State pursuing online fall*. Inside Higher Ed. https://www. insidehighered.com/news/2020/05/14/cal-state-pursuing-online-fall

Cole, D. (2010). The effects of student-faculty interactions on minority students' college grades: Differences between aggregated and disaggregated data. *Journal of the Professoriate, 3*(2), 137–160.

Coronavirus update (Live): Worldometer. (2021). https://www.worldometers.info/coronavirus/

DeWitz, S. J., Woolsy, M. L., & Walsh, W. B. (2009, January/February). College student retention: An exploration of the relationship between self-efficacy beliefs and purpose in life among college students. *Journal of College Student Development, 50*(1), 19–34. https://doi.org/10.1353/csd.0.0049

Drummond, G. (2008). Success in online education: Creating a roadmap for student success. *Distance Learning, 5*(4), 43.

Dweck, C. S. (2006). *Mindset: The new psychology of success.* Random House.

Dweck, C. S. (2007). Boosting achievement with messages that motivate. *Education Canada, 47*(2), 6–10.

Elliot, K. M., & Shin, D. (2002). Student satisfaction: An alternative approach to assessing this important concept. *Journal of Higher Education Policy and Management, 24*(2), 197–209. https://doi.org/10.1080/1360080022000013518

Fuentes, M., Ruiz Alvarado, A., Berdan, J., & DeAngelo, L. (2014). Mentorship matters: Does early faculty contact lead to quality faculty interaction? *Research in Higher Education, 55*(3), 288–307. https://doi.org/10.1007/s11162-013-9307-6

Gill, R. (2002). Change management--or change leadership? *Journal of Change Management, 3*(4), 307–318.

Glazier, R. A. (2016, October 1). Building rapport to improve retention and success in online classes. *Journal of Political Science Education, 12*(4), 437–456. https://doi.org/10.1080/15512169.2016.1155994

Gluckman, N. (2020, April 7). Campus zero. *The Chronicle of Higher Education.* https://www.chronicle.com/interactives/covid-closures-part-1

Gresh, K. S., & Mrozowski, S. (2000). Faculty/student interaction at a distance: Seeking balance. EDUCASE 2000: Thinking IT through, Nashville, TN.

Gumport, P. J., & Sporn, B. (1999). Institutional adaptation: Demands for management reform and university administration. In J. Smart (Ed.), *Higher education: Handbook of theory and research* (pp. 103–145). Agathon Press.

Harrell, I. L. (2008). Increasing the success of online students. *Inquiry, 13*(1), 36–44.

Hayes, J. (2018). *The theory and practice of change management* (5th ed.). Palgrave Macmillan.

International Business Machines Corporation. (2017). *IBM SPSS.* (Version 25.0) Armonk, NY.

Johnson, G. M. (2019). On-campus and fully-online university students: Comparing demographics, digital technology use and learning characteristics. *Journal of University Teaching & Learning Practice, 12*(1), 4.

Juillerat, S. L., & Schreiner, L. A. (2004). The role of student satisfaction in the assessment of institutional effectiveness. In T. Banta (Ed.), *Hallmarks of effective outcomes assessment* (pp. 50–55). Jossey-Bass.

Kezar, A. (2003, December 1). Achieving student success: Strategies for creating partnerships between academic and student affairs. *NASPA Journal, 41*(1), 1–22. https://doi.org/10.2202/1949-6605.1302

Kuh, G. D., Kinzie, J., Buckley, J. A., Bridges, B. K., & Hayek, J. C. (2006). *What matters to student success: A review of the literature.* http://citeseerx.ist.psu.edu/viewdoc/download?doi=10.1.1.169.4913&rep=rep1&type=pdf

Lewis, G. (2010). I would have had more success if . . . : Student reflections on their performance in online and blended courses. *American Journal of Business Education, 3*(11), 13–21. https://doi.org/10.19030/ajbe.v3i11.58

Matthews, K. E., Cook-Sather, A., Acai, A., Dvorakova, S. L., Felten, P., Marquis, E., & Mercer-Mapstone, L. (2019). Toward theories of partnership praxis: An analysis of interpretive framing in literature on students as partners in teaching and learning. *Higher Education Research & Development, 38*(2), 280–293.

Miltiadou, M., & Savenye, W. C. (2003). Applying social cognitive constructs of motivation to enhance student success in online distance education. *AACE Journal, 11*(1), 78–95.

Orozco, M., Fowlkes, J., Jerzak, P., & Musgrove, A. (2012). Zero to sixty plus in 108 days: Launching a central elearning unit and its first faculty development program [Article]. *Journal of Asynchronous Learning Networks, 16*(2), 177–192. https://doi.org/10.24059/olj.v16i2.255

Pascarella, E. T., & Terenzini, P. T. (2005). *How college affects students: A third decade of research.* Jossey-Bass.

Rabourn, K. E., BrckaLorenz, A., & Shoup, R. (2018). Reimagining student engagement: How nontraditional adult learners engage in traditional postsecondary environments. *Journal of Continuing Higher Education, 66*(1), 22–33. https://doi.org/10.1080/07377363.2018.1415635

Restauri, S. L. (2006). *Faculty-student interaction components in online education: What are the effects on student satisfaction and academic outcomes?* Capella University.

Roddy, C., Amiet, D. L., Chung, J., Holt, C., Shaw, L., McKenzie, S., Garivaldis, F., Lodge, J. M., & Mundy, M. E. (2017). Applying best practice online learning, teaching, and support to intensive online environments: An integrative review. *Frontiers in Education, 2*, 59. https://doi.org/10.3389/feduc.2017.00059

SAP. (2013). *Qualtrics.* Provo, UT.

Smollan, R., Sayers, J. G., & Matheny, J. A. (2010). Emotional responses to the speed, frequency and timing of organizational change. *Time & Society, 19*(1), 28–53.

Umbach, P. D., & Wawrzynski, M. R. (2005). Faculty do matter: The role of college faculty in student learning and engagement. *Research in Higher Education, 46*(2), 153–184. https://doi.org/10.1007/s11162-004-1598-1

Winger, A. (2016). *What do the numbers really mean? An examination of learning analytics related to online courses and university student retention and success.* ProQuest Dissertations Publishing.

Wood, G. (2020, April 27). There's no simple way to reopen universities. *The Atlantic.* https://www.theatlantic.com/ideas/archive/2020/04/colleges-are-weighing-costs-reopening-fall/610759/

Yukselturk, E., & Bulut, S. (2007). Predictors of student success in an online course. *International Forum of Educational Technology & Society, 10*(2), 71–83.

Bios

David Edens, Ph.D., is an Assistant Professor in Nutrition and Food Science at Cal Poly Pomona. Dr. Edens was the former Chef Director for the Culinary Arts Programs at the Art Institute of California—Hollywood and Department Chair of Advanced Culinary Arts at Le Cordon Bleu Los Angeles. Dr. Edens has published and presented in the area of student success within the culinary student population, for-profit sector, under-served populations, and international students. E-mail: dredens@cpp.edu

Emily Kiresich, Ph.D., RD, is an Assistant Professor in Nutrition and Food Science at California Polytechnic State University, Pomona. She is also a Registered Dietitian with 12 years of experience in clinical nutrition; full-time for six years, and consulting and part-time for the past six years. She is a former Lecturer for California State University, Long Beach, for eight years where she served as Director for both the Didactic Program in Dietetics and the Individualized Supervised Practice Pathway Internship for three years. Dr. Kiresich has published and presented in the areas related to public health. E-mail: ejkiresich@cpp.edu

10 Chinese College Students' Experiences of Using the Learning Management System and Their Sense of Online Classroom Community during the COVID-19 Pandemic

Xi Lin, Mingyu Huang, and Qingchuan Zhang

Abstract

This study examines Chinese college students' experiences of using the learning management system (LMS) including their technology anxiety (ANX) of using an LMS, perceived ease of use of an LMS (PEU), computer self-efficacy (CSE), and their sense of classroom community (CCS) in synchronous, asynchronous, and blend of both synchronous and asynchronous online courses during the COVID-19 pandemic. This study further investigates the relationship between CCS, ANX, PEU, and CSE using ANX, PEU, and CSE as predictors. Results indicate that students' ANX and CSE are associated with their CCS regardless of the learning formats. It is expected that this study would enlighten Chinese higher education professionals to enhance students' online learning experience and establish a supportive online community.

Keywords

online learning; perceived ease of use; sense of classroom community; technology anxiety; higher education

Introduction

Distance learning has been identified as an efficient way to deliver educational opportunities to a wide range of audiences in a flexible and convenient way (Croxton, 2014; Yamagata-Lynch, 2014), especially during the COVID-19 pandemic (Adedoyin & Soykan, 2020; Lassoued et al., 2020). Universities in China have established online programs but specifically for continuing or vocational education (Li & Zhang, 2009). In higher education, however, face-to-face instruction predominates, while online teaching is used as a supplement to in-person courses. At the end of 2019, universities in China shut campuses in response to COVID-19, and all schools moved from face-to-face to online teaching and learning in early February during the 2020 Spring semester. This was the first time that all college courses were completely delivered online across the nation, and it was also the first time that many Chinese college students were taking courses online. To improve students' online learning experiences, building a sense of classroom community is significant as the feeling of being a member of the community positively influences student engagement, performance, and retention (Stubb et al., 2011; Trespalacios & Uribe-Florez, 2020). Meanwhile, students' experiences of using the online learning management system (LMS) additionally influence their sense of classroom community, especially those who are taking online courses for the first time. As a result, this study investigates (1) Chinese college students' experiences of using an LMS and their sense of classroom community (CCS) in synchronous, asynchronous, or a blend of both synchronous and asynchronous online courses, and (2) the relationship between college students' experiences of using an LMS and CCS in synchronous, asynchronous, or a blend of both online courses.

Literature Review

Online Course Formats and Students' Sense of Classroom Community

Building a sense of classroom community in online learning environments is important. Scholars identified that a sense of classroom community is the feeling of membership and belonging within a group (Yuan & Kim, 2014). Berry (2017) further discussed that "in a learning community, students work with peers, instructors, and staff to learn collaboratively and support each other in pursuing academic, social, and emotional goals" (p. 2). When students experience a sense of community, they will receive academic and social benefits in an online classroom (Lai, 2015). Additionally, a sense of community also enhances classroom participation and students' abilities to manage stress and emotional well-being (Stubb et al., 2011).

However, the different course formats may contribute to students' sense of classroom community within an online context. Generally, there are three types of online courses: asynchronous, synchronous, or a blend of both online learning formats (Shoepe et al., 2020). Synchronous online learning refers to the learning activity that both students and instructors engage in learning at the same time through audio or video conferencing (Ruiz et al., 2006). In synchronous online environments, students develop a strong connection with their instructor and peers, and they are often engaged in classroom activities (Clark et al., 2015; Yamagata-Lynch, 2014). In other words, the real-time lectures and the instance interaction enhances students' engagement in learning because the real-time communication could shorten students' feelings of distance with their peers and the instructor so as to build a strong sense of community (Abdelmalak, 2015; Francescucci & Rohani, 2019; Pattillo, 2007; Watts, 2016).

In asynchronous learning environments, however, the learning activities do not happen in real time. Instead, instructors use emails and online discussion boards to develop interaction (Ruiz et al., 2006). Students have more flexibility in this learning format as they do not have to be online at the same time, and they are able to manage their learning process at their own pace (Hrastinski, 2008; Pang & Jen, 2018). In terms of conducting the discussion activity in asynchronous online learning environments, students can fully express their thoughts as they have more time to think before discussing topics in greater detail as well as responding to others (Brierton et al., 2016).

A combination of both synchronous and asynchronous online course formats has been considered as an efficient learning approach (Gregory, 2003). The mix of these two formats could bring various benefits to student learning. For instance, asynchronous learning environments allow the instructor to provide additional content to students who need extra time without slowing down the class. On the other hand, when synchronous teaching and learning happens, the instructor could read students' body or facial language to determine whether they understand the learning content or they need more assistance (Horvitz et al., 2019). Moreover, the blended online learning format has been proved to be more efficient than a single asynchronous and synchronous teaching method in some cases (Ge, 2012; Xie et al., 2018).

Experiences of Using Technology and Students' Sense of Classroom Community

The use of an LMS may additionally impact students' sense of classroom community in online learning environments (Haar, 2018). For example, Rideout and colleagues (2008) investigated the influence of implementation of an LMS on 34 pre-service teachers in Canada, and they found that these participants received a high sense of classroom community when interacting with their peers, professors, and supervisors through the online platform. They also discovered that the experiences of using an LMS were the primary predictor of learners' sense of community. In other words, interactions would be encouraged through various activities such as group discussion, announcements, and instructional videos in an LMS, and these activities would help establish a strong online community (Aldosemani et al., 2016).

Meanwhile, students' perspectives of using an LMS would influence their online learning experiences, which may further impact their sense of classroom community. Generally, most previous studies focus on how students' anxiety of using technology affects their interaction with this technology (Agbatogun, 2010; Tuncer, 2012). Students with technology anxiety usually experience feelings of frustration, the potential of embarrassment, disappointment, and fear of the unknown (Tuncer, 2012). Specifically, students with a high level of technology anxiety often have a low level of academic performance, and they intend to avoid using the technology for academic purposes (Mooney, 2007). In contrast, students who have a low level of technology anxiety are more likely to have a positive experience towards using technology such as an LMS

(Stiller & Köster, 2016). Additionally, students would have a better attitude towards using the technology if they find that the technology could be useful in their studies (Heinecke & Adamy, 2010).

Scholars identified perceived ease of use (PEU) as an important factor that influences the intentions of students to adopt a technology, as well as their satisfaction with using this technology (Abdel-Maksoud, 2018; Juha-Matti & Niklas, 2014; Teo, 2011). For example, Juhary (2014) investigated whether students' PEU has a significant influence on their attitude towards using an LMS, and the results indicated that PEU had influenced students' attitudes towards an LMS. Specifically, a positive PEU results in a positive attitude towards using an LMS. Similarly, Ajijola and colleagues (2019) explored PEU of an LMS among distance learners, and they found that students with positive PEU of an LMS often hold positive perceptions towards adopting an LMS. Distance learners who have a positive PEU also hold a positive perceived usefulness of an LMS. Moreover, the degree of PEU of an LMS would further influence learners' academic performance and learning outcomes within the context of online learning (Sun et al., 2008).

Additionally, computer self-efficacy (CSE) also influences students' online learning experiences. Self-efficacy refers to an individual's "ability to organize and implement the course of action required to achieve specific accomplishments" (Bandura, 1977, p. 3), and CSE refers to individual's beliefs in their ability to use technology to solve problems, make decisions, and create and use electronic information (Hagger et al., 2005). In other words, CSE is a combination of self-confidence and skill, and it is defined as individuals' perceptions of their ability to use technology to complete a task (Bandura, 1977; Compeau & Higgins 1995; Gupta, 2017). The CSE is identified to have a positive impact on students' learning outcomes, as well as their adoption and attitudes towards using the technology (Compeau et al., 2006). Previous studies discovered that a high level of CSE improves college students' learning, while a low level of CSE impacts their use of skills for learning (Schlebusch, 2018).

While most previous studies focus on influences of technology anxiety, PEU of technology, and CSE on college students' attitudes of adopting technology and their learning outcomes, it is possible that these factors would meanwhile impact students' sense of online classroom community, specifically when using an LMS. Therefore, this study investigates:

1)   Chinese college students' experiences of using an LMS and their sense of classroom community (CCS) in synchronous, asynchronous, or blended online courses;
2)   the relationship between college students' experiences of using an LMS and CCS in synchronous, asynchronous, or blended online courses.

Methods

A convenience sampling procedure was used to recruit participants. College students in two northeastern universities in China were invited to participate in the study. An invitation email with the link to the survey was sent through these universities and lasted for one week. A total number of 211 students participated in the survey with 187 usable responses (usable response rate equals 88.6%). All the students have taken synchronous, asynchronous, and blended online course formats using the LMS provided by their universities during this time. The LMS that bring used was Rain Classroom, which integrates the information publishing before class, the real-time answering, and multi-screen interaction in class (Li & Song, 2018). This software has been used in over 2,300 Chinese universities (Lew, 2018). By using this online learning platform, students and their instructors conduct major tasks including having synchronous online courses, watching the pre-recording course lectures, conducting online discussion, taking online quizzes, and completing assignments.

Students were asked to think about a course format before answering the survey. Data reported that among those who completed the survey, 52 (27.8%) of them expressed their feelings towards synchronous online courses, 41 (21.9%) of them shared their thoughts regarding asynchronous online courses, and 95 (50.8%) of them conveyed their experiences about blended courses that use both synchronous and asynchronous formats.

Instrument

The instrument for measuring students' online classroom community was adopted from the Classroom Community Scale (Rovai, 2002). This scale is a 20-item 5-point Likert-type scale, ranging from 1 (strongly disagree) to 5 (strongly agree). This questionnaire assesses students' overall classroom community with two subscales: connectedness and learning, each with 10 items. Connectedness refers to students' feelings of the community "regarding their connectedness, cohesion, spirit, trust, and interdependence" (Rovai, 2002, p. 206). Three items were reversed, and a higher score indicates a higher level of connectedness. Sample questions include "I feel that students in this course care about each other," "I feel isolated in this course," and "I feel confident that others will support me." Learning refers to

> the feelings of community members regarding interaction with each other as they pursue the construction of understanding and the degree to which members share values and beliefs concerning the extent to which their educational goals and expectations are being satisfied. (Rovai, 2002, pp. 206–207)

Seven items were reversed, and a higher score indicates a higher level of interaction with community members when sharing the understanding of the course content. Sample questions include "I feel that I am encouraged to ask questions," "I feel that it is hard to get help when I have a question," and "I feel that this course does not promote a desire to learn."

The instrument for measuring students' experiences of using the LMS was adopted from Saadé and Kira's (2009) measurement. This assessment includes PEU of technology with 4 items, ANX with 4 items, and CSE with 10 items. PEU and ANX are 5-point Likert-type scales, ranging from 1 (strongly disagree) to 5 (strongly agree). CSE was revised into a 5-point Likert scale to make it consistent with other surveys. PEU refers to the degree that students expect an LMS to be easy to use, such as "I think that learning to navigate the online course components using an LMS will be easy for me," and "I think that I will find it easy to get the online course components in an LMS to do what I want them to do." A higher score indicates an easier degree of using an LMS for learning. ANX presents students' anxiety of using an LMS for online learning, such as "I feel apprehensive about using the LMS," and "I hesitate to use the LMS for fear of making mistakes I cannot correct." All items were reversed. Thus, a higher score implies a lower level of anxiety in using an LMS. Finally, CSE refers to students' confidence in using an LMS for online learning. Sample questions include "I could complete the required tasks using the LMS if there was no one around to tell me what to do as I go," and "I could complete the required tasks using the LMS if I had seen someone else using it before trying it myself." A higher score refers to a higher level of belief in their capability of using an LMS.

A few modifications such as minor wording changes were made to the original items so that to make them fit into the context of this study. The original internal consistency Cronbach's alpha of connectedness, learning, PEU, ANX, and CSE were 0.92, 0.87, 0.89, 0.93, and 0.78, respectively (Rovai, 2002; Saadé & Kira, 2009). The Cronbach's alpha for each factor in this study were 0.85, 0.89, 0.90, 0.82, and 0.94, respectively.

Procedure

The recruited students clicked on the survey link provided in the invitation email. They then read the informed consent and decided whether to participate in the study or not. The survey was anonymous which would take approximately eight to ten minutes to complete. Students were able to withdraw from doing the survey by closing the website at any time. The original items were in English and needed to be translated into Chinese. To guarantee the validity of the Chinese version of the measure, a standard translation and back-translation procedure was used (Hambleton & Patsula, 1998).

Data Analysis

Data were analyzed through SPSS version 27. Descriptive analysis was used to examine the students' perspectives of using an LMS, and regression analysis was applied to investigate the relationship between the experiences of using an LMS and students' sense of classroom community in synchronous, asynchronous, or blended online courses. The alpha level was set at 0.05.

Harman's single factor score was examined, and the total variance (ranges from 14.1% to 37.2%) for a single factor is less than 50%. Thus, results indicated that common method bias did not affect the data (Podsakoff et al., 2003).

Results

RQ1: What Are Chinese College Students' Experiences of Using an LMS and Their Sense of Classroom Community (CCS) in Synchronous, Asynchronous, or Blended Online Courses?

Descriptive analysis was conducted to examine college students' experiences of using an LMS for online learning (see Figure 10.1). Overall results show that students hold a positive attitude towards PEU of an LMS ($M = 3.49$, $SD = 0.81$), and a neutral attitude of the anxiety to use an LMS ($M = 3.01$, $SD = 0.81$). However, students hold a higher degree of self-efficacy in using an LMS for online learning ($M = 4.21$, $SD = 1.01$).

In synchronous online courses, students have a positive attitude towards the easiness of using an LMS ($M = 3.49$, $SD = 0.92$). They also hold a slightly low degree of anxiety towards using an LMS ($M = 3.29$, $SD = 0.83$), while they have high self-efficacy in terms of using the LMS for online learning ($M = 4.19$, $SD = 1.23$). In asynchronous online courses, students' attitude towards the ease to use an LMS is slightly positive ($M = 3.26$, $SD = 0.75$). They also have high self-efficacy towards using an LMS ($M = 3.94$, $SD = 0.87$). However, they hold a high level of anxiety to use an LMS ($M = 2.74$, $SD = 0.80$), which indicates that students are slightly anxious when using an LMS in an asynchronous online

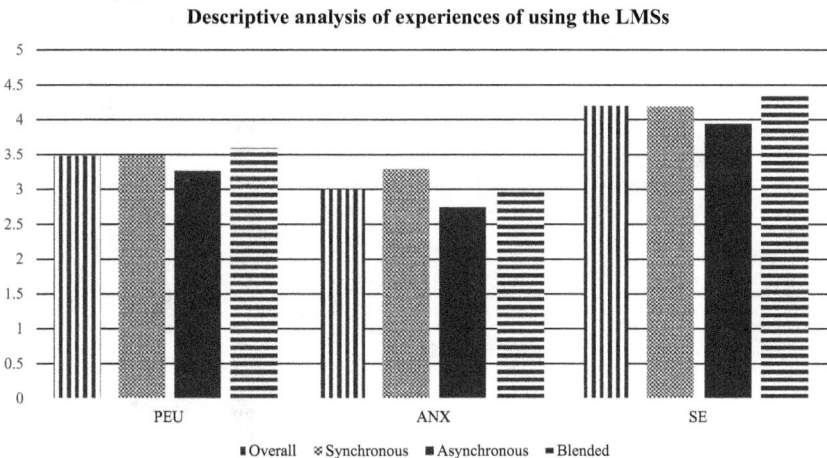

Descriptive analysis of experiences of using the LMSs

■ Overall ⊗ Synchronous ■ Asynchronous ▬ Blended

Figure 10.1 Descriptive analysis of experiences of using an LMS.

environment. Similar to asynchronous online courses, students are worried about using an LMS when in blended online courses ($M = 2.97, SD = 0.77$). Yet, they think a LMS is easy to use ($M = 3.60, SD = 0.74$) and they are confident in using an LMS for online learning ($M = 4.34, SD = 0.93$).

RQ2: What Is the Relationship between College Students' Experiences of Using an LMS and CCS in Synchronous, Asynchronous, or Blended Online Courses?

A series of multiple regression analyses using a stepwise procedure were conducted to investigate the relationship between students' experiences of using an LMS and their sense of classroom community in three learning formats (see Table 10.1). Asynchronous and blended online courses were dummy coded as 1 and 0, respectively, using synchronous online courses as a reference category. Specifically, when a synchronous online course was set as a reference group, the asynchronous online course was coded as 1, and the rest were coded as 0. Similarly, using synchronous online courses as a reference group, blended online courses were coded as 1, and the rest formats were coded as 0.

Results indicated that only the level of ANX and CSE are associated with the level of connectedness, $F_{(2,186)} = 55.3, p < 0.001$. Thirty-seven and five percent of the variance in the level of connectedness can be accounted for by the linear combination of the levels of ANX and CSE ($R^2 = 37.5\%$).

Table 10.1 Multiple regression results ($N = 187$)

DV	R^2	F	df	p	Predictors	β	t	p
Connectedness	0.375	55.31	2,186	<0.001	Tech anxiety	0.16	3.74	<0.001
					Computer self-efficacy	0.27	8.15	<0.001
					Ease to use	0.16	1.77	0.08
					Asynchronous (*coded as* 1)	0.09	1.48	0.14
					Blended (*coded as* 1)	−0.01	−0.09	0.93
Learning	0.438	71.75	2,186	<0.001				
					Tech anxiety	0.34	7.89	<0.001
					Computer self-efficacy	0.21	6.07	<0.001
					Ease to use	0.09	1.04	0.30
					Asynchronous (*coded as* 1)	0.02	0.39	0.80
					Blended (*coded as* 1)	0.05	0.86	0.39

Note: Synchronous online course was set as a reference group.

For every unit the level of ANX increases, the level of connectedness increases by 0.16 unit while the level of CSE remains the same (b = 0.16, t = 3.74, p <0.001). Additionally, for every unit the level of CSE increases, the level of connectedness increases 0.27 unit when the level of ANX unchanged (b = 0.27, t = 8.15, p <0.001). However, the regression results indicate that learning formats and PEU do not significantly influence students' connectedness.

Similarly, only the levels of ANX and CSE are related to students' levels of learning, $F_{(2,186)}$ = 71.75, p <0.001. 43.8% of the variance in the level of learning can be accounted for by the linear combination of the levels of anxiety and self-efficacy (R^2 = 43.8%). To be specific, when the level of CSE stays the same, for every unit the level of ANX increases, the level of learning increases by 0.34 unit (b = 0.34, t = 7.89, p <0.001). Meanwhile, for every unit the level of CSE increases, the level of learning increases by 0.21 unit when the level of ANX remains the same (b = 0.21, t = 6.07, p <0.001). However, the regression results show that learning formats and PEU do not significantly influence students' learning.

Discussions and Conclusions

Regarding Chinese college students' experiences of using an LMS and their sense of classroom community in synchronous, asynchronous, or blended online courses, results of the study indicate that students hold a positive PEU of an LMS and they are confident to use an LMS for online learning, regardless of the course formats. However, some students expressed their anxiety towards using an LMS for online learning especially in asynchronous online courses. It is possible that these students were not well prepared for fully online courses without real-time support from their instructors during the transition from face-to-face to online learning. However, further study should be conducted to explore this finding.

In terms of the relationship between college students' experiences of using an LMS and their sense of community in different online formats, results show that the learning format does not influence students' sense of online classroom community. These findings argue with previous conclusions that students in synchronous online courses or blended online courses usually feel a stronger classroom community than in asynchronous online courses (Abdelmalak, 2015; Clark, et al., 2015; Francescucci & Rohani, 2019; Ge, 2012; Pattillo, 2007; Watts, 2016; Xie et al., 2018). Although previous studies identified PEU as an important factor that influences students' intentions and attitudes of using an LMS (Abdel-Maksoud, 2018; Juha-Matti & Niklas, 2014; Teo, 2011), students' PEU of an LMS does not influence their sense of online classroom community according to this study.

However, students' sense of classroom community is affected by their ANX and self-efficacy of using an LMS for online learning. Previous studies discovered that a low level of ANX and a high CSE would lead to a positive attitude towards using an LMS (Agbatogun, 2010; Schlebusch, 2018; Tuncer,

2012). This study further indicates that students who have a lower degree of ANX while a higher level of confidence in using an LMS for online learning usually have a stronger sense of classroom community. Moreover, these students hold a stronger feeling "regarding their connectedness, cohesion, spirit, trust, and interdependence" (Rovai, 2002, p. 206). Similarly, students who are less anxious and more confident in using an LMS for online learning have a stronger feeling of "community members regarding interaction with each other as they pursue the construction of understanding and the degree to which members share values and beliefs concerning the extent to which their educational goals and expectations are being satisfied" (Rovai, 2002, pp. 206–207).

In conclusion, while online courses were often used as a supplement to traditional face-to-face classes in Chinese universities, the COVID-19 pandemic has forced higher education institutions to use distance learning as a main course delivery method (Lin & Gao, 2020). This study specifically examined Chinese college students' experiences of using an LMS focusing on the relationship between their ANX, PEU, and CSE of using an LMS with their sense of classroom community. Findings indicate that positive attitudes toward using an LMS will positively influence students' sense of community in online courses. Therefore, to improve Chinese college students' sense of classroom community in online learning environments, educators should pay attention to reduce their anxiety about using an LMS while enhancing their confidence to use an LMS for online learning. For example, instructors could show students how to efficiently use an LMS step by step on the first day of the online class. Online office hours should be arranged to help students with any questions related to using an LMS. Graduate teaching assistants should be assigned to help answer questions raised by students as well. Additionally, instructors should provide students with adequate support resources such as the contact information of the university IT personnel, so that to help students with any technology-relevant challenges when using an LMS for online learning. Finally, the Ministry of Education of the People's Republic of China has proposed the "Guidance on the Organization and Management of Online Teaching in the Higher Education Institutions During Epidemic Prevention and Control Period" (Ministry of Education, 2020) which requires national and local governments to support colleges and universities, together with the society, to joint implementation of online education (Zhu & Liu, 2020). Therefore, related policy and strategies should be proposed to encourage online learning and the development of LMSs so as to enhance students' online learning experiences.

Limitations and Future Study

Several limitations exist in the study. First, this study should take instructors' characteristics into consideration. It is possible that the different teaching styles and their levels of familiarity with online teaching may impact college students' feelings of classroom community. Additionally, this study should compare students' sense of classroom community in STEM (e.g., math, physics) and non-STEM fields (e.g., English, higher education). It is possible that more interactive activities would be arranged in non-STEM courses that would create a stronger classroom community, while instructors may often apply teacher-centered lectures in STEM courses. Therefore, future studies should compare students' sense of classroom community in different areas. Moreover, students' previous experiences of taking online courses may influence their experiences of using an LMS as well as their sense of classroom community. As a result, future studies should control for their previous online learning experiences. Additionally, students were not recruited from a specific course, therefore, the different ways that the instructors using an LMS for online teaching may influence students' online learning experiences. Thus, future studies should take the course curriculum design into consideration. Lastly, this study recruited participants from two first-tier four-year public universities located in Beijing, a well-developed city in China. However, universities with lower ranks and in rural areas may have few instructors who have experience in using technology, fewer online resources, and limited technology support. Students in those universities probably have contrasting feelings towards online learning compared to those studying in first-tier universities located in well-developed provinces. Therefore, future studies should explore college students' online learning experiences who are studying in lower ranked universities and those located in less-developed provinces so as to indicate more comprehensive conclusions.

References

Abdel-Maksoud, N. F. (2018). The relationship between students' satisfaction in the LMS "Acadox" and their perceptions of its usefulness, and ease of use. *Journal of Education and Learning, 7*(2), 184–190.

Abdelmalak, M. M. M. (2015). Web 2.0 technologies and building online learning communities: Students' perspectives. *Online Learning, 19*(2). http://dx.doi.org/10.24059/olj.v19i2.413

Adedoyin, O. B., & Soykan, E. (2020). Covid-19 pandemic and online learning: The challenges and opportunities. *Interactive Learning Environments*, 1–13. https://doi.org/10.1080/10494820.2020.1813180

Agbatogun, A. (2010). Self-concept, computer anxiety, gender and attitude towards interactive computer technologies: A predictive study among Nigerian teachers. *International Journal of Education and Development Using ICT, 6*(2), 55–68.

Ajijola, E. M., Ogunlade, O. O. S., Abdulsalam, A., Buraimoh, O. F. A., & Gboyega, A. (2019). Perceived usefulness and perceived ease of use of learning management system among distanve learners' in South-West, Nigeria. In *Conference Proceedings of the AITIE 3rd International Conference and Workshop on Innovation, Technology and Education* (ICWITE, Abuja 2019) (p. 223).

Aldosemani, T. I., Shepherd, C. E., Gashim, I., & Dousay, T. (2016). Developing third places to foster sense of community in online instruction. *British Journal of Educational Technology, 47*(6), 1020–1031.

Bandura. A. (1977). Self-efficacy: Toward a unifying theory of behavioral change. *Psychological Review, 84*, 191–215.

Berry, S. (2017). Building community in online doctoral classrooms: Instructor practices that support community. *Online Learning, 21*(2), 1–22. https://doi.org/0.24059/olj.v21i2.875

Brierton, S., Wilson, E., Kistler, M., Flowers, J., & Jones, D. (2016). A comparison of higher order thinking skills demonstrated in synchronous and asynchronous online college discussion posts. *NACTA Journal, 60*(1), 14–21.

Clark, C., Strudler, N., & Grove, K. (2015). Comparing asynchronous and synchronous video vs. text-based discussions in an online teacher education course. *Online Learning, 19*(3), 48–69.

Compeau, D., Gravill, J., Haggerty, N., & Kelley, H. (2006). Computer self-efficacy. In P. Zhang & D. F. Galletta (Eds.), *Human-computer interaction and management information systems: Foundations* (pp. 225–261). Routledge.

Compeau, D. R., & Higgins, C. A. (1995). Computer self-efficacy: Development of a measure and initial test. *MIS Quarterly, 19*(2), 189–211.

Croxton, R. A. (2014). The role of interactivity in student satisfaction and persistence in online learning. *Journal of Online Learning and Teaching, 10*(2), 314.

Francescucci, A., & Rohani, L. (2019). Exclusively synchronous online (VIRI) learning: The impact on student performance and engagement outcomes. *Journal of Marketing Education, 41*(1), 60–69. https://doi.org/10.1177/0273475318818864

Ge, Z. G. (2012). Cyber asynchronous versus blended cyber approach in distance English learning. *Educational Technology & Society, 15*(2), 286–297.

Gregory, V. L. (2003). Student perceptions of the effectiveness of Web-based distance education. *New Library World, 104*(10), 426–431.

Gupta, S. (2017). Reducing computer anxiety in self-paced technology training. Proceedings of the *50th Hawaii International Conference on System Sciences*, Hawaii.

Haar, M. (2018). Increasing sense of community in higher education nutrition courses using technology. *Journal of Nutrition Education and Behavior, 50*(1), 96–99.

Hagger, M. S., Chatzisarantis, N. L., Barkoukis, V., Wang, C. K. J., & Baranowski, J. (2005). Perceived autonomy support in physical education and leisure-time physical activity: A cross-cultural evaluation of the trans-contextual model. *Journal of Educational Psychology, 97*(3), 376.

Hambleton, R. K., & Patsula, L. (1998). Adapting tests for use in multiple languages and cultures. *Social Indicators Research, 45*(1–3), 153–171. https://doi.org/10.1023/A:1006941729637

Heinecke, W., & Adamy, P. (Eds.). (2010). *Evaluating technology in teacher education: Lessons from the preparing tomorrow's teachers for technology (PT3) program.* IAP.

Horvitz, B. S., Garcia, L. R., Mitchell, R. G., & Calhoun, C. D. (2019). An examination of instructional approaches in online technical education in community colleges. *Online Learning, 23*(4), 237–252.

Hrastinski, S. (2008). Asynchronous and synchronous e-learning. *Educause Quarterly, 31*(4), 51–55.

Juha-Matti, S., & Niklas, E. (2014, May). *Students' perceptions of learning management systems. An explorative case study of upper secondary school students* (Bachelor of Information Systems Thesis). University of Gothenburg Department of Applied Information Technology Gothenburg, Sweden.

Juhary, J. (2014). Perceived usefulness and ease of use of the learning management system as a learning tool. *International Education Studies, 7*(8), 23–34.

Lai, K. W. (2015). Knowledge construction in online learning communities: A case study of a doctoral course. *Studies in Higher Education, 40*(4), 561–579. https://doi.org/10.1080/03075079.2013.831402

Lassoued, Z., Alhendawi, M., & Bashitialshaaer, R. (2020). An exploratory study of the obstacles for achieving quality in distance learning during the COVID-19 pandemic. *Education Sciences, 10*(9), 232–245. https://doi.org/10.3390/educsci10090232

Lew, L. (2018, April). Tsinghua University is using the cloud to make it rain in the classroom. *Technode.* https://technode.com/2018/04/19/rain-classroom/

Li, H., & Zhang, H. (2009). The current status and future development of modern distance education in China. *Higher Education and Research, 8*, 28–31.

Li, X., & Song, S. (2018). Mobile technology affordance and its social implications: A case of "Rain Classroom". *British Journal of Educational Technology, 49*(2), 276–291. https://doi.org/10.1111/bjet.12586

Lin, X., & Gao, L. (2020). Students' sense of community and perspectives of taking synchronous and asynchronous online courses. *Asian Journal of Distance Education, 15*(1), 169–179.

Ministry of Education of P.R. China. (2020). Guidance on the organization and management of online teaching in the higher education institutions during epidemic prevention and control period. http://www.moe.gov.cn/jyb_xwfb/gzdt_gzdt/s5987/202002/t20200205_418131.html

Mooney, M. E. (2007). *Computer anxiety and web-based course management systems: Does design matter?* (Doctoral dissertation, Purdue University).

Pang, L., & Jen, C. C. (2018). Inclusive dyslexia-friendly collaborative online learning environment: Malaysia case study. *Education and Information Technologies, 23*(3), 1023–1042. https://doi.org/10.1007/s10639-017-9652-8

Pattillo, R. E. (2007). Decreasing transactional distance in a web-based course. *Nurse Educator, 32*(3), 109–112. https://doi.org/10.1097/01.NNE.0000270224.38543.2f

Podsakoff, P. M., MacKenzie, S. B., Lee, J.-Y., & Podsakoff, N. P. (2003). Common method biases in behavioral research: A critical review of the literature and recommended remedies. *Journal of Applied Psychology, 88*(5), 879–903. https://doi.org/10.1037/0021-9010.88.5.879

Rideout, G., Bruinsma, R., Hull, J., & Modayil, J. (2008). Online learning management systems (LMS) and sense of community: A pre-service practicum perspective. *Canadian Journal of Learning and Technology/La revue canadienne de l'apprentissage et de la technologie, 33*(3), 1–18.

Rovai, A. P. (2002). Development of an instrument to measure classroom community. *Internet and Higher Education, 5*, 197–211. https://doi.org/10.1016/S1096-7516(02)00102-1

Ruiz, J. G., Mintzer, M. J., & Leipzig, R. M. (2006). The impact of e-learning in medical education. *Academic Medicine, 81*(3), 207–212. https://doi.org/10.1097/00001888-200603000-00002

Saadé, R. G., & Kira, D. (2009). Computer anxiety in e-learning: The effect of computer self-efficacy. *Journal of Information Technology Education: Research, 8*(1), 177–191.

Schlebusch, C. L. (2018). Computer anxiety, computer self-efficacy and attitudes towards the internet of first year students at a South African University of Technology. *Africa Education Review, 15*(3), 72–90.

Shoepe, T. C., McManus, J. F., August, S. E., Mattos, N. L., Vollucci, T. C., & Sparks, P. R. (2020). Instructor prompts and student engagement in synchronous online nutrition classes. *American Journal of Distance Education*, 1–17. https://doi.org/10.1080/08923647.2020.1726166

Stiller, K. D., & Köster, A. (2016). Learner attrition in an advanced vocational online training: The role of computer attitude, computer anxiety, and online learning experience. *European Journal of Open, Distance and E-Learning, 19*(2), 1–14.

Stubb, J., Pyhältö, K., & Lonka, K. (2011). Balancing between inspiration and exhaustion: PhD students' experienced socio-psychological well-being. *Studies in Continuing Education, 33*(1), 33–50. http://dx.doi.org/10.1080/0158037X.2010.515572

Sun, P., Tsai, R., Finger, G., Chen, Y., & Yeh, D. (2008). What drives a successful E-Learning? An empirical investigation of the critical factors influencing learner satisfaction. *Computers & Education, 50*(4), 1183–1202. https://doi.org/10.1016/j.compedu.2006.11.007

Teo, T. (2011). *Technology acceptance in education: Research and issues.* Sense Publishers. http://dx.doi.org/10.1007/978-94-6091-487-4.

Trespalacios, J., & Uribe-Florez, L. J. (2020). Developing online sense of community: Graduate students' experiences and perceptions. *The Turkish Online Journal of Distance Education, 21*(2), 57–72.

Tuncer, M. (2012). Investigation of effects of computer anxiety and internet attitudes on computer self-efficacy. *International Journal of Social Science, 5*(4), 205–222.

Watts, L. (2016). Synchronous and asynchronous communication in distance learning: A review of the literature. *Quarterly Review of Distance Education, 17*(1), 23–32.

Xie, H., Liu, W., & Bhairma, J. (2018, December). Analysis of synchronous and asynchronous E-learning environments. In *2018 3rd Joint International Information Technology, Mechanical and Electronic Engineering Conference* (JIMEC 2018). Atlantis Press.

Yamagata-Lynch, L. C. (2014). Blending online asynchronous and synchronous learning. *The International Review of Research in Open and Distributed Learning, 15*(2). https://doi.org/10.19173/irrodl.v15i2.1778

Yuan, J., & Kim, C. (2014). Guidelines for facilitating the development of learning communities in online courses. *Journal of Computer Assisted Learning, 30*(3), 220–232. http://dx.doi.org/10.1111/jcal.12042

Zhu, X., & Liu, J. (2020). Education in and after Covid-19: Immediate responses and long-term visions. *Postdigital Science and Education, 2*, 1–5.

Bios

Xi Lin, Ph.D., is an Assistant Professor at East Carolina University. Her research focuses on online and distance learning as well as game-based learning. She also explores cross-cultural experiences especially the adaptation of international students and faculty in the US institutions. Email: linxi18@ecu.edu

Mingyu Huang, Ph.D., is an Assistant Professor at Beijing Dance Academy. Her research focuses on arts management, artistic bilingualism learning, and online learning. She is also interested in the adaptation of international art students and artists studying and living in China. Email: huangmingyu@bda.edu.cn

Qingchuan Zhang, Ph.D., is an Assistant Professor at the University of Science and Technology Beijing. He is the author of one book and more than ten articles. His research focuses on semantic computing, natural language processing, and data mining. Email: zqc1982@126.com

11 Pedagogical Implications of COVID-19

A Case Study of What Faculty Learned about Teaching Well by Teaching Remotely during the COVID-19 Pandemic

Kim Manturuk and Grey Reavis

Abstract

On January 30, 2020, Duke Learning Innovation (DLI) began the Keep Teaching Initiative to assist Duke Kunshan University, and later Duke University, faculty through the transition to remote teaching due to the COVID-19 pandemic. Throughout the process, DLI heard about the challenges faculty faced, but also their success stories. For many faculty members, remote instruction gave them an opportunity to be more experimental in their pedagogy and try new ways of engaging students, leading them to adopt new approaches to campus-based teaching. In this case study, we conducted semi-structured interviews of Duke and Duke Kunshan faculty to understand how they transformed their teaching as a result of their remote teaching experiences. We describe the themes that emerged around flexible pedagogy and student engagement strategies. We also highlight implications for policy and practices that improve student learning outcomes and support more flexible pedagogy to create more resilient learning environments in the future.

Keywords

COVID-19; Remote Learning; Face-to-Face Learning; Pedagogy; Case Study

Introduction

On January 30, 2020, Duke Learning Innovation (DLI) began the Keep Teaching initiative to assist Duke Kunshan University, and later Duke University, faculty through the transition to remote teaching due to the COVID-19 pandemic. This initiative involved three primary components: (1) a collection of curated resources to help instructors quickly transition from in-person to remote teaching, (2) training and support on technology tools and platforms to facilitate online teaching, and (3) daily drop-in office hours with DLI's team of teaching consultants.

As a result of this comprehensive outreach to faculty members at both universities (Duke Kunshan and Duke), we heard a lot about the instructor experiences during the transition to remote instruction, both positive and negative. As the semester drew to a close, we began to notice a trend of instructors sharing things they had tried during remote instruction that worked so well that they wanted to keep those parts of their course even when they returned to in-person teaching. After collecting these anecdotes for several weeks, we decided to build a case study of pedagogical lessons learned from the remote teaching experience with an emphasis on lessons that would carry over to the traditional, face-to-face teaching experience. This chapter summarizes that case study and presents recommendations for how university instructors can build resilience and flexibility into their courses.

Literature Review

Remote instruction at the college level is not new. In 1957, New York University and CBS created Sunrise Semester, a series of college-level classes delivered weekly on television. Almost as soon as it began, professors teaching Sunrise Semester classes quickly realized that teaching remotely was not the same as teaching in person. Early lectures often came across as canned, and professors were advised to create student engagement by allowing their personalities to come through during their recorded lectures (McDonald, 2004). While college students no longer watch classes on television, the options for online remote instruction have grown rapidly; as of 2010, over 30% of U.S. students reported having taken at least one online class (Platt et al., 2014).

With this growth in online learning has come a robust body of research on remote teaching pedagogy, much of it focused on strategies to increase student engagement. Studies have consistently found that interaction is important for fostering engagement, and there are many effective ways to create an interaction (Dixson, 2010). These strategies include incorporating active learning opportunities (Freeman et al., 2014; Maki & Maki, 2007; Phillips, 2005), providing opportunities for discussions and collaboration among students (Gayton & McEwen, 2007; Robinson & Hullinger, 2008), giving and soliciting feedback frequently (Arend, 2007; Dennen et al., 2007), and offering varied student assessments (Barber et al., 2015).

Yet in spite of this large body of research, very few studies have attempted to apply conclusions from research on remote instruction to the face-to-face learning experience. Rather, many studies have implicitly treated in-person learning experiences as optimal and sought to improve online learning by applying findings from research on traditional classes to the online space. This approach is often fruitful (for an excellent example, see Darby & Lang, 2019), but we believe that there is an overlooked opportunity to apply findings from research on remote teaching to the in-person context because the few studies that exist show improvement to the face-to-face experience.

In fact, there is some precedent for applying findings about remote learning to the in-person experience. When Massive Open Online Classes (MOOCs) became widely available in 2011, many researchers identified potential and actual ways that MOOCs could transform the university experience. Campus instructors who designed and taught MOOCs frequently found that the experience changed the way they taught their on-campus classes (Waldrop, 2013). Docq and Ella (2015) found that some university instructors who taught MOOCs, "evolve[d] from a focus on the content to be taught to a focus on the learning process of every student." Looking at more concrete outcomes, another research team found that instructors who taught MOOCs subsequently added more interactive learning experiences and scaffolded learning activities into their campus-based classes (Manturuk & Ruiz-Esparza, 2015).

In this chapter, we use a case study approach to explore how the lessons learned from the rapid shift to remote learning during the 2020 spring semester can be leveraged to inform and improve the on-campus teaching and learning experiences. In doing this, we hope to contribute to a nascent yet growing body of literature that views remote instruction not as inferior to in-person learning, but as a unique learning modality. This theoretical approach to remote learning facilitates drawing on lessons learned from all teaching modalities to improve pedagogy broadly conceived, regardless of the mode of delivery.

Theoretical Framework

Online instruction and its many forms, including hybrid courses and MOOCs, are viewed as innovations within higher education. Research shows that some faculty and some students are resistant to this innovation (Allen & Seaman, 2016). Rogers' (1995) Model of the Innovation-Decision Process suggests that various characteristics of a decision maker and their perceptions of an innovation influence whether a decision maker will adopt and implement an

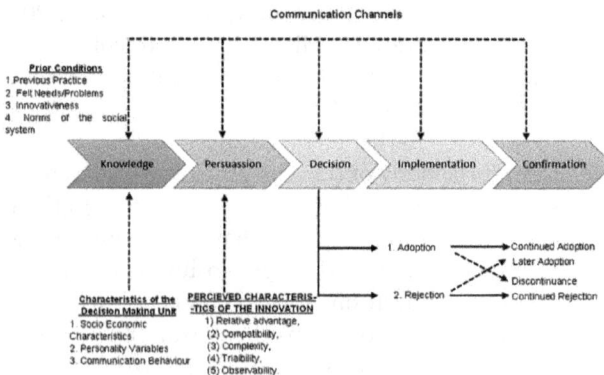

Figure 11.1 Model of the innovation-decision process.

innovation (see Figure 11.1). In the framework, a user moves from (1) having knowledge about an innovation, (2) to being persuaded that the innovation is an advantage, (3) to deciding to adopt or reject it, (4) to implementing it, and (5) lastly to confirming whether their decision to implement it should be continued (Rogers, 1995).

In the context of our case study at Duke, undergraduate learning was taking place in-person, and online learning was a rare occurrence; thus, many of the faculty and students at the universities may have had some knowledge about online learning, but few would have engaged in an innovation-decision process around online learning. However, a disruption to the traditional in-person course model occurred in spring 2020 when campuses were closed due to COVID-19. Suddenly, all faculty and students had to consider their perceptions of remote teaching and learning and decide how much to invest in its adoption and implementation. Anecdotally, we know that there were varying levels of faculty adoption and implementation of online learning tools and strategies during the second half of the spring semester. This case study seeks to understand how implementation took place and whether faculty were confirmed in their decision to implement those tools and strategies.

Method

We began hearing about new teaching practices emerging from remote learning through word-of-mouth during the spring and summer of 2020. Based on hearing these stories, we formalized a research study to access how these anecdotes are reflected in actual practice. Drawing on Merriam's (1998) method, we designed a bounded case, employed purposeful sampling, and iterative data collection and analysis. Our case study is bounded by the experience of teaching a face-to-face undergraduate course in spring 2020 and having to translate that class to an online format due to the COVID-19 campus closure. We collected data to build this case study by conducting semi-structured interviews with Duke Kunshan University and Duke University faculty members following the end of the spring 2020 semester. We recruited faculty members for this study by invitations sent through email to instructors who taught a course in spring 2020 and who had contact with either the Duke Kunshan Center for Teaching and Learning or Duke University Learning Innovation. We explained that we were looking to interview people who had identified ways that they planned to change how they taught in the future as a result of their remote teaching experience. In particular, we sought the perspectives of faculty who fully adopted and implemented online learning techniques in the second half of the spring semester and indicated that they may implement them in the future.

We conducted a total of 11 interviews over a 2-week period. Three of the participants were Duke Kunshan faculty, and eight participants were Duke University faculty, one of whom was teaching in a study abroad program during the spring semester. The participants included faculty from natural sciences, social sciences, and humanities, and faculty members at a wide range of academic ranks from junior professors of the practice to senior tenured professors. The interviews were semi-structured; all the interviews asked participants to share how they had changed their teaching during the remote instruction period and to describe what had worked well and what had not. Beyond that, the researchers followed the subject trajectories mentioned by the participants (Creswell, 2014).

After the interviews were completed, the interviews were transcribed verbatim. The researchers first coded the interviews and then compared notes, outlining the themes that had emerged. We created a spreadsheet listing each theme that came up during the interviews and added rows for sub-themes and examples of each one. Because this is a case study, we did not look only for commonalities across interviews. Rather, we were interested in finding the variety of experiences that instructors shared to gain as complete a picture as possible of the effective practices and pedagogies that had emerged from the remote teaching experience.

Participants

Our interview participants included instructors from a diverse range of disciplines including physical sciences (e.g., chemistry, biology), social sciences (e.g., statistics, public policy), humanities (e.g., languages, theater), and graduate/professional schools (e.g., law, medicine). We interviewed faculty members of different ranks (e.g., assistant professor, full professor, professor of the practice), some of whom were new to teaching and some who had several decades of experience. Most of the interview participants were teaching at their respective campuses when remote instruction began, but one person had been teaching abroad.

We note that our sample is not a representative sample of instructors at the two universities. The goal of a case study is to collect information from key informants who can describe different aspects of the case. For this research, we were specifically looking for instructors who had been teaching during the spring 2020 semester and who had to quickly switch to remote instruction. Within that large population, we used purposeful sampling to recruit instructors who had significantly changed how they taught in response to the pandemic (Creswell, 2014). We also used snowball sampling when participants mentioned colleagues that had shared similar experiences (Merriam, 1998).

Trustworthiness

To ensure trustworthiness in our research study, we first reflected on our own bias, especially because we both work with consultants and faculty through Duke Learning Innovation who have shared anecdotal experiences with us. In addition, one researcher taught a face-to-face undergraduate course at another university in spring 2020 that had to move online due to COVID-19 campus closure. To ensure that we did not allow our experiences to overly influence the data analysis, we used intercoder reliability as we coded interviews individually and then discussed themes together. We also asked a peer debriefer to review our results (Creswell, 2014)

Results

Throughout our interviews, we found that most participants found confirmation of their adoption and implementation of online tools and strategies. Three main themes emerged when we asked instructors to describe what they had learned from their remote teaching experiences. These were:

> *Pedagogical flexibility*: Remote teaching required instructors to be flexible in how they taught because students were learning from a wide variety of locations with different time zones, different access to the internet, and different physical spaces in which to work.
> *Expansive but Simple Communication*: Instructors had to explore new communication channels as regular face-to-face interaction with students was often not possible.
> *Authentic Assessment*: Most instructors quickly found proctored, multiple-choice exams to be impractical or even impossible in remote teaching, so they explored how to do assessment in new and often more authentic ways.

We will describe each of these in more detail below, followed by recommendations for how to implement the lessons learned from remote teaching into campus teaching.

Pedagogical Flexibility

When universities shifted to remote instruction, there was little advance warning. Students had to quickly leave campuses, and most, but not all, went home. Students were suddenly in learning environments with different time zones, inconsistent access to reliable high-speed internet, and often limited access to resources and quiet spaces. As a result, all the instructors we interviewed noted that simply moving their usual teaching practice to an online format was not possible. The instructors who felt their teaching was the most successful under these difficult circumstances were those that practiced pedagogical flexibility. Rather than trying to design a remote learning pedagogy that would work for every student, these instructors found success by meeting students where they were, with the resources they had. This generally meant giving students multiple ways to interact and learn new material, exploring new mediums for communication, and prioritizing student wellness.

Flipped Class Models

Almost all the instructors we interviewed quickly adopted a flipped class model of teaching, and they reported that students responded very well to this approach. Some instructors would pre-record lectures and then use synchronous class times for activities just as they would in a campus-based flipped class. Other instructors took pedagogical flexibility farther by recording short lecture videos during online class sessions and giving the students the option to attend class or watch the videos later. Some instructors also tried this for class activities—students who could attend a synchronous session participated in the activity and students who could not attend watched the activity later and did a similar activity on their own. Student feedback to this approach was favorable. Students really liked being able to listen to a lecture or participate in an activity during a live session, but then go back and re-watch the session later and take notes.

Student-Centered Deadlines

The instructors we interviewed generally did not make significant changes to their syllabi when they shifted to remote instruction. They kept the same assignments, projects, and assessments that they had planned for the campus classes. However, several of them noted the need to offer more flexibility in when those activities would happen. Because many students moved at least once and often more often during the remote instruction period, due dates became problematic. This was compounded by students not knowing in advance when they would have access to an internet connection or a quiet space in which to take a test or complete an assignment. Instructors found that they needed to offer students more flexibility in deadlines and due dates. One instructor noted, "I thought I was being flexible at the start by giving a day grace period…but as the semester went on, I had to extend that period." Instructors also talked about the importance of letting students communicate with them when they had extenuating circumstances that necessitated a change in a deadline. One described that "I guess one of the big adaptations I had to do was deadlines. Every deadline got spread and stretched to accommodate peoples' situations, which fluctuate much more widely when they are on campus."

Pedagogies of Care

Most instructors we interviewed talked about the importance of checking in with students to see how they were doing and find out if they needed any help connecting with university support resources. As several people noted, students could not be successful in learning if they were in crisis. The nature of the pandemic meant that some students experienced stress related to both physical and mental health, so checking in with students was critical. One faculty member described why adopting a pedagogy of care was a critical part of her ability to teach successfully:

> It's a real human problem. How do we make sure our students are feeling safe? How are we modeling kindness? And those aren't "bonus extras,"

actually. You know, the science tells us that when we are kind and the students feel cared for and as if they belong, the learning outcomes increase.

Expansive but Simple Communication

Throughout the remote instruction period, students received a lot of emails—official university updates, housing information, and notifications of new policy changes on a seemingly daily basis. Faculty members too quickly found that they were receiving many more emails than they could keep up with, and often by the time they read a message it was outdated. This "avalanche of emails" experience prompted several instructors to think about better and more effective ways they could communicate with, and get information from, their students.

The most universal communication success story we heard from instructors was the use of online chat tools as a way for students to interact and ask questions. Students overwhelmingly appreciated having the ability to ask a question during class by typing it into a chat window instead of having to speak in front of a room. Several instructors told us that the number of students who were actively engaged during class time increased when they had the opportunity to engage through online chat. This was an especially effective way to help students engage with guest speakers; students were less intimidated typing a question or comment to a guest speaker than they typically felt having a similar engagement face-to-face.

Other communication strategies that instructors shared with us that were effective during remote instruction included:

- Using online platforms for small group discussions was easier than trying to manage such discussions in a physical classroom where many discussions would be happening at the same time in the same space. One instructor shared that breakout discussions were richer because groups had more private spaces for conversation.
- Online office hours were very popular with students because they did not have to spend a significant amount of time traveling to a physical office to ask what they anticipated would be a quick question. Many faculty members saw office hours visits increase dramatically when they moved online.
- Short surveys were an effective way for instructors to take the pulse of a class and find out if a new approach or experiment was working or not. Students generally seemed comfortable giving honest feedback on short check-in surveys.

Authentic Assessment

Almost every instructor we interviewed shared that they had to re-think and redesign their course assessments. They quickly found that it simply was not feasible to administer traditional multiple-choice exams when teaching online. But other assessment plans were rendered impractical as well. For example, language faculty shared that inconsistent internet access among students made it impossible for students to be assessed on their conversational skills the way they would be in an in-person class session. A public policy faculty member shared that the primary summative assessment in their course was a group presentation to the class, something that would be difficult to impossible under the circumstances. Instead, the instructor had students record presentations. Then the instructor, along with other students, watched them and gave feedback. This approach allowed for a more thoughtful assessment of the presentation, and better feedback, because reviewers could watch the presentation more than once instead of having to rely only on their notes to write feedback.

As instructors re-designed their assessments, many shared that the process pushed them to think more critically about how and why they were evaluating student learning. Having to create new assessments led one faculty member to go back to the learning objectives and make sure the assessments were closely aligned with the course content. During the interview, they said, "So the first thing that I do is to strip this down to the learning objectives. What do I want them to know how to do a year from now?" They went on to describe how they developed assessments that evaluated students on their ability to perform those tasks, not their ability to recall facts and details. Another instructor described this process as "shifting from 'what' questions to 'why' questions."

Finally, instructors shared experiences of giving student teams more autonomy over how they were evaluated. In a particularly striking example, one instructor shared that she gave small groups of students leeway to decide as a team what types of artifacts they wanted to create at the end of the semester to demonstrate their learning. She was impressed by the quality of work that students produced, telling us,

> [the final projects] were amazing. There were teams that created videos and teams that created podcasts and teams that created zines and comic books. So that showed us that the students were appreciative of having the opportunity to connect with their peers.

Discussion and Conclusions

The abrupt switch to remote instruction, and the limitations associated with that, pushed many faculty instructors to implement new ways of teaching, communicating, and assessing learning. In institutions with very high levels of research activity, such as Duke University, many faculty have not experienced formalized pedagogical training and may not receive recognition for their efforts to improve their pedagogical practice. All but one of our participants had contact with a teaching and learning center either at Duke Kunshan University or Duke University, but we do not know the extent to which they engaged with those centers around pedagogical or technological innovations. We do know that they had to reconsider their course delivery and assessments to finish the semester successfully. To accomplish this task, they had to implement online learning.

While implementing these changes in the midst of the pandemic was difficult, some of those changes represented improvements that instructors can bring back to campus when in-person instruction resumes. Remote instruction highlighted the importance of flexibility and student-centered pedagogies that allow students to be active participants in identifying when and where they can best learn. New communication channels, especially online chats, and web-based meetings helped introverted students feel more comfortable asking questions and interacting, leading to more engagement during class time and office hours. When proctored, multiple-choice exams were not an option, instructors found that authentic assessments that emphasized applying knowledge to create artifacts or solve problems were more rewarding for both themselves and their students.

There were also some important lessons learned from strategies that did not work out well during remote instruction. Almost every instructor we interviewed had a story about some technology failing or some activity just not working out online. One of the requests that several instructors raised along these lines was that they should have all their students appear on video during synchronous class sessions. This generally emerged from a desire to see students' faces and respond to their body language, but an unintended consequence was that this requirement highlighted socioeconomic inequality among students within a class. One instructor who experienced this said:

> You know there are a lot of students who families are economically well off. But then there are also students who are here on financial aid and will never talk about the realities of their family life. But, you know, Zoom brings us into one another's homes and some homes are really beautiful and lavish and other homes are very simple. And, you know, just the insecurities about revealing one's private space to a world of people on a Zoom call...[that is] something I tried, you know, I want to be sensitive to.

While we know that socioeconomic inequality exists, bring a class into students' homes changed that from an abstract concept to something that was a visible part of a learning experience. By highlighting this, remote instruction has led to a new conversation on the two campuses involved in this case study about how to minimize visible signs of inequality and be more sensitive to, and aware of, the experiences of lower-income students.

Our results further confirm that innovative pedagogical strategies, such as active learning, are valuable, and understanding those strategies is an asset in times of disruption. When faculty had better perceptions of these innovative strategies and had at least considered adopting them in the past, they were better prepared to implement them in this crisis. Further, when implemented effectively, these strategies proved themselves effective enough to be adopted for further use even when classes return to an in-person format.

Implications

Remote teaching during the pandemic was the catalyst for many positive changes in how university instruction happened at Duke Kunshan University and Duke University. Some instructors used the disruption to finally implement innovations that they wanted to adopt. Every instructor we interviewed shared at least one change they made during the spring 2020 semester that they plan to incorporate in their usual teaching practice in the future. One instructor who tried a flipped class pedagogy for the first time, summarized this by saying, "[I] always wanted to do this; [last semester] I was forced to do this, and I will do it in the future."

In conclusion, based on our case study of successful remote teaching at two campuses, we present the following recommended practices to create a more flexible and resilient learning environment for students:

1. Be pedagogically flexible: provide your course content through several different channels and in several different formats. This creates ways for students to remain engaged with a class even if they experience an unexpected absence and gives instructors that opportunity as well.
2. Make communication simple: give students lots of different ways to talk to you, from one-on-one meetings and online office hours to short chat messages and feedback surveys. Students who feel comfortable with a communication medium are more likely to use it.
3. Assess students authentically: create assessments that allow students to demonstrate their knowledge, skills, and abilities in ways that are relevant to them.

Beyond these evidence-based practice recommendations, we propose that researchers move away from frameworks that implicitly prioritize in-person modes of instruction as normative or optimal. Most pedagogical studies of remote instruction have emphasized exploring ways to improve the online learning experience, often by applying principles and practices from in-person teaching. This case study suggests that while this approach has merit, there is also much to be gained by exploring ways in which pedagogies native to remote instruction can improve the in-person learning experience. While this case study was exploratory in nature, we hope that future research will continue this productive approach and further explore how remote learning pedagogies can improve campus-based learning.

We cannot know whether we will ever face another pandemic as we did in the spring of 2020. However, there is a good chance that some of our universities will face unexpected events or changes that will require rapid changes in how and where we teach. Adopting flexible pedagogies, multi-channel communications, and authentic assessments now can make it much easier to be responsive to unexpected changes in the future. These practices can also create more student-centered learning experiences on campuses in general.

References

Allen, I. E., & Seaman, J. (2016). *Online report card: Tracking online education in the United States.* Babson Survey Group.

Arend, B. D. (2007). Course assessment practices and student learning strategies in online courses. *Journal of Asynchronous Learning Networks, 11*(4), 3–17. http://dx.doi.org/10.24059/olj.v11i4.1712

Barber, W., King, S., & Buchanan, S. (2015). Problem based learning and authentic assessment in digital pedagogy: Embracing the role of collaborative communities. *Electronic Journal of e-Learning, 13*(2), 59–67. https://files.eric.ed.gov/fulltext/EJ1060176.pdf

Creswell, J. W. (2014). *Research design: Qualitative, quantitative, and mixed methods approaches.* Sage.

Darby, F., & Lang, J. M. (2019). *Small teaching online: Applying learning science in online classes.* Jossey-Bass.

Dennen, V. P., Aubteen Darabi, A., & Smith, L. J. (2007). Instructor–learner interaction in online courses: The relative perceived importance of particular instructor actions on performance and satisfaction. *Distance Education, 28*(1), 65–79. https://doi.org/10.1080/01587910701305319

Dixson, M. D. (2010). Creating effective student engagement in online courses: What do students find engaging?. *Journal of the Scholarship of Teaching and Learning,* 1–13. https://www.learntechlib.org/p/54817/

Docq, F., & Ella, H. (2015). Why make MOOCs? Effects on on-campus teaching and learning. Experience track: Proceedings of the European MOOC Stakeholder Summit, 18–20. https://hdl.handle.net/2078.1/159530

Freeman, S., Eddy, S. L., McDonough, M., Smith, M. K., Okoroafor, N., Jordt, H., & Wenderoth, M. P. (2014). Active learning increases student performance in science, engineering, and mathematics. *Proceedings of the National Academy of Sciences - PNAS, 111*(23), 8410–8415. https://doi.org/10.1073/pnas.1319030111

Gayton, J., & McEwen, B. C. (2007). Effective online instructional and assessment strategies. *The American Journal of Distance Education, 21*(3), 117–132. https://doi.org/10.1080/08923640701341653

Maki, R. H., & Maki, W. S. (2007). Online courses. In F. T. Durso (Ed.), *Handbook of applied cognition* (2nd ed., pp. 527–552). Wiley & Sons, Ltd.

Manturuk, K., & Ruiz-Esparza, Q. M. (2015). On-campus impacts of MOOCs at Duke University. *EDUCAUSE Review.* https://er.educause.edu/articles/2015/8/on-campus-impacts-of-moocs-at- duke-university

McDonald, S. (2004). Sunrise semester: Distance learning before the Internet. The Back Table. Archives and Special Collections at New York University. https://wp.nyu.edu/specialcollections/2014/05/13/sunrise-semester- distance-learning-before-the-Internet/

Merriam, S. B. (1998). *Qualitative research and case study application in education* (2nd ed.). Jossey-Bass Publishers.

Phillips, J. M. (2005). Strategies for active learning in online continuing education. *The Journal of Continuing Education in Nursing, 36*(2), 77–83. https://doi.org/10.3928/0022-0124-20050301-08

Platt, C. A., Amber, N. W., & Yu, N. (2014). Virtually the same?: Student perceptions of the equivalence of online classes to face-to-face classes. *Journal of Online Learning and Teaching, 10*(3), 489. https://jolt.merlot.org/vol10no3/Platt_0914.pdf

Robinson, C. C., & Hullinger, H. (2008). New benchmarks in higher education: Student engagement in online learning. *Journal of Education for Business, 84*(2), 101–109. https://doi.org/10.3200/joeb.84.2.101-109

Rogers, E. M. (1995). *Diffusion of innovation* (4th ed.). The Free Press.

Waldrop, M. M. (2013). Campus 2.0. *Nature, 495*(7440), 160. https://www.nature.com/news/online-learning-campus-2-0-1.12590

Bios

Kim Manturuk, Ph.D., is the Associate Director of Research, Evaluation, and Development in Learning Innovation at Duke University. Her research interests include survey design, higher education evaluation, and teaching and learning in the postsecondary classroom. E-mail: kim.manturuk@duke.edu

Grey Reavis, M.A., is the Research Project Coordinator in Learning Innovation at Duke University and pursuing a Ph.D. in Higher Education at North Carolina State University. Their research interests include critical quantitative methods, identity in the classroom, and LGBTQ+ communities in higher education.

12 International Students in Times of Corona in the United States

A Duoethnography of Foreignness

Wu Xie and Musbah Shaheen

Abstract

The COVID-19 pandemic has become a representation of different countries and cultures. In the U.S., it seemed to assert American elitism and white supremacy. The "go back to your country" trope became rampant, and Asians in the U.S. scrambled to ensure their health and safety both from the virus and from the social response it unleashed. Higher education was profoundly affected by COVID-19 and associated challenges. This volume has likely addressed the educational, financial, and political ramifications of COVID-19 on higher education. However, missing from the conversation are stories representing experiences of internationals. This chapter is a duoethnography about foreignness, demonstrating how COVID-19 in the U.S. perpetuated a postcolonial ideology that impacts the experiences of those deemed foreign by western standards. We use our lived experiences and narrative to illustrate how COVID-19 did not create this sense of foreignness, but intensified its presence and effects.

Keywords

international students; belonging; foreignness; duoethnography; postcolonialism; neo-racism

Introduction

As the Coronavirus and associated COVID-19 spread globally, the world went into a frenzy. The pandemic, and the response to it, have become cultural phenomena (Mansouri, 2020) not only because COVID-19 inspired a plethora of online memes (Romano, 2020) but also because it became a representation of different countries and cultures. In the U.S., it asserted American elitism, especially in its earlier stages; outrage was directed towards China, first for their lack of immediate response (Kuo, 2020), then for what was seen as excessive Draconian measures to curb the spread (Page, 2020). Stories of discrimination, harassment, and violence towards Asians emerged in the media (Zho, 2020). The "go back to your country" trope became rampant (Escobar, 2020), and Asians in the U.S. scrambled to ensure their health and safety both from the virus and from the social response it unleashed.

Higher education was profoundly affected by COVID-19 and associated challenges. Students departed, demanding tuition refunds, and questioning their return in the fall (Dickler, 2020). Many colleges and universities are struggling financially and facing the possibility of closure, merger, or bankruptcy (Carey, 2020). This volume has likely addressed the educational, financial, and political ramifications of COVID-19 on higher education. However, missing from the conversation are stories representing experiences of internationals. As a cultural artifact, COVID-19 resulted in two phenomena. The first is hostility towards those who appeared Asian, including and mainly international students—this includes the numerous news stories about anti-Asian prejudice. The second phenomenon is harder to pinpoint: the pandemic and the response to it from individuals, groups, and governments were tools for western elitism to reassert its dominance, reminding all of us internationals in the U.S. that we are foreign. This chapter is a duoethnography about foreignness. It is about being colonized and pushed into western ways of thought. Our goal is to demonstrate how COVID-19 in the U.S. perpetuated a postcolonial ideology that has impacted and will continue to impact the experiences of those deemed foreign by western standards. COVID-19 did not create this sense of foreignness. It did, however, intensify its presence and effects.

Analytical Framework

Because of the personal nature of this duoethnography, we were intentional about how we approached the data to uncover new insights of which we may not have been aware. For that purpose, we adopted postcolonialism and neo-racism as analytical frameworks. The development of postcolonial studies is largely attributed to the work of Edward Said on Orientalism, a construct premised on positioning a "fundamentally ontological and epistemological distinction...between 'the orient' and 'the occident'" (Said, 1978, p. 2). Orientalism creates and authorizes a dichotomous distinction between being Occident and of being Orient leading to the enactment of hierarchical binaries of civilized/savage, rational/nonrational, developed/undeveloped (Prasad, 1997; Said, 1978). This conceptual maneuver justifies western colonialism as a moral obligation to civilize inferior non-westerners and essentializes the dominance of western thoughts. Occidentalism becomes the ambivalent production of "that otherness which is at once an object of desire and derision" (Bhabha, 1994, p. 67). Although western entities perceive the East as inferior and undesirable, westerners simultaneously desire Easterners' knowledge without allowing them to tell their own stories (Bhabha, 1994; Spivak, 1988). Further, esterners tell stories about the East that do not represent Eastern historical truths (Said, 1978). Centering and elevating the west as the default encourages mimicry of their western colonizers: "*almost the same, but not quite... almost the same, but not white"* (Bhabha, 1994, p. 89, italics in the original).

Postcolonialism deconstructs western hegemony that subjugates the colonized economically, culturally, and ideologically (Christophers, 2007; Iwowo, 2014) and actively disrupts the Occident/Orient unbalanced binary. Postcolonialism for analyzing the data in this project meant that we asked the data fundamental epistemological and ontological questions to make meaning out of the lived narratives, bringing the duality of East and west to the forefront, leading us to question whether the way we interpret a phenomenon is entrenched in western-washed colonial remnants that make Eastern realities— our realities—inapplicable and irrelevant. Postcolonialism allowed us to go back in our analysis to the basics: why do we believe what we believe?

Racism in contemporary society is racism without races (Balibar, 2007; Balibar & Wallerstein, 1991). The definition of race itself varies based on the perspective of a particular discipline. Biologists, for example, often approach race from an essentialist perspective, making race fixed and attributed to physical phenotype, while Social scientists and researchers adopt a socially constructed definition of race that foregrounds the ways in which people make meaning of race and interact within and across racial categories (Hochman, 2021; Wagner et al., 2017). Racism, thus, holds numerous meanings as to how it is experienced, observed, and perpetuated (Banton, 2015). Globally, the connection between race/racism and culture/multiculturalism is one that has been increasingly highlighted (Modood, 2011), suggesting that elements beyond observed characteristics and interactions construct interactions across races (Modood, 1997, 2005a, 2005b). The overarching theme of *neo*-racism is no longer based on biological differences, but on nationality, language, and culture (Balibar, 2007; Lee & Rice, 2007). The underlying principle of the utility of "culture" is Janus-faced flexibility: the universality of culture can be deployed as a signifier for inclusion, while at the same time cultural difference can get escalated to the point of irreconcilable divergence, setting solid grounds for separation, discrimination, and exclusion (Rangan & Chow, 2016).

In the contemporary political climate of the U.S., a combination of multiculturalism and ethnic foundationalism has been on the rise during the last decade. Specifically, there has been a tendency to replace the term "race" with aspects of cultural diversity such as nationality, cultural heritage, language, lifestyle, behavior, and more, as a way of avoiding "race" and its biological and eugenic connotations (Balibar, 2007). However, the utility of cultural diversity provides racism with highly generative, sophisticated, and flexible new forms to persist in contemporary society. Seeing how neo-racism may be implicated in the study of foreignness allows us in our analysis to break the artificial boundaries of race, ethnicity, nationality, and culture. In a neo-racism framework, one does not need to be of the dominant race (i.e., white) to display prejudice against others and to hold others to the westernized standards of being and knowing. A neo-racism perspective allows us to analyze the data outside of biological and phenotypic manifestations of race, to broaden our awareness as racialized, cultured, and internationalized beings. The combination of postcolonialism and neo-racism provides an opportunity to look at racial, ethnic, and cultural experiences through a lens that is not western-centric, but that acknowledges the role that systemic manifestations of western dominance motivate our views of culture vis-à-vis experiences of foreignness triggered by a large-scale global event.

Literature Review

Institutions of higher education in the U.S. have increased their efforts to recruit international students as part of an overall move towards globalization in higher education. The Institute for International Education (IIE) indicates that over 1 million international students studied in the U.S. in the 2019–2020 academic year (5.5% of total enrollment; IIE, 2017, 2020). Although the COVID-19 pandemic coincided with a 1.8% decrease in international student numbers, it remains larger than that recorded in the 2016–2017 academic year. The overwhelming field of study for international students was science, technology, engineering, and math in 2019, followed by business and management and the social sciences. The international student population is a growing demographic despite the restrictions that have been imposed on international travel and education. In 2020, the top three places of origin for international students were China (34.7% of total), India (10.9%), and South Korea (5.7% of total). In the past three years, institutions have witnessed a decline in new international student enrollment due to obstacles related to procuring visas, and competition from other countries such as Canada, China, and Australia (NAFSA, 2020; Redden, 2018, 2019), not to mention shifts in the sociopolitical climate in the U.S. which presented anti-immigration rhetoric and policies under the Trump administration (Burmila, 2019; Dreid, 2016; Patel, 2018). And yet, the U.S. has historically hosted the largest proportion of global students. In 2016, a report from IIE indicates that the majority of students who study abroad globally come to the U.S. (25%) followed by the United Kingdom (12%), China (10%), France (8%), Australia (7%), Russia (7%), Canada (6%), and Germany (6%). As for U.S. students, in 2018–2019, it was estimated that over 347 thousand U.S. students studied abroad, the majority of whom studied in Europe (193,422), Latin America and the Caribbean (47,954), and Asia (40,602). The top nation destinations for U.S. students studying abroad are the United Kingdom, Italy, Spain, Mexico, and France. The majority of these students are white (69% in 2019) followed by Hispanics (11%), Asians (9%), and Black or Africa American (6.4%).

A substantial body of literature pertaining to international students in American postsecondary institutions has historically emphasized the various perceived deficits that international students face as they adapt to social and academic life, often neglecting the resilience, motivation, and capability of this pool of students (de Wit, 2020; Shaheen, 2019). Regardless of the perspective on the source and perpetuating factors, the reality remains that international students face difficulties in classroom curricular, co-curricular, and social engagement. For example, faculty often misunderstand and misinterpret the engagement in classroom settings of international students, attributing silence as a sign of disinterest and incompetence when it might stem from a difference in cultural attitudes towards student-teacher interactions (Bjork et al., 2020; Wekullo, 2019). International students—particularly those from Asian and Middle Eastern countries—face an unwelcoming college campus climate marked by well-documented hostility and discrimination (e.g., Azim & Happel-Parkins, 2019; Quinton, 2019; Yeo et al., 2019). It is important to note that "international student" is a legally defined category of students who are not U.S. citizens or permanent residents (NAFSA, 2020), and yet international students hold multiple social identities that color their experiences. Notably, the top countries from which international students hail (China, India, and South Korea) are not majority-white nations. (Hackett et al., 2015; IIE, 2020). When international students express opinions that differ from mainstream white cultural beliefs, U.S. nationals sometimes perceive the American sociocultural system to be under threat (Suspitsyna & Shalka, 2019). The state of international students in the U.S. is related to dominant social systems, motivated by racism and xenophobia.

Research Method

Duoethnography is a research methodology in which two authors use their experiences to explore and explain a shared phenomenon (Norris & Sawyer, 2012). In a duoethnography, the researchers are equal partners. They become the subjects and instruments. Their narratives become data (Breault, 2016). We chose duoethnography to legitimize storytelling as a way of understanding social issues. We have felt stifled—our stories were viewed as "too unique" or "ungeneralizable." Our ways of thinking have been uninvited in classrooms, our peers and professors have micro-aggressed us, and we have felt foreign. It is our shared sense of foreignness that brought this duoethnography together. Duoethnograpahy uses our similarities and differences to make more significant meaning, broader than a single autoethnography could. Therefore, duoethnography needs to be conducted intentionally and responsibly (Ashlee & Quaye, 2020; Breault, 2016).

Our methodological design was based on the tenets defined by Norris and Sawyer (2012), as well as previous scholars who used duoethnography in the higher education setting (e.g., Ashlee & Quaye, 2020; Hummel & Toyosaki, 2015; Snipes & LePeau, 2017). Duoethnography is dialogical where "the voices of each researcher are made explicit throughout the narrative" (Breault, 2016, p. 778), resisting metanarratives—the assumption that there is a single version of someone's story (Norris & Sawyer, 2012), and prioritizing differences. Duoethnography relies on telling and retelling stories while resisting supporting a universal truth (Ashlee & Quaye, 2020; Breault, 2016; Norris & Sawyer, 2012). In our data collection, analysis, and presentation, we ensured that both our voices occupy adequate space and time. The narrative is not just the stories we share about ourselves but also how we responded to each other. We looked for points of connection and reflected on points of departure. Our stories are presented in their raw forms to demonstrate the messiness of our experiences. Most importantly, duoethnography requires trust. We could not have completed this project without trusting each other with our stories, our time, and our deepest thoughts.

Data Collection and Analysis

During our first meeting about this project, we talked via Zoom about our vision for this work, the frameworks we want to use, and our hopes and fears going into the research process. Following Ashlee and Quaye's (2020) example, we each wrote narrative responses to two questions: (1) What does it mean to be Chinese or Syrian in the U.S.? and (2) do I belong here? We kept the questions broad to capture different ways of reflecting and writing, Musbah being more narrative and Wu more analytical. We read each other's narratives and made written comments before the second meeting. During the second Zoom meeting, we reflected on the process of writing and asked clarifying questions. We began to recognize and discuss commonalities and differences that emerged. After the second meeting, we read the transcripts and/or listened to the audio while taking notes and jottings to capture our immediate reactions (See Jones et al., 2014). We then came up with shared ideas that stood out in the data that included feelings we experienced (e.g., sadness, anger, and frustration), incidents we encountered (e.g., microaggressions, discrimination, and hostility), and memories we shared (e.g., interactions we had before the pandemic). These shared ideas functioned as open codes (See Corbin and Strauss, 2008) which we then continued to refine by reading and re-reading the transcripts. We repeated this process one more time by reading the transcripts (or listening to the audio) and refining our thematic findings. In the next meeting, our goal was to distill our open codes into thematic clusters which became the three themes we present below. The themes revolved around the personal implications of the COVID-19 pandemic, the political violence that accompanied the pandemic and its development, and the omnipresent nature of prejudice that we encountered long before the pandemic started.

The duoethnographic approach was iterative—we allowed our stories, thoughts, and reflections to guide the conversations, which strengthened our mutual trust. Adhering to the tenets of duoethnography, we maintained the connection with the central phenomenon, that is feelings of foreignness in times of COVID-19. It was perhaps the most challenging aspect of data collection and analysis. We both know much about foreignness as something we have experienced our entire lives. Nevertheless, we needed to focus on this particular historical moment. This methodology was useful because it allowed us to start with feelings we know we felt during the pandemic but were not sure what they meant. As a result, we emerged from the data collection analysis with a deeper understanding of ourselves and the world around us. Before we present the findings of the analysis, we want to share with the reader excerpts from our written reflections.

Narratives

Do I belong in Syria? Do I belong in the U.S.? Do I belong to the Academy? Belonging feels so amorphous and unquantifiable. If I say that I feel that I belong in the U.S., does that mean I have the right to claim the benefits of being in the U.S.? When I start to feel like "I belong," the fact remains that, technically, I don't. What good is it to feel belonging if I am at risk of being hauled back on a plane at any given moment? I am not American, but there is something about this place that draws me. Something compels me to be here. Typically, one of the first remarks that people make is: "wow your English is so good! You don't even have an accent!" It doesn't bother me that much—having an accent is not a bad thing. But people expect people like me to sound different. How could it be that I speak perfect English? They often ask if we spoke English at home, which we didn't. My story with the language has everything to do with belonging. I wanted to be prepared not only to succeed in the U.S. but also to blend in. This blending in is the biggest mind (expletive). To me, part of belonging is not being seen as foreign, to blend in. But people will always see me as foreign. My immigration status becomes a form of "small talk" in gatherings. I ask myself, what is the threshold of years required for one to be considered equal to those who were born here? Being born somewhere else is beyond my control. That can never change. Therefore, I will never be enough. Enoughness seems to mean being purely and unequivocally American. I feel trapped between a Syria that would not recognize me and an America that will forever see me as foreign

—Musbah

I am from China. I position myself at an in-between angle, influenced by the amalgamation of Confucianism and western culture. I am a transnational individual who has felt at home in Oregon, the States, and Hefei, China. I am here, pursuing a Ph.D. degree in Higher Education and Student Affairs at Ohio State for a reason, that is social justice. However, the question of "Do I really belong here?" has constantly been hovering over me since the very beginning. By here, I mean any spaces in the States, including classrooms, offices, local communities. The responses to the questions might be full of ambiguity or merely negative. It seems self-contradictory by saying that I feel a sense of being at home in Oregon while articulating a sense of alienation wherever I am. The reason is that I am always reminded that I am a foreigner; I don't belong to any spaces that are supposed to belong to Americans and other white international students. After having a glance at me entering a space, some people instantly and subconsciously treat me with a certain attitude, manifested in eye contacts, speech patterns, and physical distances they keep from me. When I disrupt westerners' imagination for Chinese people influenced by the U.S. propaganda, living my life in an 'assertive' way and being very vocal about my opinions, which western society values, I evoke criticism for not conforming to westerners' stereotypical images of Chinese women as feminine and submissive. A more explicit manifestation of the reminder that I don't belong is indicated in an insensitive statement from a white woman, "Where did you live in China? You need to find your roots," following my expression of feelings of belonging to Oregon. So, being a Chinese woman in the States means that living my life can evoke irrational contempt and hatred, and that my feelings are subject to be defined by privileged American people.

—Wu

Findings

The data we collected in our duoethnography through written narratives and recorded discussions demonstrated that our experiences as international students before and amidst the COVID-19 pandemic are similar yet very divergent based on our other identities and experiences. Musbah, a Middle Eastern man in his late twenties, and Wu, a Chinese woman in her thirties. In the data emerged three thematic findings. First, COVID-19 and the response to it from government, groups, and individuals personally affected us in different ways. Second, we saw COVID-19 as a means of enacting a xenophobic social and political agenda. Third, our experience of the pandemic did not surprise us but was a reflection of broader issues we saw and experienced.

COVID-19 and the Response to It Are Personal

COVID-19 affected everyone who fell ill, lost loved ones, or lost a job. For us, the pandemic had deep emotional and personal connotations that extended to our presence in the U.S. and experiences as internationals. Wu, in particular, felt more on edge in public. She said, "I try my best not to go out during this time as I am fearful of any potential harassment I might encounter once I show up in public spaces." Even when doing something as simple and mundane as buying groceries, Wu felt the need "not to speak in Chinese and not to let people figure out my nationality based on accent." Musbah did not describe similar anxiety. During our discussions, Musbah reflected on how Wu's Chinese background was particularly salient in this example, while Musbah "felt off the hook" when navigating a public space because his presence did not feel like a risk to onlookers. In response to Wu's story, Musbah said

> When people look at me, they see foreign, but in this instance, they see the *right* type of foreigner… For Wu, it seemed like, in times of COVID-19 she felt like a target. We have the same citizenship status… But she is an Asian woman, and I am a White-passing man. That makes a huge difference.

COVID-19 pandemic also affected Wu's connection with the Chinese community, the same community she had felt isolated from. Wu talked about how the Chinese student community banded together using an "emergency support group on WeChat" the purpose of which was to share urgent information. The group's creators included this guidance, "In a state of emergency, please call 911 first and then share location to the group chat so that any group members are aware of the occurrence of an emergency and get to the location. Let's stick together!."

In making sense of how this group brought Wu a sense of solidarity with the Chinese community, Wu realized that "when encountering racist, xenophobic harassment, violence, we cannot fully rely on schools, police, or any other authorities and the safe way to protect ourselves is to band together and rely on one another." Both of us had felt foreign before the context of COVID-19, both within our communities and with the larger American society. Nevertheless, the pandemic intensified and morphed our feelings of lack of belonging differently based on our national, racial, and ethnic identities.

Waves of Political Violence amidst COVID-19

The omnipresence of xenophobic attitudes could be seen in political responses to the pandemic and its ramifications. For example, soon after the pandemic outbreak, the Trump administration issued the Proclamation on the Suspension of Entry as Nonimmigrants of Certain Students and Researchers from the People's Republic of China. For Wu, this proclamation

> pulled me into an anxiety whirl where I know I am viewed by U.S. society as outsiders and as not rightfully belonging. Being a Chinese person in the States at this time means that our lives can be recklessly discarded.

For Wu, references to COVID-19 as the China virus by government officials, choosing to halt travels from China and not Europe even when Europe was showing more severe infection rates, demonizing the Chinese government for its response to the pandemic as unnecessarily draconian, and announcing the Proclamation collectively were:

> a striking mirror of … history in the late 19th century and early 20th century, where Chinese people in the States were treated as medical scapegoats and discriminatory laws were designed to expel those already in the States and to discourage other Chinese people from immigrating to the States…Being a Chinese person in the States one hundred years ago meant that they were held responsible for any mishaps in general as a result of being perceived as a filthy menace to white civility.

Musbah, who was unaware of many of the things that Wu shared about the history of discrimination against Chinese people, expressed a sense of guilt reflecting that "if I really cared about solidarity, I would have known this happened. Because I am not from China, I think this isn't a priority. That's why I feel guilty. I don't do what I preach." Our dialogue was crucial for unpacking the power dynamic that exists between us due to the identities we hold. Yet, our mutual rapport allowed us to be honest and reflective. In response to Musbah's feelings of guilt, Wu said, "you were not aware of how personal it can get for Asians, especially for Chinese people when it comes to this pandemic...This made me think about the meaning of voicing my narrative and challenging systemic issues in higher education."

Further, regulations from Immigration and Customs Enforcement (ICE), which revoked visas for international students if their campuses went to an entirely online format, enraged us. Musbah exclaimed, "it makes zero sense... no sense at all to send international students back. Like, they're not working or taking money. We would sit on our asses and eat pizza and spend money. I don't understand." Wu concurred but noted that "this shouldn't be just about economic benefit" and that threatening to send students home impacts their sense of worthiness and belonging. Wu commented that "things weren't that much better before" and that "ICE regulations mirror previous neglect of international students."

From the initial conversations about the effect that COVID-19 had on us, we knew that the pandemic came as a new tool utilized to exclude and stigmatize internationals. In Musbah's words, "when COVID-19 ends, the problem is not going to end. It is just going to look different." and "the powers that be will always find ways to exclude people who aren't American and aren't white. Before it was the Arabs and Muslims, then it was Mexicans. Now it's Asians' turn again." We were frustrated and angered by living through another example of pervasive xenophobia in the U.S. political and social contexts.

COVID-19 Speaks to Modern Western Colonial Relations and Neo-racism

The events occurring in response to the pandemic, including ICE policy, and the Proclamation, are not isolated events. As Wu asserted, "It's not new. I'm not surprised. You're not surprised. The systemic issues are so embedded and so prevalent for a long time." Before COVID, we had experienced these dynamics of postcolonial thought and neo-racism. We firmly believed that COVID-19 revealed, exposed, and intensified systemic oppression that existed before the pandemic. Many things had just been insidiously hidden.

Americans have been intensely interested in knowing us as one from China and one from Syria. Musbah narrated, "the most intriguing thing about me is from Syria." Similarly, Wu recalled being asked, "do women in China marry someone totally because of money?" in a restroom during class break time and being asked, "Do Chinese people tend to burp in public?" during a project meeting. It is likely that coveting mainstream approval leads to

Wu's complicated relationship with the community of Chinese international students. Wu "was sometimes struggling with finding a fit in my own community—Chinese international students' community." Musbah had a similar experience as he emphatically responded by saying: "I avoid Syrian people like the plague...the people who hold the keys to the culture like food and stuff would probably not like how I think or who I am."

Two years of working and studying in the States made Wu aware of the fact that "no matter how hard I attempted to run away from being seen as one that reflects the Chinese image, regardless, westerners would label me as a forever inferior foreigner." Wu has since then started decolonizing her mind by giving constant attention to the processes in which Americans attempt to colonize the "Orient." She pointedly asserted that

> What has been so intriguing to witness all the time is the fact that people (in most cases, by people, I'm referring to white Americans) can quickly and tacitly find a way to mitigate their internal dissensions and develop a united identity to confront me who is deemed as an inferior threat or peril to their privileged body and mind.

Seeing an undercurrent of discrimination and othering veiled in multicultural America, Musbah shared a similar sentiment, "there would always be someone who would delegitimize my belonging as a function of my background and citizenship status. White America's obsession with White America will never grant me belonging even if it ever grants me citizenship."

Reflective of how westerners (Americans in this instance) enact insidiously emotional violence against us as international students, who are forever "Other" is the striking statements that Wu and Musbah heard. Wu heard from a white woman, "Where is your hometown in China? You need to find your roots," following Wu's expression of feelings belonging to Oregon. In a similar vein, following Musbah's opinions about politics and election in the U.S., a white man responded, "as one born here, I actually know how this works." Consequentially, being non-white international students in the States means that westerners define our feelings and label our pursuit belonging in the States as illegitimate and thus denied by Americans.

Discussion

We conducted this duoethnography in the midst of the pandemic. Everything around us was changing and evolving rapidly; it was challenging to keep up. For example, the changes in ICE policies on international students were announced halfway through our data collection efforts. We needed to discuss that policy, which shifted our entire meaning-making process. The goal of this duoethnography is not to have recorded chit-chats, but to arrive at a better understanding of ourselves and of the world as it converged around COVID-19. By the time our words are likely in ink, more and more have already changed.

This duoethnography speaks to the force of the systems of power that surround us on a large scale. Following a duoethnographic approach, we learned from each other's differences and bonded over our similarities. We challenged each other's perspectives with empathy to illuminate a web of social relations characterized by race, class, gender, and power in the U.S.

Our experiences demonstrate how westerner's perceive us as both subjects of knowledge, be it for entertainment or serious eagerness to understand the "other," and objects of derision, a duality that is prevalent in postcolonial thought (Bhabha, 1994). Our attempts to belong – to be less foreign – like Musbah's desire to blend in, and Wu's efforts to disguise the marks of her Chinese culture, led us to an important realization: no matter what, Americans will forever label us as inferior foreigners. It is what Bhabha (1994) describes as "*almost the same but not quite…almost the same but not white*" (p. 89, italics in the original). Besides, the ontological difference between us and the community surrounding us prompts westerners to feel obligated to remind us that, we are inferior not just in terms of nationality but also our forms of knowledge (Prasad, 1997; Said, 1978) and that they, westerners, have every right to tell stories about everyone (Bhabha, 1994; Spivak, 1988), including international students whom they do not possess direct experience or knowledge.

Westerners feel entitled to represent us to tell our stories sometimes as a way of advancing in academic careers while the genuine dedication to trying not to see us as "other" is missing from their work. What is even more irritating is that our real-life stories are misrepresented and distorted in narratives emerging from a bevy of settings, including the workplace, personal life, popular media resources, and academia, which accurately speaks to what the seminal scholar in postcolonialism Said (1978) has to say regarding the fact that the stories westerners tell about us as easterners do not represent actual histories or life.

It is our cultures, not our skin color (Balibar, 2007; Balibar & Wallerstein, 1991) that legitimize the reality of exclusion we experience. The rationale is that after all, how we are treated does not stem from our biological differences but instead from cultural differences—nationality, immigration status, language, behaviors, lifestyles (Balibar, 2007). This form of racism without races, neo-racism, represents an insidiously effective form of racialization developed by modern colonizers to govern people who are not Anglo-Saxons, like us. Depending on needs and settings, Americans leverage the flexible nature of culture to either promote inclusion and diversity (e.g., us being tokenized, representing diversity) or discriminate against us due to the so-called irresponsible divergence between our culture and mainstream culture.

COVID-19 served as a tool to advance the narrative of cultural incompatibility. Some responses to the pandemic were to blame it on eating exotic animals (Campbell, 2020), which has always been an image imposed on Eastern cultures (Reuter, 2016). The incompatibility with western culture, which is implied in statements like "go back to your country," shifts to become that of cultural incompatibility. The depth of the chiasm depended on the closeness to whiteness that allowed Musbah to be "of the hook," to exist, move, and function without fear, and made Wu's trips to the supermarket excruciatingly stressful.

Implications

After the completion of data collection and analysis (and perhaps throughout the process to various degrees), we got frustrated not knowing what to do next. We uncovered many of our feelings and experiences and connected them to the broader context, and yet we could not articulate what we think needs to be done. Through reflection, we came to conclude that what we need is solidarity–both in our praxis on the ground and in our scholarship in the academy.

Amidst the COVID-19 pandemic, waves of political violence targeted at people of color in the U.S. prompted us as junior scholars to reflect on whom we are standing together with and what we are going to do on our micro-level on a daily basis. The whole collaboration of developing the book chapter is an exemplar of building solidarity across lines of race, nationality, and other social identities. We are standing with people of color whose cultural values are marginalized in the west. Reflective of such stance, we call on higher education educators to invest in programs and practices about supporting international students in understanding the complex relationships among race, gender, nationality, other social identities, and power in U.S. college communities and U.S. society as well as in getting involved with not only academic communities but also campus communities. In the meantime, we call for more efforts in exposing the apolitical positionality of American higher education when it comes to supporting international students because the fates of international, more accurately, international students of color are subject to be controlled by U.S. white supremacy as well as international politics as demonstrated in our chapter.

Based on emerging ideas/findings from our study, we are interested in a more nuanced understanding of different ways international students of color encounter, internalize, and resist the force of being "othered" in the U.S. Future studies should explore the roles that aspects of the social identity and values of international students of color impact the processes. We are also interested in seeing more studies analyzing practice and research in higher education through the lens of postcolonialism to challenge the dominant Eurocentric forms of knowledge.

Conclusion

Higher education has long grappled with issues of diversity, inclusion, and social justice for many years. Fortunately, educators have embraced an international perspective that acknowledges and celebrates cultural diversity as evident by the swaths of U.S. students who study abroad every year, which undoubtedly yields positive outcomes. However, these programs are not immune to the paradigmatic assumptions of western thought (see Chakravarty et al., 2020 for a discussion of neo-colonialism in U.S. study abroad programs). The real dilemma seems to be not just getting students to interact and become comfortable with diversity. The challenge for educators, and for society writ large, is to disrupt hegemonic ways of thinking that exclude, alienate, and privilege some over others. When a calamity like the COVID-19 pandemic occurs, the fundamental ways in which people see each other and interact across lines of difference become rooted in prejudiced dominant ontologies. The Coronavirus reminded all that the U.S. is far from being the melting pot some would like it to be. Much more work is yet to be done.

References

Ashlee, A. A., & Quaye, S. J. (2020). On being racially enough: A duoethnography across minoritized racial identities. *International Journal of Qualitative Studies in Education*. https://doi.org/10.1080/09518398.2020.1753256

Azim, K. A., & Happel-Parkins, A. (2019). Veiled aggression: Saudi women international students' experiences of microcolonization in the United States. *International Journal of Qualitative Studies in Education, 32*(1), 1–20.

Balibar, E. (2007). Is there a "neo-racism"? In T. D. Gupta, C. E. James, R. C. A. Maaka, G. E. Galabuzi, & C. Andersen (Eds.), *Race and racialization: Essential readings* (pp. 85–88). Canadian Scholars Press.

Balibar, E., & Wallerstein, I. M. (1991). *Race, nation, class: Ambiguous identities*. Verso.

Banton, M. (2015). Race. *The Wiley Blackwell encyclopedia of race, ethnicity, and nationalism*. https://doi.org/10.1002/9781118663202

Bhabha, H. K. (1994). *The location of culture*. Routledge. https://doi.org/10.4324/9780203820551

Bjork, C., Abrams, A., Hutchinson, L. S., & Kyrkjebo, N. I. (2020). "Don't change yourselves": International students' concepts of belonging at a liberal arts college. *Journal of International Students, 10*(3), 553–570.

Breault, R. A. (2016). Emerging issues in duoethnography. *International Journal of Qualitative Studies in Education, 29(6)*. http://doi.org/10.1080/09518398.2016.11 62866

Burmila, E. (2019, March 27). *The Trump administration is driving away international students*. The Outline. https://theoutline.com/post/7247/the-trump-administration-is-driving-away-international-students?zd=2&zi=tadh77do

Campbell, C. (2020, January 24). The west blames the Wuhan Coronavirus on China's love of eating wild animals. The truth is more complex. *Times*. https://time.com/5770904/wuhan-coronavirus-wild-animals/

Carey, K. (2020, May 26). Risky strategy by many private colleges leaves them exposed. *N.Y. Times*. https://www.nytimes.com/2020/05/26/upshot/virus-colleges-risky-strategy.html

Chakravarty, D., Good, K., & Gasser, H. (2020). "Exploring your world, exploring other cultures:" How neocoloniality and neoliberalism inform U.S. education abroad programs. *Equity & Excellence in Education, 53*(1–2), 121–136.

Christophers, B. (2007). Ships in the night: Journeys in postcolonialism and cultural imperialism. *International Journal of Cultural Studies, 10*, 283–302. https://doi.org/10.1177/1367877907080145

Corbin, J. M., & Strauss, A. (2008). *Basics of qualitative research: Techniques and procedures for developing grounded theory.* SAGE Publications.

de Wit, H. (2020). Internationalization of higher education. *Journal of International Students, 10*(1), i–iv. https://doi.org/10.32674/jis.v10i1.1893

Dickler, J. (2020, May 6). Demand for refunds intensifies among college students. *CNBC.* https://www.cnbc.com/2020/05/06/demand-for-refunds-intensifies-among-college-students.html

Dreid, N. (2016, November 11). *International students wonder what a Trump administration will mean for them.* The Chronicle of Higher Education. https://www.chronicle.com/article/International-Students-Wonder/238395

Escobar, N. (2020, March 4). When xenophobia spreads like a virus. *NPR.* https://www.npr.org/2020/03/02/811363404/when-xenophobia-spreads-like-a-virus

Hackett, C., Connor, P., Stonawski, M., Skirbekk, V., Potančoková, M., & Abel, G. (2015). *Global population projections by religion: 2010–2050* (pp. 99–116). Pew Research Center. https://brill.com/view/book/edcoll/9789004297395/B9789004297395-s004.xml

Hochman, A. (2021). Janus-faced race: Is race biological, social, or mythical? *American Journal of Physical Anthropology,* 1–12. https://doi.org/10.1002/ajpa.24169

Hummel, G. S., & Toyosaki, S. (2015). Duoethnography as relational whiteness pedagogy: Human orientation toward critical cultural labor. *International Review of Qualitative Research, 8*(1), 27–48. https://www.jstor.org/stable/10.1525/irqr.2015.8.1.27

Institute of International Education. (2017). *A world on the move.* https://www.iie.org/Research-and-Insights/Project-Atlas/Research-Special-Reports-and-Analyses

Institute of International Education. (2020). *Open doors.* https://opendoorsdata.org/

Iwowo, V. (2014). Postcolonial theory. In D. Coghlan & M. Brydon-Miller (Eds.), *The SAGE encyclopedia of action research* (pp. 632–633). SAGE Publications. http://dx.doi.org/10.4135/9781446294406

Jones, S. R., Torres, V., & Arminio, J. (2014). *Negotiating the complexities of qualitative research in higher education: Fundamental elements and issues* (2nd ed.). Routledge.

Kuo, L. (2020, April 17). China denies cover-up as Wuhan coronavirus deaths revised up 50%. *The Guardian.* https://www.theguardian.com/world/2020/apr/17/china-denies-cover-up-as-wuhan-coronavirus-deaths-revised-up-50

Lee, J. J., & Rice, C. (2007). Welcome to America? International student perceptions of discrimination. *Higher Education, 53,* 381–409. https://doi.org/10.1007/s10734-005-4508-3

Mansouri, F. (2020, May 29). The socio-cultural implications of COVID-19. *UNESCO.* https://en.unesco.org/news/socio-cultural-implications-covid-19

Modood, T. (1997). "Differences", cultural racism and antiracism. In P. Werbner & T. Modood (Eds.), *Debating cultural hybridity: Multicultural identities and the politics of anti-racism* (pp. 154–172). Zed Books.

Modood, T. (2005a). *Multicultural politics: Racism, ethnicity and Muslims in Britain.* University of Minnesota Press.

Modood, T. (2005b). Racism, Asian Muslims, and the politics of difference. In T. Modood & C. Calhoun (Eds.), *Multicultural politics: Racism, ethnicity, and Muslims in Britain* (pp. 1–23). University of Minnesota Press.

Modood, T. (2011). Multiculturalism, ethnicity and integration: Some contemporary challenges. In T. Modood & J. Salt (Eds.), *Global migration, ethnicity, and Britishness* (pp. 40–64). Palgrave Macmillan.

NAFSA. (2020, March). *Losing talent 2020: An economic and foreign policy risk America can't ignore.* https://www.nafsa.org/sites/default/files/media/document/nafsa-losing-talent.pdf

Norris, J., & Sawyer, R. (2012). Toward a dialogic method. In J. Norris, R. Sawyer, & D. Lund (Eds.), *Duoethnography: Dialogic methods for social, health, and educational research* (pp. 9–40). Left Coast Press.

Page, J. (2020, March 24). China's progress against Coronavirus used Draconian tactics not deployed in the west. *The Wall Street Journal.* https://www.wsj.com/articles/the-west-is-misinterpreting-wuhans-coronavirus-progressand-drawing-the-wrong-lessons-11585074966

Patel, V. (2018, November 13). *Is the 'Trump effect' scaring away prospective international students?* The Chronicle of Higher Education. https://www.chronicle.com/article/Is-the-Trump-Effect-/245067

Prasad, A. (1997). Provincializing Europe: Towards a postcolonial reconstruction: A critique of Baconian science as the last stand of imperialism. *Studies in Cultures, Organizations & Societies, 3*(1), 91–117. https://doi.org/10.1080/10245289708523489

Quinton, W. J. (2019). Unwelcome on campus? Predictors of prejudice against international students. *Journal of Diversity in Higher Education, 12*(2), 156. https://doi.org/10.1037/dhe0000091

Rangan, P., & Chow, R. (2016). Race, racism, and postcoloniality. In G. Huggan (Ed.), *The Oxford handbook of postcolonial studies.* Oxford University Press. http://doi.org/10.1093/oxfordhb/9780199588251.001.0001

Redden, E. (2018, November 13). *New international enrollments decline again.* Inside Higher Education. https://www.insidehighered.com/news/2018/11/13/new-international-student-enrollments-continue-decline-us-universities

Redden, E. (2019, November 18). *Number of enrolled international students drops.* Inside Higher Education. https://www.insidehighered.com/admissions/article/2019/11/18/international-enrollments-declined-undergraduate-graduate-and

Reuter, K. (2016, July 28). Eating wild animals: Commonplace, cultural, complicated. *The Conversation.* https://www.conservation.org/blog/eating-wild-animals-commonplace-cultural-complicated

Romano, A. (2020, May 7). Choose your quarantine meme house. *Vox.* https://www.vox.com/2020/5/7/21238720/quarantine-house-meme-best-quarantine-memes

Said, E. (1978). *Orientalism.* Penguin Books.

Shaheen, M. (2019). Call me by my name: It's Musbah. *About Campus, 24*(4), 15–20. https://doi.org/10.1177/1086482219875733

Snipes, J. T., & LePeau, L. A. (2017). Becoming a scholar: A duoethnography of transformative learning spaces. *International Journal of Qualitative Studies in Education, 30(6),* 576–595. http://doi.org/10.1080/09518398.2016.1269972

Spivak, G. C. (1988). Can the subaltern speak? In C. Nelson & L. Grossberg (Eds.), *Marxism and the interpretation of culture* (pp. 271–313). University of Illinois Press.

Suspitsyna, T., & Shalka, T. R. (2019). The Chinese international student as a (post)colonial other: An analysis of cultural representations of a US media discourse. *The Review of Higher Education, 42*(5), 287–308. https://doi.org/10.1353/rhe.2019.0053

Wagner, J. K., Yu, J.-H., Ifekwunigwe, J. O., Harrell, T. M., Bamshad, M. J., & Royal, C. D. (2017). Anthropologists' views on race, ancestry, and genetics. *American Journal of Physical Anthropology, 162*, 318–327.

Wekullo, C. S. (2019). International undergraduate student engagement: Implications for higher education administrators. *Journal of International Students, 9*(1), 320–337.

Yeo, H. J. T., Mendenhall, R., Harwood, S. A., & Huntt, M. B. (2019). Asian international student and Asian American student: Mistaken identity and racial microaggressions. *Journal of International Students, 9*(1), 39–65.

Zho, L. (2020, April 21). How the coronavirus is surfacing America's deep-seated anti-Asian biases. *Vox.* https://www.vox.com/identities/2020/4/21/21221007/anti-asian-racism-coronavirus

Bios

Wu Xie is a second-year Ph.D. student in the Higher Education and Student Affairs program at Ohio State. She currently serves as a graduate research associate at the Quantitative Methodology Center within the College of Education and Human Ecology. Wu's research interests include internationalization of higher education, organizational behavior and theory in higher education, and STEM education, with a personal penchant for both qualitative methods and quantitative methods. Regarding internationalization, her ongoing scholarship gives attention to international students amid a changing sociopolitical and geopolitical climate. Wu received two M.S. degrees in Electrical Engineering from Nanjing Tech University and The University of Nottingham before working as an electrical engineer. Following that, she completed an M.Ed. in College Student Services Administration from Oregon State University. Email: xie.1089@osu.edu

Musbah Shaheen is a Ph.D. candidate in Higher Education and Student Affairs at The Ohio State University. He is a research associate for the College Impact Laboratory (CoIL) in the College of Education and Human Ecology. Musbah has a B.A. from Vanderbilt University and an M.Ed. in Higher Education and Student Affairs from the University of Vermont. Email: shaheen.59@osu.edu

Index

www.ingramcontent.com/pod-product-compliance
Lightning Source LLC
Chambersburg PA
CBHW050116280326
41933CB00010B/1123